D1165611

MR. POLK'S WAR

American Opposition and Dissent, 1846–1848

MR. POLK'S WAR

*American Opposition and
Dissent, 1846–1848*

JOHN H. SCHROEDER

The University of Wisconsin Press

Published 1973
The University of Wisconsin Press
Box 1379, Madison, Wisconsin 53701

The University of Wisconsin Press, Ltd.
70 Great Russell Street, London

First printing

Printed in the United States of America

For LC CIP information see the colophon

ISBN 0-299-06160-4

For Sandra

★ *Contents*

★ *Illustrations*

★ *Introduction*

A POPULAR AMERICAN MYTH suggests that the American people have patriotically suspended their political differences when their nation was at war. United, they have met the crisis at hand. To do otherwise would be disloyal, unpatriotic, un-American. And to criticize administration policy publicly in time of war would offer encouragement to the enemy, endanger national security, and unnecessarily jeopardize the lives of more American men on the battlefield. Only after the emergency has been met, the enemy defeated, and peace restored should criticism of foreign policy resurface and the nation return to politics as usual.

Throughout the nineteenth and twentieth centuries—from the War of 1812 down to the Vietnam War—wartime presidents and their supporters have consistently attempted to utilize these arguments to strengthen their war efforts by creating a united home front. To stimulate patriotic sentiment and to engender overwhelming national support for their war policies, wartime administrations have sought to discourage antiwar spokesmen. But in addition to its avowed nationalistic purpose, this patriotic rationale has offered wartime presidents a tempting political weapon which they have used with little hesitation. While pleading for the suspension of antiadministration criticism under the guise of unselfish national unity, various presidents have simultaneously sought to silence and discredit their political opponents by labeling their criticisms as disloyal, unpatriotic, and helpful to the enemy.

The idea that partisanship and antigovernment criticism should be suspended during the crisis of war has, however, always been a controversial one. Administration attempts to stifle dissent have usually had the opposite effect. To assertions that administration policy should be unanimously endorsed once the fighting begins, lest domestic criticism of the president offer "aid and comfort" to the enemy, dissenting politicians have responded with resentment and scorn. While traditionally reaffirming their determination to support American forces in the field, antiwar politicians have asserted their own constitutional right and duty to examine, question, and criticize administration war policy and objectives. True patriotism, they have rightly maintained, does not consist in blind support for any war policy; rather it consists in the constant scrutiny and, if need be, the exposure and reversal of an unwise, destructive, or unjust national course.

With the exception of World War II, American wars in the past have generated a host of antiwar politicians and activists. Nor have dissenting activities been confined to a small minority of radical pacifists, political extremists, and religious zealots. Men of conservative, as well as radical, political orientation have spoken out. During the nineteenth century, two major political parties, the Federalists during the War of 1812 and the Whigs during the Mexican War, assumed active and vocal antiwar positions. So, too, have Democrats, as well as Republicans, denounced American participation in various wars during the present century. Throughout American history, then, opponents of war have been outspoken and articulate and have encompassed a broad spectrum of political opinion.

The strength and character of respective antiwar movements have varied from conflict to conflict according to the special circumstances and nature of each war. Traditionally, a number of related but distinct factors have determined the intensity of the opposition. Most basic and influential have been the causes of war and the necessity for American involvement. In those rare instances when the aggression or belligerence of a foreign power has genuinely forced war on the United States, the American people have responded with united determination. As a result, when war has offered the only means of preserving American security or protecting vital American interests, the opposition has been weak. For example, the Roosevelt administration eventually entered World War II with practically no domestic dissent because the issues were clear-cut. Although sharp differences on foreign policy had existed before 1941, the Japanese attack on Pearl Harbor unified the nation. After December 7, 1941, there was simply no choice but to confront Japanese and German military aggression with force. Likewise, in 1951, the Communist invasion of South Korea forced war on the United States. With South Korea about to be crushed militarily by North Korean aggression, the Truman administration had no viable alternative but to commit American arms.

Conversely, those wars which have evoked the most intense opposition have been those in which the causes and necessity for American involvement have been debatable. The War of 1812, the Mexican War, and the Vietnam War all have provided cases in which the president was unable to convince an overwhelming majority of Americans that war was either advisable or imperative. In 1812, the New England states strongly rejected the Madison administration's argument that the violation of American neutral rights and commercial interest dictated war with England. In the Vietnamese conflict, its complex causes and the questionable rationale of American participation resulted in the unyielding opposition of numerous Americans.

Closely related to the crucial factors of cause and necessity has been the issue of American war objectives. In American history, war goals have been variously intertwined with and distinct from the causes of American involvement. Responding to the threats of Japan and Germany in World War II, the Roosevelt administration was able to create a policy which combined high-minded idealism with the war goal of national security. In World War I, President Wilson weakened domestic opponents of the war by convincing the American people that the involvement of the United States was not only imperative to national interests but also central to an idealistic crusade for international democracy and justice. More frequently, however, the question of war goals has been distinct from American entry into war. In Korea, unified domestic support of the Truman administration began to disintegrate after the initial defensive objectives of the war had been changed dramatically by General MacArthur's invasion of North Korea and drive toward the Chinese border. In 1898, sharp dissent surfaced once President McKinley's imperialistic objectives became evident, and then, after peace with Spain, intensified when the administration was forced to fight a brutal guerrilla war in the Philippines to secure control of America's new possession. In contrast, President Abraham Lincoln during the Civil War was able to mollify some antiwar critics when he issued the Emancipation Proclamation. If this flawed document did not satisfy all antislavery objections by immediately freeing any slaves, it did allay some criticism by committing the federal government to the war objective of ending slavery.

Domestic opposition has also been affected by several less important factors, including the related elements of American military success and the length of a conflict. In such instances as World War II, when the necessity has been strong and the cause just, these factors have not strongly influenced antiwar sentiment. When the prowar rationale has been debatable, however, the American people have been impatient at seemingly interminable and indecisive conflicts. This has been particularly true in so-called limited wars like that waged in Vietnam to sustain a questionable Asian policy. Similarly, in Korea by early 1951, the confused nature of this limited war and the developing military stalemate sharply increased domestic criticism and growing popular disillusionment with the Truman administration's policy. In contrast, the relatively short duration, and the consistent success of American arms, which characterized the Spanish-American War and World War I, significantly reduced domestic dissent during these conflicts.

A final element influencing antiwar sentiment has been the existence, or absence, of unpopular and undemocratic war-related measures. Traditionally, military conscription laws, increased federal taxes, abridgement of civil liber-ties, and government suppression of dissent have tended to infuriate war crit-ics and intensify their dissent. The New York Draft Riots of 1863 and the attempts to resist conscription during the Vietnam War have demonstrated how requisite war measures can weaken public support for administration pol-icy. Likewise, government attempts to restrict freedom of expression and muzzle public dissent have had similar effects during these two wars. World War I, of course, represents an exception. Here the Wilson administration was largely successful in its attempts to intimidate and quell some opposition, because the American people were willing to accept Wilson's definition of the war as a crusade for democracy. As a result of the administration's effective propaganda campaign in behalf of the war effort, Americans themselves ex-pressed widespread intolerance of war dissenters and accepted the legal sup-pression of dissent as necessary. Unpopular and repressive wartime policies, however, have provided useful symbols on which the opposition could focus its activities. In the Mexican and Spanish-American Wars, which did not re-quire such repressive and controversial measures, the opposition was deprived of a potent device. Hence it could not broaden its popular appeal by dramatiz-ing the pernicious effects of war on the nation.

Though sizable and outspoken, American antiwar dissent traditionally has been a study in frustration. Dissenters have consistently been unable to shorten wars, restrict war goals, or alter an administration's war policy. Only two con-flicts offer notable exceptions. In the War of 1812, overwhelming opposition in New England contributed to the failure of American military strategy. In addition to the many New England civilians who openly assisted and supplied the enemy, numerous well-trained New England militia units were unavailable to the Madison administration for the strategically important inva-sion of Canada. In the Vietnam War, widespread dissent and public disillu-sionment have combined with an unsuccessful military policy, based on a shaky rationale, to reverse American policy.

This general failure of American antiwar movements stems from a variety of factors. First, it is virtually impossible for antiwar groups and politicians to prevent the outbreak of hostilities. The opposition is obviously powerless to restrain a foreign power like Germany or Japan, already bent on armed ag-gression. But it is also extremely difficult for critics to prevent war when the president himself seems inclined toward one. With his dominance of Ameri-can foreign policy and his broad prerogatives as commander in chief, the pres-ident can (willfully or not) exacerbate a deteriorating international situation in which serious tension and differences already exist. Through his own pur-poseful maneuvers, or unintentional blunders, he can place the United States in a position where a war seems the only alternative to national dishonor. Of-ten such cases have been precipitated by a provocative incident, such as the attack on American soldiers along the Rio Grande in 1846, the bombardment of Fort Sumter in 1861, or the Gulf of Tonkin incident in 1964. All brought a period of tension and conflict to a head by temporarily outraging and unifying American opinion. The president can then go before Congress, declare a state of national emergency, and request the authority and means to meet the crisis. When the president requests a declaration of war and the authority to take appropriate military action, Congress can hardly refuse. At this crucial point, the chief executive holds strong cards. A national emergency requiring immediate action exists, and the time necessary for careful investigation of the circumstances surrounding the outbreak of fighting cannot be expended. During such dramatic crises, few congressmen have had the courage to deny a president's request to relieve embattled American troops, protect the nation's honor, repel an "invasion," or declare outright war, no matter how suspicious the situation.

Second, once the nation has been plunged into war, political opponents face an equally difficult problem. They must seek the means of reversing government policy without deserting or undermining American forces already under fire. If, as he traditionally has, the president refuses to heed antiwar demands, the most direct and potent constitutional power which Congress can employ to change administration policy is its control over appropriations and manpower. By refusing to authorize the money and men required to sustain a successful war effort, Congress can theoretically force the president to abandon his prosecution of the war and withdraw American troops. In practice, however, this congressional prerogative has never provided a realistic or effective antiwar tactic. A widely accepted tenet of American patriotism provides that American forces, once committed to battle, must be fully supported. Even those antiwar politicians who have been most vocal and have most firmly maintained their right to question and criticize administration war policy have also consistently reaffirmed their patriotism by voting the requisite men, money, and supplies.

In addition to lacking an effective antiwar weapon, the opposition has rarely been able to present viable alternatives to existing policy. War, of course, tends to make its own laws and to narrow the range of diplomatic alternatives. Once on the tiger's back, one cannot dismount easily. Belligerents are rarely unwilling, and they readily fight until some military conclusion, whether it be defeat, victory, or stalemate, has been reached rather than seek peace through negotiation. So while dissenters in the United States might urge primary emphasis on negotiations rather than armed force, the enemy has rarely been as reasonable as war critics would like. In fact, with the exception of the Spanish in 1898, virtually all of America's opponents have preferred fighting to treating with the hated Americans.

Lacking viable means of opposition and without feasible policy options, antiwar movements have necessarily been minority movements. Despite the volume of antiwar sentiment, such dissent has rarely expressed the opinions of an American majority. Only the Vietnam War has presented a striking exception. Admittedly a majority of Americans during the War of 1812, the Mexican War, and the Korean War were exasperated with American involvement at one point or another. But this public frustration was never translated into a consuming activist opposition to war. Disillusioned as they might have been, most Americans saw no other alternative to continued, if sullen, support for adminstration war policy.

Representative of this persistent war debate in American history is the Mexican War. With notable exceptions and variations, the motivations, composition, arguments, and ultimate failure of the opposition between 1846 and 1848 are characteristic of other antiwar movements. In the opinion of its numerous critics, the Mexican War was unnecessary, impolitic, illegal, and immoral. Furthermore, the outbreak of hostilities was shrouded by highly suspicious circumstances. War critics charged that a secretive, evasive, and highhanded president himself had provoked Mexico into firing the first shots. And once under way, the war soon manifested the Polk administration's intention to obtain territory by invasion, conquest, and plunder. Horrified by such an immoral spectacle, opponents argued that the most basic democratic precepts of the United States were being violated in her thirst for land.

Emerging from such dubious beginnings and questionable motives, the war generated a forceful and broad domestic opposition. Dissenters included Whigs, Democrats, reformers, and clergymen. They ranged from the intense individualism of Henry David Thoreau to the devoted partisanship of Whig Robert Winthrop; from the abolitionist extremism of William Lloyd Garrison to the proslavery conservatism of Democrat John C. Calhoun; and from the high-minded idealism of Theodore Parker to the political expediency of Daniel Webster. In accord with the wide spectrum of opponents was a corresponding diversity in their respective motivations, tactics, and criticisms.

Many and dedicated, but unable to overcome obstacles which all opponents of war must confront, they failed. Angry as they were at the outbreak of fighting, most antiwar Whigs and Democrats dared not further endanger General Zachary Taylor's beleaguered forces by voting against President Polk's request for formal war, nor could they withhold the means to wage it. Then, once war existed, political opponents of the administration could not agree on an acceptable or workable means of shortening and limiting the conflict. Outside the Congress, dissenters were likewise ineffective. Concentrated in the northeastern region of the country, these critics were unable to dramatize adequately the evils of a foreign war which was, in fact, fought by willing volunteers, not by draftees, and financed by government loans, not by increased taxes. Write, speak, and petition as they might, the opposition, then, never enlisted enough public support to force the president to reconsider or to alter his objectives.

In addition to fitting into the continuity of American antiwar dissent, the controversy over the Mexican War provides an excellent index to the particular tensions and issues which divided the American people during the mid-1840s. Most directly, debate over the war highlighted a basic disagreement on the ends, means, and basic philosophy of American expansionism. The Mexican conflict also manifested and hastened the process of political change in the United States. Before 1846, slavery had usually been secondary to more dominant and traditional national issues like the tariff and fiscal policy, as well as subordinate to the primary considerations of national party unity which characterized the "second American party system." But after 1846, the crucial and related issues of slavery and expansionism increasingly dominated the political stage. Sectional antagonism, party splintering, and the decline of traditional partisan issues would characterize the new American politics as the nation marched toward civil strife.

American historians, of course, have not ignored the opposition to the Mexican War.[1] A number of scholars have treated the topic as it related to their own studies on the war itself, on leading figures of the day, on American expansionism, and on the politics of the 1840s. Other American historians have studied the opposition within the framework of their own studies on social and intellectual developments. But antiwar dissent from 1846 to 1848 has not heretofore been treated in a detailed and comprehensive manner. This study is an attempt to fill that void.

In introducing this volume, I wish to acknowledge the assistance of numerous individuals who contributed to the study. I owe a considerable debt of gratitude to the staffs of the following libraries: Manuscript Division of the Library of Congress, Alderman Library of the University of Virginia, Massachusetts Historical Society, Houghton Library of Harvard University, William R. Perkins Library of Duke University, Southern Historical Collection at the University of North Carolina, New York Public Library, New York Historical Society, and State Historical Society of Wisconsin. For permission to reprint several cartoons, I want to thank the Newberry Library of Chicago.

I appreciate the helpful comments, criticisms, and suggestions offered by the following individuals: Professors Bernard Mayo, Norman A. Graebner, Richard E. Ellis, and William J. Gilmore. I also want to thank Mrs. Mary Schoultz, Mrs. Hazel Kay, and Miss Kathy Poplawski for their good cheer

1. For a brief summary of the opposition, see Frederick Merk, "Dissent in the Mexican War," in *Dissent in Three American Wars*, Samuel Eliot Morison, Frederick Merk, and Frank Freidel (Cambridge, Mass.: 1970), 35–63.

and their able job of typing the manuscript. I am especially indebted to three individuals whose efforts have substantially enhanced the quality of this volume and hastened its completion. In directing this study as a doctoral dissertation, Professor Willie Lee Rose gave generously of her knowledge and time. Questioning, criticizing, and encouraging, Professor Rose read the entire manuscript in its several drafts to help bring order to confusion. My colleague Reginald Horsman read the manuscript carefully, asked numerous penetrating questions, and recommended a variety of significant revisions. Finally, I am most deeply indebted to my wife, Sandra Barrow Schroeder, for her encouragement, patience, and confidence. As she well knows, her contribution as an uncompromising stylistic critic, careful typist, and meticulous proofreader has been indispensable.

John H. Schroeder

Milwaukee, Wisconsin
April 1973

MR. POLK'S WAR

American Opposition and Dissent, 1846–1848

1

★ *War—"By the Act of Mexico"*

WORD OF THE ATTACK reached the White House about six o'clock in the evening of Saturday, May 9, 1846. On April 25, 1846, a detachment of Mexican troops crossed the Rio Grande and ambushed two companies of American soldiers on the left bank of the river.[1] In the ensuing skirmish, eleven Americans were killed, five wounded, and the remainder taken captive. Since he had expected this news for several days, President James K. Polk seized the moment and called his cabinet into session for the second time that day. Earlier in the afternoon, although dissenting views had been heard, the cabinet had acquiesced in Polk's recommendation that a war message be sent to Congress during the next week. Now, upon being reconvened and informed of the developments on the Rio Grande, the cabinet unanimously supported the president's decision to send a war message to Congress on Monday. That same evening Polk began to draft the statement which he completed the following day, Sunday. He also conferred throughout the day with advisers and congressional leaders to ensure rapid and smooth treatment of his recommendations on Capitol Hill.

President Polk's decision to send a war message to Congress, even before he received word of the hostilities on the Rio Grande, and his decisive actions in the hours immediately after the news arrived, demonstrated unmistakably that Polk readily embraced war. In fact, war with Mexico well suited the president's plan for territorial expansion. In 1844 the orthodox Jacksonianism of Polk, the former governor of Tennessee, had been acceptable to all factions of the Democratic party, which had nominated him as a dark horse. But combined with his Jacksonian views on such domestic issues as the tariff and monetary policy was an aggressive continental vision. Polk campaigned as an avowed expansionist and upon his inauguration, he announced to Secretary of the Navy George Bancroft that, in addition to reducing the tariff and estab-

---

1. At that time, the Rio Grande was also known and frequently referred to as the Rio del Norte.

3

lishing an independent treasury, he intended to settle the Oregon question and to acquire California. At this time, in March 1845, Polk had already assumed that Texas would soon be added to the Union, since the joint resolution of annexation had been passed by Congress and accepted by outgoing President Tyler.

A slight man with piercing eyes and compressed lips, James K. Polk was an individual of unwavering personal integrity, intense determination, and great diligence. But because of his narrow partisanship, lack of candor, and proclivity for secrecy and evasiveness, Polk was never a popular president. His public image was neither dynamic nor forceful, and during his presidency he was continually handicapped by a lack of popular support and by disunity within his own party. At the same time, as his most perceptive biographer has noted, the new president was "superbly fitted to initiate and direct the drive to the Pacific." A firm believer in American superiority and national destiny, the president was both "literal-minded and unimaginative," qualities which made him insensitive to the moral implications of aggressive expansion or slavery.[2] He refused to concede that the slavery question was closely related to expansion into the Southwest, and throughout the war with Mexico he adamantly maintained that the two issues were not legitimately related. Rather Polk labeled the extension of slavery an "abstract question," which when considered in connection with territorial expansion was "not only mischievous but wicked."[3]

After his inauguration, President Polk's expansionist goals found a favorable reception in both the cabinet and the Congress. In selecting his cabinet, Polk assured a positive acceptance for his objectives by appointing men of like mind from around the country. Robert Walker of Mississippi, George Bancroft of Massachusetts, William Marcy of New York, and vacillating James Buchanan of Pennsylvania, all shared their chief's continental dreams. The Democrats also enjoyed a majority of 144 to 77 in the House and 30 to 24 in the Senate of the Twenty-ninth Congress which convened in December 1845. In addition, a number of the party's congressional leaders were young and aggressive expansionists from the Northwest and Southwest. Men like Stephen Douglas and Jefferson Davis in the House and Lewis Cass and William Allen in the Senate were anxious to hasten the nation's drive to the Pacific. Combining a long-standing sense of national mission with ideas of territorial growth, the Democratic expansionists in Congress spoke not only of extending the country's borders, but also of expanding the "area of freedom"

---

2. Charles Sellers, *James K. Polk Continentalist, 1843–1846* (Princeton, N.J., 1966), 214.

3. Milo M. Quaife, ed., *The Diary of James K. Polk, 1845–1849*, 4 vols. (Chicago, 1910), 2: 308.

and spreading the blessings of democratic self-government across the continent.

But unfortunately for the president, factional dispute weakened the Democratic majorities in both Houses. Factions led by Thomas Hart Benton, John C. Calhoun, and Martin Van Buren were suspicious or critical of the Polk administration and of one another. In the Senate, Benton and his followers were ambivalent toward the administration. The Missourian was offended when Polk selected the House proposal rather than his own plan to annex Texas, and he was critical also of the president's reckless Mexican policy and apparent determination to have all of Oregon, whatever the cost. At the same time, Benton was bitterly antagonistic toward Calhoun and the disunionist threat which Benton believed the South Carolinian and his followers posed. In short, Polk could neither depend on Benton's support nor expect his opposition.

Nor were Calhoun and his coterie in Congress committed to supporting the administration. Conservative in outlook and piqued at not having been offered the position of Secretary of State by Polk, Calhoun believed that Polk's aggressive Oregon and Mexican policies promised war with both England and Mexico and ultimate disaster for the nation. Emerging from a brief retirement, Calhoun returned to the Senate in December 1845 hoping to modify the precipitous course of the administration. But Calhoun's position was complicated by his role as chief defender of the South and his continuing ambition for the presidency. He believed that if he played a major role in helping to prevent war with both England and Mexico, he would emerge as a strong contender for the presidency in 1848.

Democratic party discipline was further weakened by the hostility of the Van Burenites toward the administration. This strong party faction had loyal followers in Ohio, Pennsylvania, and New England, as well as New York, where they were concentrated and known as the Barnburners. Bitter over the rejection of their chief by the Democratic Convention in 1844, resentful because Polk's key cabinet appointments ignored their leading members, and suspicious of the president's sympathy toward their conservative New York Democratic rivals, the Hunkers, the Van Burenites eyed Polk with hostility and vowed to regain control of the party in 1848. In addition, these antislavery politicians resented the prosouthern orientation of the Polk administration. With Van Buren in temporary retirement, this wing was led in the House by Preston King of New York and in the Senate by John Dix of New York and John M. Niles of Connecticut.

At the same time, despite the threat of disunity within his own party, Polk was not seriously challenged by the outnumbered Whig opposition in Congress. Although their leadership in the Senate was strong, with only Henry Clay absent from a glittering list of names which included Daniel Webster, John J. Crittenden, John Berrien, Willie Mangum, Thomas Corwin, and John Clayton, the Whigs were a distinct minority. Not only were the Whigs outnumbered almost two to one in the House, but they also suffered from their own internal divisions. A tiny but ever-vigorous group of antislavery Whigs subjected the party to increasing sectional stress. Led by aged John Quincy Adams and fiery Joshua Giddings of Ohio, these radicals continually attempted to agitate the explosive slavery question in Congress. Although only a tiny minority in the party, about a dozen of these Whig radicals from Ohio and New England frequently attempted to embarrass their conservative fellow Whigs who were determined to avoid the slavery question and thereby preserve the tenuous national unity of the party. Most Whigs were extremely cautious on the slavery issue, realizing that the political ties which bound northerners like Daniel Webster and Robert Winthrop of Massachusetts with southerners like John Berrien and Alexander Stephens of Georgia would be dissolved once the slavery issue was allowed to supersede such traditional domestic issues as the tariff, land policy, and financial questions. Before the mid-1840s, the antislavery radical Whigs had achieved only isolated victories, but they gained more adherents and posed a greater threat to conservative Whigs with the passing of each succeeding Congress.

Despite the threat of internal division within the Democratic and Whig parties, the structure of national politics in the fiercely partisan 1840s promised to assist the Polk administration. By this time the "second American party system" had matured. At all levels of political activity and in every state, both Whig and Democratic party machinery was fully developed and functioned more effectively than ever before. On national issues, politicians divided along party rather than sectional lines. With each passing year, sectional stress within the major parties increased as tension over the issue of slavery increased, but as late as 1846 partisan lines remained firm as the traditional issues of the Jacksonian era remained dominant. In Congress, party discipline was high; few congressmen deserted their party on key votes. On the unsettled issues of the 1830s partisanship was understandable, and into the 1840s the national bank, a protective tariff, and the distribution of land sales revenue were dominant issues on which Whigs and Democrats continued to disagree. Partisan lines also remained taut on issues like expansion which had come to dominate national politics by the mid-1840s.

As a party, the Democrats were aggressive exponents of Manifest Destiny and sought to implement their visions by annexing Texas and by acquiring all of the jointly held Oregon country. In contrast, the Whigs refused to be moved by the doctrine of Manifest Destiny. Traditionally conservative on matters of foreign policy, the Whigs cautioned against a headlong rush to the Pacific. In 1844 Whig presidential candidate Henry Clay warned of the dangers inherent in annexing Texas. In Congress, the Whig party unsuccessfully attempted to block the annexation of Texas and by 1845 was predicting that disastrous consequences would follow an attempt to demand all of Oregon. At the same time, most Whigs denied that they were categorically opposed to future expansion and claimed that they favored a gradual, orderly process of national growth which sought to avoid war with other nations while ensuring the eventual acquisition of valuable harbors on the Pacific. In short, theirs was a commercially oriented expansionism designed to secure frontage on the Pacific without recourse to war.

Although the Whig party accepted the principle of national expansion, most Whigs found ample reason to criticize various projects of expansion whenever they were presented. By 1846, the Whig party had assumed an antiexpansionist posture and had already presented a considerable volume of antiexpansionist arguments based on theoretical and practical as well as political grounds. For example, Whigs warned that the inevitable result of annexing Texas or demanding the entire Oregon territory would be war with either Mexico or England, or quite possibly with both nations. Northern Whigs denounced the annexation of Texas as a thinly veiled plot to extend slavery and the power of the slave South; at the same time, conservative southern Whigs criticized the proposed addition of Texas because they believed it would diminish the strength of slavery in the older slave states. The antiexpansionist opposition also denounced the pending annexation on constitutional grounds. Contending first that the annexation of another sovereign state was illegal, Whig opponents later objected to annexation by the joint resolution of Congress as a usurpation of the Senate's treaty-making power.

On more theoretical grounds, the Whig party constantly emphasized that limits should be placed on the size of the American republic and warned that unrestricted expansion would ultimately lead to the undermining of republican government in the United States. The Whigs argued that if the nation continued to grow geographically, it would soon resemble a vast empire more closely than a small republic. With the creation of a continental empire would come the perversion of the republican form of government and the replacement of the federal system with an all-powerful central government, a virtually unlimited executive, and a formidable military establishment. Thus, when the Mexican War began in 1846, the Whig party had already developed a considerable body of antiexpansionist arguments which they would extend, reshape, and intensify during the months ahead under the pressure of war with Mexico.

Once inaugurated, Polk had moved decisively to realize his continental objectives. He quickly accepted and then implemented the joint resolution annexing Texas. Meanwhile, ignoring the strength of existing British claims to Oregon and the quarter-century willingness of the United States to divide the territory at the forty-ninth parallel, Polk asserted in his inaugural address that the nation's claim to all of Oregon was "clear and unquestionable."[4] Later, in his first annual message to Congress in December 1845, the president reaffirmed this claim and recommended that the United States terminate the existing convention for joint occupation of Oregon. This message aroused great excitement across the nation, and a lengthy congressional debate ensued in the early months of 1846 before the president's recommendation was adopted in April 1846.

On Mexican affairs, Polk was equally aggressive. On March 28, 1845, while the annexation of Texas was pending, Mexico severed diplomatic relations with the United States and threatened reprisals against Texas. Polk responded on several fronts. In an effort to encourage Texas to accept annexation, he assured leaders of the Lone Star Republic that the administration would uphold their exaggerated claims to the Rio Grande, even though the Nueces River, about 150 miles to the north, had been the traditional border of Texas and had been widely recognized as such by both the United States and Mexico. In June, before annexation had been approved by Texas, Polk also ordered General Zachary Taylor and his small army of 1,500 men to advance just beyond the Nueces to Corpus Christi, in disputed territory. In August, the size of the American force was doubled in response to a reported Mexican buildup along the Rio Grande.[5]

At the same time, Polk had been working through special agents to reestablish diplomatic relations with Mexico. Specifically, he sought Mexican assurance that a regular United States minister would be received and "unsettled questions" negotiated. In the early autumn of 1845 the precarious José Herrera regime in Mexico indicated that it would receive a special commissioner to discuss the outstanding Texas question, as well as the more than $2 million in claims it owed to United States citizens. To these overtures, Polk responded in a manner which made the reception of a United States minister impossible for any Mexican regime hoping to retain power. The president dispatched John Slidell to Mexico, not as a special commissioner, but as "Envoy Extraordinary and Minister Plenipotentiary" to reopen regular diplomatic relations. In addition, Slidell was instructed to negotiate not only the Texas border dispute and the claims questions, but, more critically, the Mexican cession of New Mexico and, if feasible, Upper California. The president hoped to use the outstanding claims issue as a lever to obtain New Mexico and Upper California, with the United States assuming the outstanding claims and paying Mexico a fair

---

4. James D. Richardson, ed., *A Compilation of the Messages and Papers of the Presidents, 1789–1902*, 10 vols. (Washington, D.C., 1903), 4: 381.

5. The best account of the coming of the war from the American point of view is Sellers, *Polk*, 215–34, 259–66, 330–39, 398–407.

equivalent for whatever territory was ceded. Finally, Slidell was accompanied by William Parrott, as secretary of the legation. Because of Parrott's previous transactions with the Mexicans, the Herrera regime found him particularly offensive. In its tottering position, the regime did not dare accredit a regular minister from the United States until the Texas question had been resolved and, preferably, some form of apology exacted from the United States. Nor could the Mexican government negotiate the cession of additional territory to the contemptible Americans. Consequently, for several weeks the Herrera regime refused to receive Slidell. Early in 1846, Herrera was overthrown and his government supplanted by the more bellicose one of Mariano Paredes. Finally, in March 1846, Slidell requested his credentials and departed for the United States.

Polk did not wait until diplomatic channels had been explored before taking action. On October 16, 1845, even before Slidell had departed for Mexico, Polk ordered General Taylor to march from Corpus Christi and approach the Rio Grande. By January Taylor had not yet advanced, and in explicit language Polk again ordered the advance. Moving his troops in February and arriving opposite the Mexican town of Matamoros in late March, Taylor encamped here and established a fortification with cannons pointed toward the small Mexican settlement. Meanwhile a naval blockade of Matamoros had been established. When word of Slidell's rejection reached Washington in April, Polk resolved on war, but, because of the seriousness of the Oregon crisis, postponed action. Finally, with Slidell's return to Washington, the president called a cabinet meeting on May 9 to discuss war with Mexico. It was only hours later that word from the Rio Grande gave Polk the incident he needed to ensure the war he sought.

During his first year in office, President Polk had followed a dual Mexican policy to achieve his continental designs. While publicly committed to peaceful diplomacy, Polk maneuvered to ensure war if necessary to gain his objectives. Hoping to coerce Mexico peacefully into recognizing the Rio Grande as the Texas border and ceding New Mexico and California to the United States, the administration worked through the channels of diplomacy. But Polk's was a militant policy designed not to resolve outstanding issues like the claims question, but rather to use this dispute to achieve his territorial objectives, whatever the cost. If Mexico would not peacefully acquiesce in Polk's demands, then war would be the alternative. And the president did not shrink from war. Polk's diplomatic maneuvering also promised to win support for a war with Mexico if and when it became necessary. When the president asked Congress for war, he could claim that all diplomatic alternatives had been exhausted and that the only remaining course was war with the unreasonable and intransigent Mexicans. This situation would not have given Polk a strong case, but the hostilities on the Rio Grande added the ingredient of a national crisis which he needed to mobilize public opinion and to stampede a doubting Congress.

Despite the provocative nature of the administration's Mexican policy in the early months of 1846, political observers in the United States largely ignored Mexican affairs while focusing on the ominous Oregon question and the immediate threat of war with England. In Washington, with Congress involved in a prolonged debate over Oregon, Polk's Mexican activities were neglected by politicians of both parties as the nation drifted toward war. Such men as Calhoun, Benton, the Van Burenites, and Joshua Giddings were disturbed by the situation along the Rio Grande, but chose to remain silent. Nor was the nation's press more attentive. Newspapers carried regular reports on the Mexican situation, but few warned of the impending war.[6]

On Monday, May 11, a tense Congress received the president's message which reviewed the deteriorating relations between the United States and Mexico and asked Congress to recognize the existence of war. To win the support of Congress and the country, Polk depicted the United States as a long-suffering nation which had patiently endured a series of "insults" and "injuries" at Mexican hands, while at the same time it had left "no effort untried to effect amicable adjustment" of existing difficulties. The president reviewed the series of grievances one by one: Mexico had consistently refused to pay several million dollars in outstanding damage claims owed to citizens of the United States; the Mexican government had been unwilling to recognize the annexation of Texas or to concede that the legitimate border of Texas was the Rio Grande; Mexico had aggravated an already serious situation by refusing to discuss the outstanding disputes; and two successive regimes had refused even to receive the American envoy, John Slidell.[7]

In the face of Mexico's belligerent posture and after continued Mexican threats to invade Texas, Polk argued, it had been necessary to take precautionary action. The advance of American troops to Corpus Christi and then to the Rio Grande was justified as a defensive measure. Once there, claimed Polk, the Americans had been instructed to "abstain from all aggressive acts" toward Mexico and her citizens, but Mexican troops in the area had "assumed a belligerent attitude" which resulted directly in the attack of April 25. By this final unwarranted act, Mexico had exhausted the "cup of forbearance," invaded American territory, and "shed American blood upon the American soil." Since fighting had commenced, the two nations were now at war. Polk continued: "As war exists, and, notwithstanding all our efforts to avoid it,

---

6. See for example, *Charleston Mercury,* 6 February, 25 April 1846; *New York Tribune,* 20 April 1846; *National Intelligencer* (Washington, D.C.), 23 April, 2 May 1846; *Augusta Daily Chronicle and Sentinel* (Georgia), 14 April, 7 May 1846.

7. Richardson, *Messages of the Presidents,* 4: 442, 439.

exists by the act of Mexico herself, we are called upon by every consideration of duty and patriotism to vindicate with decision the honor, the rights, and the interests of our country." The president requested that Congress now act promptly to recognize the existence of war and to provide "the means of prosecuting the war with vigor, and thus hastening the restoration of peace."[8]

In seeking the support of a Congress which included not only a critical Whig opposition but also such dissident Democrats as Calhoun and Benton, Polk attempted to present the strongest possible case for war, a case which would be irrefutable and would force his supporters and critics alike to accept his recommendations. But in so doing, Polk grossly overstated his argument and his message abounded in half-truths, distortions, and falsehoods.

Crucial to Polk's version of the outbreak of hostilities was his assertion that the Rio Grande was and traditionally had been the rightful border of Texas. Obviously, Polk's charge that Mexico had invaded and attacked American troops on American soil was predicated on his claim that the Rio Grande, not the Nueces River 150 miles to the north, was the true border. To substantiate his claim, Polk cited a series of facts. In 1836, the Congress of the independent Texas republic had formally "declared" the Rio Grande to be the border; the disputed area between the Nueces and Rio Grande had been formally represented in the Congress of Texas; and the area was presently "included within one of our Congressional districts." Furthermore, the Congress of the United States had, by an act of December 1845, recognized this boundary "with great unanimity" by including it within "our own revenue system" and by appointing a revenue officer to reside in the district.[9]

Here Polk was on shaky ground because the Rio Grande had never been the recognized border of Texas, and the area between the Rio Grande and Nueces was, at best, disputed territory. Not only Mexico, but also such leading American politicians of both parties as Thomas Hart Benton, former Secretary of State John Calhoun, and former presidents John Quincy Adams and Andrew Jackson had recognized this fact for years prior to 1846. Mexico had always controlled the area between the Nueces and the Rio Grande, and loyal Mexican citizens continued to inhabit the sparsely settled desert region. The claim of the United States fully accepted the overblown assertions of the Republic of Texas, specifically its 1836 unilateral claim to the Rio Grande. However, the boundary was purposely left undefined in the joint resolution which annexed Texas to the United States in 1845.[10] In his message to Congress in December 1845, Polk picked an inauspicious moment to insist that the true

---

8. Ibid., 441, 442, 443.

9. Ibid., 440.

10. The best discussion of the disputed Texas border is included in Chapter VI, "The True Boundary," of Frederick Merk's *The Monroe Doctrine and American Expansionism, 1843–1849* (New York, 1966), 133–60.

border was the Rio Grande. Because the message was devoted largely to the explosive Oregon issue, the president's remarks on Mexican affairs evoked little notice in Congress or the press. The administration's claim in the Texas border issue, then, was a weak one, unfounded in fact. If the Rio Grande was not the border of Texas, but within Mexican territory, it could hardly be argued that Mexico had provoked war by shedding American blood on American soil. Indeed, the reverse was true; President Polk had incited war by sending American soldiers into what was disputed territory, historically controlled and inhabited by Mexicans.

In addition to the Texas border question, Polk distorted the true nature of Slidell's diplomatic mission to Mexico in 1845. Although Polk claimed that the Slidell mission represented a sincere attempt to resolve existing differences peacefully, Polk's diplomacy was clearly coercive in manner. Already deeply aggrieved by the annexation of Texas, no Mexican regime could have then negotiated the cession of Mexican territory in New Mexico and California. Yet Slidell's instructions provided that he negotiate for the cession of New Mexico and California, and further stipulated that Mexico must accept the annexation of Texas as an established fact. In other words, the United States would consider giving neither an apology nor reparation. Also, while the Mexican government asked that a special commissioner be dispatched to resolve outstanding grievances and thus prepare for the restoration of regular diplomatic relations, Polk insisted on sending Slidell as a regular minister, not a special commissioner. Finally, although the Mexicans had labeled Polk's former secret agent in Mexico, William Parrott, as obnoxious and objectionable, Polk insisted on designating Parrott as secretary of the legation in Mexico. In short, because it was highly improbable that the Mexican government would agree to Polk's unreasonable demands, the failure of Slidell's mission was virtually assured even before the American diplomat left the United States in 1845. That Polk himself anticipated the inevitable failure of the Slidell mission was evinced by his orders to General Taylor to advance American troops to the left bank of the Rio Grande in January 1846, almost three months before news of Slidell's final failure reached Washington. Thus, long before diplomatic channels were exhausted, President Polk had moved to ensure hostilities on the Rio Grande.

A peculiar feature of the president's message was his request that Congress not declare war, but rather recognize that war already existed. Yet neither nation had declared war on the other, and the minor hostilities which had transpired on the Rio Grande did not automatically constitute a state of war any more than the Chesapeake Affair in 1807 had placed the United States and Great Britain at war. Finally, the motives of the intensely partisan president were suspect. Polk had not asked for the power to repel the "invasion," but for the authority to prosecute a war which did not yet exist to a "speedy and successful termination." Once embodied in the war bill, this phrase empowered the president, with the full blessing of Congress, to wage the conflict for whatever ends he deemed advisable. He was in no way restricted merely to resolving the border dispute or to ensuring that Mexico would pay her outstanding claims.[11]

The disciplined Democratic majority in the House responded with alacrity and high-handed efficiency to Polk's May 11 war recommendations. First, the voluminous official documents, which accompanied the war message and purportedly sustained the call for war, were tabled over the strenuous objections of the incredulous Whig opposition. By this maneuver, doubting opponents of the president were prevented from examining the weak factual basis of Polk's recommendations before they were acted on by the House. Next the House proceeded immediately to consideration of a bill providing volunteers and appropriations to meet the crisis on the Rio Grande. Once the bill was read, debate was quickly limited to two hours, more than three-fourths of which was spent reading selected portions of the accompanying documents. This time-consuming procedure completed, Democrat Linn Boyd of Kentucky, acting for the administration forces, proposed a crucial amendment to the bill under consideration which not only provided for 50,000 volunteers and $10 million, but asked also for recognition of the existence of a state of war to eliminate the need for a formal declaration. The Boyd amendment empowered the administration to prosecute the existing war to a "speedy and successful termination," and wrote the president's version of the existing situation into the enabling bill by declaring in a brief preamble that war existed "by act of the Republic of Mexico."[12]

Thus the Democratic leadership determined to use the crisis on the Rio Grande to force Whig support of a war with Mexico, by fusing Polk's partisan objectives with national patriotism. By insisting on writing a formal recognition of war and Polk's version of the entire emergency into the bill for men and supplies to relieve Taylor's army on the Rio Grande, the Democrats purposely offered the opposition a harsh decision. If the Whigs and doubting Democrats chose to affirm their patriotism by voting volunteers and funds to meet the emergency, they would simultaneously endorse what they believed to be questionable claims by the president that war already existed and false contentions that the rightful border of Texas was the Rio Grande and that therefore Mexico was responsible for the war. Yet by voting against the war bill and refuting the assertions of the president, the opposition would be denying support to an embattled American army in the field and exposing themselves

11. Richardson, *Messages of the Presidents*, 4: 443.
12. *Congressional Globe*, 29th Congress, 1st Session, 1846, 792.

to the politically fatal charge of disloyalty. The war bill shrewdly denied the opposition the option it desperately sought: the chance to reject the manifest falsehoods of the president's message and to vote reinforcements for General Taylor's tiny army.

Confronted by this dilemma, an angry Whig opposition, with the support of several southern Calhounite Democrats, struggled frantically to evade the entire issue. Although bitterly opposed to the Boyd amendment and war with Mexico, Whig and Democratic opponents were eager to vote reinforcements. Accordingly, a series of hurried motions sprang from House Whigs. Their object was to provide reinforcements but restrict their use by the president, as well as to rephrase or delete the Boyd amendment with its objectionable preamble. For example, Ohio Whig Robert Schenck moved that the bill provide supplies and authorize the president to "relieve and extricate" the army from its perilous position, as well as "to prevent any invasion" of American territory, but declare that Congress would "not sanction or approve forcible occupation, under the order of the President . . . of territory between the rivers Nueces and Del Norte, by the armed forces of the United States. . . ."[13] However, this and other Whig amendments proved futile when the House accepted the controversial Boyd amendment by a partisan 123 to 67 margin. Of the dissidents, fifty-three were Whigs and most of the others were Calhounite Democrats from South Carolina and Virginia.

Pitted against a high-handed Democratic majority, the Whig and Democratic dissidents were helpless, their amendments marked for failure, their pleas to speak unrecognized by the Democratic Speaker of the House. Finally, Whig Garrett Davis from Henry Clay's home district in Kentucky was permitted to explain his request that he be excused from voting on the bill. Briefly but forcefully expressing sentiments held by most Whigs in the House at that moment, Davis decried the intemperate haste of the House proceedings. "Not a single moment" had been allowed to any Whig to say one word on this momentous question of war. Furthermore, Davis labeled the president's war message a falsehood and charged that it was not the Mexicans, but "our own President who began this war. He had been carrying it on for months." Davis affirmed his loyalty and emphasized his willingness to vote reinforcements "with hearty alacrity," but urged that once the enemy had been chastised, the American army should be withdrawn from the disputed area and the border question with Mexico should be settled on "the most liberal terms." After concluding his remarks, which had been frequently interrupted by hostile Democrats, Davis withdrew his request to be excused from voting, indicating his intention to vote reluctantly for the war bill.[14]

---

13. Ibid., 792–93.
14. Ibid., 794–95.

After Davis' protest and a similar one by Democrat Thomas Bayly of Virginia, the final vote was taken with the outcome never in doubt. The margin was 174 to 14 with numerous abstentions. All of the negative votes were cast by so-called antislavery Whigs who were known for their radicalism. For the Whigs and Calhounite Democrats it was a cruel decision. Robert Winthrop, a leading Massachusetts Whig, later wrote that the measure "presented the most difficult case for an honest man to give a satisfactory vote upon, which I have ever met with."[15] In fact, as presented, amended, and rushed to a final vote, the administration's war bill purposely offered the opposition no real choice. As sensitive politicians, most administration critics could not vote their consciences at the expense of their patriotism. Because they understood that national public opinion would be outraged and demand retribution for the attack on the Rio Grande, the opposition dared not risk charges of failing to support an endangered American army. That fear of being labeled disloyal was the foremost consideration in the minds of dissidents is indicated by the reality of the military situation on the Rio Grande. As several speakers pointed out, whatever Congress decided on May 11, volunteers could not reach General Taylor's army for several weeks.

A related consideration in the vote of some conservative Whigs was the radical political complexion of the fourteen Whigs who voted against the war bill. Representative Winthrop later explained that one reason he had voted for the war bill was that he did not want the entire Massachusetts congressional delegation to be "mixed up with a little knot of ultraists against supplies. . . ."[16] A number of conservative Whigs shared Winthrop's apprehensions and sought to avoid both the stigma of disloyalty and the taint of antislavery extremism. Motivated by their antislavery principles and their conviction that the war with Mexico was conceived and intended as a plot of the Slave Power to extend the strength and influence of slavery, the radical Whigs boldly disregarded the threat of appearing disloyal to register their protest against the blatant falsehoods of the war bill. Soon commonly referred to as the "immortal fourteen" or simply "the fourteen," the antislavery radicals were frequently compared to the Federalists who had infamously opposed the War of 1812. Throughout the war, Democratic editors and politicians bitterly attacked the fourteen as being unpatriotic, even treasonous, and sometimes referred to them as "Federalists." With the exception of aged John Quincy Adams and fervid Joshua Giddings of Ohio, these men were little known Whigs who represented antislave districts spread across the states of Maine, Massachusetts, Rhode Island, New York, Pennsylvania, and Ohio. Although they acted on firm con-

---

15. Robert Winthrop to Edward Everett, 7 June 1846, Edward Everett Papers, Massachusetts Historical Society, Boston, Massachusetts.
16. Ibid.

victions, the stand of the fourteen was likely to be well received in their home districts where opposition to the war was interpreted as a bold slap at the territorial ambitions of the Slave Power.

Action on the war bill in the Senate closely paralleled that in the House. Here the Whigs and Democrat John Calhoun attempted to delay temporarily action on the measure to allow for its careful consideration. After the bill was introduced on the afternoon of May 11, Calhoun quickly asked that there be "no haste" on a subject of such "grave importance" and urged the Senate to give the question "that high, full, and dispassionate consideration which is worthy the character of the body and the high constitutional functions which it is called on to exercise."[17] Several Whigs sustained Calhoun's sentiments and warned against intemperate haste on such a momentous issue. Like their counterparts in the House, Senate opponents were prepared to vote men and supplies to meet the emergency, but opposed to a precipitous recognition of war.

Late Monday afternoon, the opposition won a brief victory on a motion by Senator Benton of Missouri. Like Calhoun and the Whigs, Benton was at this time prepared to vote reinforcements, but he firmly objected to waging full-scale war against Mexico. Earlier he had denounced the president's aggressive Mexican policy and told Polk that he did not believe that American territory extended beyond the Nueces River. Resisting immediate action, Benton moved that the war bill be referred to committee; those portions dealing with military affairs would be examined by Benton's own Military Affairs Committee, while the sections treating foreign relations would be submitted to the Foreign Affairs Committee, whose chairman was Democrat William Allen of Ohio. When the motion carried, the dissidents gained a short-lived reprieve, but after a series of high-pressure interviews with administration advisors, Benton was persuaded to acquiesce reluctantly in the recommendations of the administration. On the following morning, May 12, his committee met, quickly approved the war bill, and dispatched it to the Senate by the time that body had convened for the day. The Committee on Foreign Affairs acted with similar alacrity. When the Senate reconvened on Tuesday, May 12, the opposition was surprised to learn that the bill was ready for immediate consideration. Calhoun and the Whigs had expected at least a forty-eight hour delay.

Now faced with the same dilemma their colleagues in the House had confronted the previous day, opponents of the administration struggled to separate the question of recognizing war from that of providing supplies by rewording the bill or deleting the preamble. The goal was to alter the bill so that opponents might vote reinforcements without endorsing the president's false claims. But each effort of the opposition was defeated. Several motions to

---

17. *Cong. Globe,* 29th Cong., 1st Sess., 1846, 783, 784.

postpone consideration of the bill were rejected. A motion by Kentucky Whig John Crittenden to restrict the reinforcements to the repelling of the apparent invasion was voted down 26 to 20. By a margin of 28 to 18, the Senate refused to delete the preamble from the bill. On each of these roll calls, party lines remained nearly firm. Only Calhoun left the Democrats to vote with the Whigs, while Whigs Henry Johnson of Louisiana, Reverdy Johnson of Maryland, and Spencer Jarnagin of Tennessee deserted their party to vote with the majority on several of the motions.[18]

Unlike the House, the Senate allowed limited debate and several critics of the administration voiced their strenuous objections to the virtually unamended House version of the war bill. Condemning the preamble to the bill, Calhoun and the Whigs denied that the Rio Grande was the border of Texas and charged that the war had been provoked by President Polk's order for General Taylor to advance to the Rio Grande. Senator John M. Clayton of Delaware contended that the advance of troops to a position within view of the Mexican town of Matamoros was "as much an act of aggression on our part as is a man's pointing a pistol at another's breast."[19] Speaking with great emotion, Calhoun declared that he would vote supplies "without an hour's delay," but it was as impossible for him "to vote that preamble as it was for him to plunge a dagger into his own heart, and more so."[20]

Despite these and other pleas for deliberation and reason, the determined administration forces refused to yield and pushed the measure to its passage by an almost unanimous 40 to 2 margin. Only John Davis of Massachusetts and Thomas Clayton of Delaware had the courage to register "nays." Before the vote, Whig Willie Mangum of North Carolina rose, asked to register his protest against the measure in the official proceedings, and then voted "aye." John Berrien of Georgia, George Evans of Maine, and Calhoun glumly abstained from voting, while Crittenden and William Upham of Vermont voted "ay, except the preamble."[21]

The president had his war and with it a harvest of partisan bitterness. Calhoun and his followers remained embittered and sullen, the Whigs furious. Already angered by the falsehoods of the war message and the preamble to the war bill, the Whigs were infuriated by the high-handed manner in which the proposal was rammed through Congress. In both Houses, supporters of the administration had arrogantly pressured, bullied, and silenced the opposition. With debate severely limited, time short, and vital documents inaccessi-

---

18. Ibid., 795–804, contains a report of the parliamentary maneuvering which preceded the vote.

19. Ibid., 786.

20. Ibid., 796.

21. Ibid., 804.

ble to them for examination, the opposition, already weak, found itself in an untenable position. It was by such tactics that Polk's claims and his call for war were superficially vindicated by the illusion of a united Congress.

Whig bitterness persisted in the weeks following passage of the war bill. In addition to the bill itself, supplementary legislation was required in order to organize and provide the volunteer forces with officers. Congress approved two such measures in June and early July. In each case, congressional action followed the general pattern established on May 11 and 12, although Congress did not move nearly so promptly as it had at that time. When finally brought to a vote on actual passage, these supplementary bills were passed without roll calls in the Senate and by overwhelming majorities in the House. However, in the maneuvering and debate which preceded the final vote, the Whigs assailed the president in partisan terms and attempted to restrict the authority necessarily granted to the commander in chief for the purpose of organizing volunteers. The volunteers were organized into battalion and regimental units on the state level, but once mustered into federal service, the volunteers came under federal control and were organized into brigades and divisions commanded by officers appointed by the president.[22]

The focal point of the Whig attack was the broad power of appointment granted to the chief executive in naming high-level officers at the brigade and division level. Fearing the partisan designs for which the Democratic president would certainly utilize his added appointive power, the Whigs in both the House and Senate vainly attempted to restrict Polk's authority. For example, in the Senate, John Crittenden of Kentucky proposed a far-reaching substitute amendment for a bill authorizing the organization of volunteers. The bill under consideration proposed to grant the president authority to organize the volunteers into brigades and divisions and "appoint such number of major generals and brigadier generals as the organization of such volunteer forces . . . may render necessary." But Crittenden's substitute moved that the appointive power be reserved largely for the individual states. Whenever the number of regiments was sufficient to form a brigade within a state, "a brigadier general . . . shall be appointed by the proper authority of the State to which they belong. . . ." The commander in chief was to be restricted to the appointment of two additional brigadier generals on an at-large basis. Although it was defeated by a 25 to 18 vote, Crittenden's amendment received the votes of all but three Whigs.[23]

The Senator from Kentucky emphasized that soldiers would "act better

---

22. See Sellers, *Polk*, 434–35, for a brief discussion of the organization of the volunteers.

23. *Cong. Globe*, 29th Cong., 1st Sess., 1846, 1026; see also the account of a similar Whig amendment in the House, ibid., 912.

and march prouder" under officers elected by themselves or commissioned by their own state governors rather than under strange officers forced upon them by federal authority. But Crittenden was less concerned with military efficiency than with party purpose. The Whigs feared that the appointment of military officers would be drawn into "the vortex of Executive patronage."[24] The ever-partisan Polk would surely attempt to strengthen his party by appointing loyal Democrats, who might or might not be competent military leaders. Events during the war justified Whig anxiety. For the most part, Polk, whenever he could, appointed Democrats to fill vacancies or new positions in the armed forces. As military experience was frequently not an important criterion, incompetence sometimes resulted. Among the brigadier generals to be named was Polk's old friend Gideon Pillow, who lacked military ability and proved to be disruptive and ineffective in the field.[25]

The partisanship which marked the early weeks of war debate set a pattern for the duration of the conflict. Angered by the events surrounding the outbreak of war, the Whigs intensified their partisan attack on the Democratic administration. While continuing to vote supplies, the Whigs directed a ceaseless barrage of invective at Polk, questioning, attacking, and ridiculing the president's every act. The same men who had opposed a recognition of war were soon denouncing the commander in chief's inadequate preparation for hostilities. Polk, they charged, had failed to provide General Taylor with sufficient reinforcements, had not prosecuted the war vigorously enough, and had lagged in his support of Generals Winfield Scott and Taylor. His organization of the volunteers, his appointment of officers, and his financing of the war came under severe censure. Whatever the issue, the target was the president. At the same time, Polk realized that the opposition, despite its vehemence, would be largely impotent. By having his version of the causes of war written into the war bill, Polk had placed the opposition in a frustrating position. Lacking the votes necessary to win official congressional rejection of the president's assertions, the politically sensitive Whig minority could only harry the administration with a barrage of verbiage while voting for every appropriation which the military campaigns required.

---

24. Ibid., 1016.

25. This evaluation of Pillow's competence as a military officer is based on Sellers, *Polk*, 437, and Justin Smith, *The War With Mexico*, 2 vols. (New York, 1919), 2: 185–86.

2

★ *Dissident Democrats and Angry Whigs*

THE COMING OF WAR provoked immediate objections from an aggregate of politicians having little else in common. Overwhelming and bipartisan as congressional approval of the war bill had been, Polk's Mexican policy, nevertheless, angered Democrats as well as Whigs. Staunch antislavery Van Buren Democrats, as well as proslavery Calhounites, objected to the war just as conservative and radical Whigs united in the chorus of dissent. But while their political views differed, so too did their reactions to the war. Confining their criticism to private channels, the Van Burenites sought a position which would allow them to weld public support with antislavery principle. Although his serious misgivings about the war remained, Calhoun saw no alternative to temporary support after his attempt to block the war bill had failed. The Whigs, meanwhile, were unrestrained, vocal, and partisan in their censure of the administration, but divided on antiwar strategy and the question of voting military supplies.

In fact, an important effect of the outbreak of war with Mexico was the increase of stress within each party. And existing factional differences continued to intensify during the conflict. Van Burenites and Calhounites might join temporarily to present a semblance of party unity, but this front was precarious. As the war progressed, Democratic unity dissolved under the related pressures of war, expansion, and slavery. A similar, though initially less serious, situation existed in the Whig party where divisions on these questions were exacerbated by the war. In May 1846 these party differences remained largely submerged, but the next two years would witness the rise of open splits among both Democrats and Whigs and would contribute to the formation of a new political party in 1848.

The initial bitterness of the Van Burenites was well expressed on May 15 by Senator John Dix of New York. Dix, who had dutifully supported Polk's call for war, confided to a fellow Van Burenite that he was "too sick of the miserable concern here. . . . It [the war] was begun in fraud last winter and I

20

think will end in disgrace. . . ."[1] The Van Burenites were particularly disturbed by the highly questionable circumstances surrounding the outbreak of hostilities. Dix explained to Van Buren that he had been "most reluctant" to vote for war because the crucial points in Polk's war message were simply "not sustained by the facts." Congress had been forced to vote "not merely on *confidence,* which is bad enough on great matters of public concern," continued Dix, "but on *faith,* which the Scripture tells us 'is the evidence of things unseen.' In short, I fear the . . . fraud is carried out to its consummation by a violation of every just consideration of national dignity, duty and policy."[2]

But the Van Burenites would have objected to war with Mexico even if Polk had been able to marshal a much stronger factual defense for his policy. Because of their antislavery convictions, their resentment of what they considered southern domination of the party, and their personal antagonism toward Polk himself, the Van Burenites had long opposed further expansion into the Southwest. These antislavery Democrats now opposed war with Mexico because they believed that such a war would probably result in the addition of more slave territory to the Union. The Van Burenites also feared the political consequences which such a war seemed to promise. As early as February 1845, Van Buren himself had cautioned the incoming Polk administration of the political dangers inherent in war with Mexico. Recognizing the pressure of rising antislavery sentiment at home and realizing that northern antislavery leaders would construe such a war, whether justifiably or not, as a conflict to extend slavery, Van Buren foresaw that many northern Democrats would then be placed in an untenable position. They must either desert their Democratic allies of the South and West on the war issue or commit "political suicide" by voting support for a southern war to extend slavery.[3]

This, of course, was precisely the position of the Van Burenites in May 1846. To resolve their dilemma, they attempted to chart a political course which would allow them to sustain the administration while not committing "political suicide" in their home states. The Van Burenites did not yet even contemplate the possibility of an open break with the administration, and for two main reasons. First, they wanted to remain loyal to the Democratic party be-

---

1. John A. Dix to Azariah Flagg, 15 May 1846, Azariah Flagg Papers, Manuscript Division, New York Public Library, New York.
2. Dix to Van Buren, 16 May 1846, Martin Van Buren Papers, Manuscript Division, Library of Congress, Washington, D.C. See also C. C. Cambreleng to Van Buren, 16 May 1846; H. D. Gilpin to Van Buren, 24 May 1846; J. R. Poinsett to Van Buren, 26 May 1846, all in Van Buren Papers; and Dix to Flagg, 6 June 1846, Flagg Papers.
3. Martin Van Buren to George Bancroft, 15 February 1845 in "Van Buren-Bancroft Correspondence, 1830–1845," ed. Worthington C. Ford, *Proceedings of the Massachusetts Historical Society* 42 (June 1909): 381–442; see esp. 439.

cause they expected to gain control of the party in 1848. Second, they initially hoped that the war might be ended promptly without the acquisition of any additional Mexican territory. Thus, in the early months of fighting, the Van Burenites asked assurances from President Polk that he sought no territory from Mexico. So long as there was no prospect of acquiring additional territory in the Southwest, the Van Burenites realized that they could fully support the war without endangering their political position at home. In response Polk was able to assuage their fears of territorial conquest temporarily by disclaiming any desire for Mexican territory.[4] However, the situation changed in August 1846 when Polk's objectives became undeniable and forced the Van Burenites to adopt a new strategy designed to preserve both their party loyalty and their political security.

In contrast to the reticence of the Van Burenites, John Calhoun charted an outspoken course in denouncing the war publicly. Now sixty-four years old and a veteran of national politics for thirty-five years, Calhoun cast a striking figure in the Senate. More than six feet tall, Calhoun's slender frame was distinguished by his square chin, unsmiling mouth, magnificent eyes, and thick graying hair. Noting his eaglelike appearance, such contemporary observers as Sarah M. Maury rarely failed to comment on his remarkable sunken eyes, "eyes so dazzling, black, and piercing that few can stand their gaze. . . . *I believe they give out light in the dark.*"[5] Although his health had begun to fail, Calhoun's mind remained as sharp and active as ever. Nor had age dulled either his egotism or his hunger for the presidency.

Calhoun's position on the war was a combination of conviction and calculation sustained by personal courage. Although he had been an active advocate of the annexation of Texas as President Tyler's Secretary of State in 1844 and 1845, Calhoun believed that war with Mexico was unnecessary, avoidable, and dangerous. A conservative on foreign policy, a constant defender of southern interests, and a staunch state's rights politician, he believed that war posed manifest evils. But closely allied to these apprehensions was Calhoun's continuing ambition for the presidency. At this time, the South Carolinian, who believed he had an excellent chance of winning the presidency in 1848, thought that his political position would be enhanced by his opposition to war with Mexico. Given these considerations of principle and political expediency, Calhoun willingly braved enthusiastic support for the war in the South and around the nation.

Beyond his antipathy to the idea of war with Mexico, Calhoun like other war critics was particularly upset by the events surrounding the outbreak of fighting. In early 1846, while national attention focused on the Oregon con-

---

4. See Chaplain Morrison, *Democratic Politics and Sectionalism; The Wilmot Proviso Controversy* (Chapel Hill, N.C., 1967), 15.

5. Sarah M. Maury, *The Statesmen of America in 1846* (Philadelphia, 1847), 181.

troversy, Calhoun clearly foresaw the increasing probability of armed conflict with Mexico. He warned in March that the administration's advance of American troops to the Rio Grande might well result in a war which a "moderate share of sagacity and firmness" could avert.[6] With the Oregon question still unresolved, Calhoun's chief fear was that war with Mexico would prevent a peaceful settlement of the Oregon issue and probably induce the British to intervene on behalf of Mexico. But Calhoun, despite his misgivings about Mexican policy, believed that his was a major role in any peaceful settlement of the Oregon dispute and, as such, it necessitated the maintenance of cordial relations with the White House. He later cited this as his reason for not publicizing his own apprehensions about Polk's Mexican policy.[7]

Once fighting commenced, Calhoun spearheaded opposition to the war bill in the Senate. His strategy was to separate the questions of military reinforcements and a declaration of war. He sought to limit the response of Congress to "repelling hostilities" while gaining precious time to deliberate carefully "on the propriety of a formal declaration of war."[8] Unable to achieve his objectives, a sullen Calhoun sat quietly on May 12 as the vote was taken. Like other opponents of war, Calhoun charged that Congress had been plunged into war against its will by a reckless president. Had Congress voted solely on the wisdom of Polk's prewar diplomacy, particularly on the advisability of marching General Taylor to the Rio Grande, "there would have been not a tenth part of Congress in the affirmative, and yet we have been forced into a war." Furthermore, claimed Calhoun, if sufficient time had been allowed to examine and discuss "the question of war deliberately . . . the vote would have been two to one against it."[9]

Calhoun's strongest immediate objections to the war itself rested on constitutional grounds. "Hostilities" had occurred, he argued, but "war" did not and could not exist until formally declared by Congress. Admittedly, the Senate should vote reinforcements without delay, but it would only "make war on the Constitution by declaring war to exist . . . when no war had been declared, and nothing had occurred but a slight military conflict between a portion of two armies."[10] In a letter of May 15, Calhoun extended his argument. The

6. Calhoun to Thomas G. Clemson, 23 March 1846, in *Correspondence of John C. Calhoun,* ed. J. Franklin Jameson, *Annual Report of the American Historical Association for the Year 1899,* vol. 2. (Washington, D.C., 1900), 2: 687. See also Calhoun to Clemson, 29 January 1846, ibid., 680–81.

7. Calhoun to Henry W. Conner, 15 May 1846, Henry W. Conner Papers, Manuscript Division, Library of Congress, Washington, D.C. See also Calhoun to A. P. Calhoun, 14 May 1846, and Calhoun to J. E. Calhoun, 29 May 1846, *Calhoun Correspondence,* 2: 690, 693.

8. Calhoun to J. E. Calhoun, 29 May 1846, ibid., 693–94.

9. Calhoun to Conner, 15 May 1846, Conner Papers.

10. *Cong. Globe,* 29th Cong., 1st Sess., 1846, 796–97.

passage of the war bill, he wrote, had done "great mischief" by divesting Congress of its war-making power and transferring that authority to the president and "even to commanders on the frontier." Here the South Carolinian was exposing a critical weakness in the system of checks and balances devised by the founding fathers. The president had dramatically demonstrated his almost unrestrained power, independent of Congress, to involve the nation in war. American troops had been maneuvered into a position along the Rio Grande which virtually guaranteed a Mexican reprisal; once the shots had been fired, Congress had no real choice but to follow the president into war. Calhoun clearly understood the importance of this precedent and accurately predicted its future consequences: "It sets the example, which will enable all future Presidents to bring about a state of things, in which Congress shall be forced, without deliberation, or reflection, to declare war, however opposed to its convictions of justice or expediency."[11]

Once war had been formally recognized, a reluctant Calhoun voted support for the military effort because he believed that troops committed to battle had to be sustained. And seeing no immediate alternative to support for administration policy, he temporarily refrained from public criticism. He continued, however, to register privately his dismay over the war and to delineate criticisms he would repeat frequently in coming months. He also vowed to hold "those responsible, who have forced the country into its present disreputable & dangerous condition."[12] Calhoun's most immediate concern was that unless the war was "speedily" terminated, it might well lead "to the interference of the Great European Powers." Although peace did not come quickly, this apprehension proved groundless. But with prolonged fighting went other serious consequences. By late July, despite the fact that Congress had reduced the tariff and was about to enact an independent treasury proposal, Calhoun feared the reversal of "thorough reform" and the derangement of the nation's domestic affairs. Admittedly, the war would "afford an opportunity for the display of patriotism and valour," but overwhelming this positive effect would be the exposure of the nation's "financial weakness," the creation of a huge public debt, the acceleration of government centralization, and the strengthening of "the Spoils principle." Furthermore the exorbitant expense of war would provide a ready pretext for protectionists to renew their agitation for high import duties.[13]

Understandably, Calhoun's desertion of the administration in May over the outbreak of war brought an expected outcry of denunciation from loyal Democrats around the nation. Nor was his stance popular in the South where news of the war was enthusiastically received. Although Calhoun received let-

---

11. Calhoun to Conner, 15 May 1846, Conner Papers.
12. Ibid.
13. Calhoun to A. P. Calhoun, 14 May 1846, *Calhoun Correspondence*, 2: 691, 702–3.

ters applauding his independent course and several Democratic papers such as the *Charleston Mercury* commended him, his war dissent and desertion of the party were sharply criticized throughout the region.[14] Near his home in Edgefield, Calhoun was publicly harangued by speakers rallying support for the war.

But Calhoun was not troubled by this adverse reaction. In addition to being convinced that his course was wise, the self-assured Senator discounted the sources from which the denunciation sprang, claiming that his posture had been weakened only "with the party and the unthinking portion of the Community. . . ."[15] Although partisan bitterness might not be easily assuaged, Calhoun believed that time and events would convert public opinion, that eventually thoughtful people around the nation would recognize the wisdom of his stance. At this time, public opinion was important to Calhoun because of his presidential aspirations. Most probably the Democratic nomination was out of reach. But the Calhoun presidential strategy was to arouse southern support and present Calhoun as a candidate of the "people" and the "Constitution" in opposition to the party nominees of the national conventions. His supporters realized that he could not expect to receive a popular majority, but the election might be deadlocked and thrown into the House of Representatives where the coveted office could be won through a coalition of Calhoun's numerous conservative Whig and Democratic friends.[16]

By the summer of 1846, Calhoun viewed his future with optimism. In July he wrote that the time had come for a "recast of the parties better suited to the exigencies of the times. We want a real honest conservative party based on broad constitutional grounds, and looking to the permanent prosperity of the country."[17] Calhoun believed that, as a national figure, he had gained stature by his independent stand on the Oregon question when he had labored diligently for a peaceful resolution of the crisis in the face of expected war with England. After a peaceful accord had been reached, Calhoun's course was praised by friends of peace throughout the nation. Viewing his opposition to the Mexican War in a similar light, the Senator minimized the effect that "mere partisans" would have on his image.[18]

An important reason for Calhoun's sanguine attitude in the face of wide-

---

14. *Charleston Mercury*, 19 May 1846; see also J. Abney to Burt, 25 July 1846 in the Armistead Burt Papers, William R. Perkins Library, Duke University, Durham, N.C.

15. Calhoun to J. E. Calhoun, 29 May 1846, *Calhoun Correspondence*, 2: 694.

16. Calhoun's presidential ambitions from 1844 to 1848 have beeen traced in Joseph Rayback, "The Presidential Ambitions of John.C. Calhoun, 1844–1848," *Journal of Southern History* 14 (August 1948): 331–56.

17. Calhoun to Henry A. S. Dearborn, 2 July 1846, *Calhoun Correspondence*, 2:700.

18. Calhoun to Mrs. Thomas G. Clemson, 11 June 1846, ibid., 695. See also Calhoun to J. E. Calhoun, 29 May 1846, ibid., 694; and Calhoun to J. E. Calhoun, 2 July 1846, ibid., 698.

spread Democratic recrimination was the praise he had received from southern Whigs. Whig editors in the South praised his courage and patriotism, while Whig politicians commended his candor. Georgia Whig Representative Alexander H. Stephens, who had abstained from voting on the war bill during the final roll call in the House, wrote that he was "beginning to think better" of Calhoun: "my admiration increases from the fact that he acted in the Senate . . . just as I did in the House,—that is, he refused to vote upon the question as it was presented; and in his speech also he said just what I should have said, in substance, if I could have had a chance."[19]

Whig praise of Calhoun rested on their agreement on the coming of war; they concurred that it was an unnecessary, unjust, and potentially disastrous conflict attributable to President Polk. But their respective responses differed. While Calhoun assumed a position of calculated public silence, after war was recognized, the Whigs sounded an insistent and vocal dissent. Whig opposition to war fit well into the context of their partisanship and political principles during the 1840s. First, the Whigs had been critical of Polk's Democratic administration from the outset. In addition, Whig hostility was intensified by Polk's own intense partisanship, by his secretive manner, and by his proposed domestic and foreign policies. Specifically they objected to the recommended tariff reduction, to the proposed reenactment of the independent treasury, and to the administration's aggressive, war-prone foreign policy. Polk's handling of the annexation of Texas and his apparent determination to have all of Oregon frightened Whigs by threatening war with both Mexico and England. The Whig antiwar position, then, was a natural result of their consistent opposition to the tone and substance of Polk diplomacy.

In assessing the causes of war, slave and free state Whigs disagreed on the importance of Texas as a basic issue. Southern Whigs a few of whom eventually supported annexation, minimized its role as a cause of war, while northern Whigs, always staunch opponents of annexation, tended to emphasize the significance of the Texas question. For example, Representative Stephens of Georgia maintained that the April 25 hostilities were not a "necessary result" of annexation, but Senator Thomas Corwin of Ohio traced the origin of war directly to the Texas question: "we are at this moment perpetrating enormous wrong upon a weak and a to us unoffending people, we have robbed her [of Texas], and now kill to secure our plunder."[20] But whatever

---

19. Alexander Stephens to Linton Stephens, 13 May 1846, Stephens Papers, Manhattanville College of the Sacred Heart, Purchase, New York (microfilm copy in Alderman Library, University of Virginia). For an example of press praise of Calhoun, see the *Richmond Whig* (Virginia), 15 May, 22 May 1846.

20. *Cong. Globe*, 29th Cong., 1st Sess., 1846, Appendix, 946; Thomas Corwin to William Greene, 16 June 1846, in "Selections from the William Greene Papers, I," ed. Belle L. Hamlin, *Quarterly Publication of the Historical and Philosophical Society of Ohio* 13 (1918): 3–38; see esp. 16.

their views of annexation as a cause of war, Whigs of all sections quickly moved beyond the Texas issue and placed full blame for the war on President Polk. Stephens averred that the conflict was "justly chargeable upon Mr. Polk," while Corwin agreed that the "President began this war."[21]

Denied an opportunity to express their dissent on May 11 and 12, the embittered Whigs directed a scathing political assault at Polk in the weeks following passage of the war bill. The Whigs emphasized arguments which they would reiterate constantly in focusing immediately on the causes and responsibility of war and on the alleged usurpations of the president. A succession of Whig speakers denied that the Rio Grande was the true border and charged that the president's order for American troops to advance to its banks represented the first real act of war.

After tracing recent United States–Mexican relations, Stephens concluded that "the whole affair is properly chargeable to the imprudence, indiscretion, and mismanagement of our own Executive." Polk had "literally provoked" an unnecessary war which "could have been easily avoided without any detriment to our rights, interest, or honor as a nation."[22] Kentucky Representative Garrett Davis indicted the chief executive for violating his constitutional authority: "I charge and arraign James K. Polk with having, as President of the United States, during the present session, usurped the power of Congress by making war upon Mexico, a nation with whom the United States were at peace."[23]

At the same time, the Whigs followed the pattern they had set on the war bill by emphatically affirming their loyalty and support for the military effort. For example, Stephens declared that "all hands to the rescue would be my motto. . . . now the fires of war are raging on our frontier, all good citizens should render their willing aid, as I most cheerfully do. . . ."[24] Davis opened and concluded his attack on the president with similar professions. "I heartily echo the sentiment . . . that in this war with Mexico, 'The star-spangled banner in triumph may wave.' I am for bringing this war to a speedy, and, on our part, triumphant close by engaging in it, if needful, with the whole power of the country, and by fighting Mexico on her territory and on ours, by land and by sea."[25]

Amidst their initial denunciations of the president and their eager professions of patriotism, few Whigs bothered to scrutinize the administration's likely war goals. An exception to this oversight was thirty-four-year-old Al-

21. Stephens to Linton Stephens, 13 May 1846, Stephens Papers; Corwin to Greene, 16 June 1846, "Greene Papers, I," 16.

22. *Cong. Globe,* 29th Cong., 1st Sess., 1846, Appendix, 946.

23. Ibid., 916.

24. Ibid., 949.

25. Ibid., 916.

exander Stephens, then in his second term in Congress. A "little slim, pale-faced, consumptive man" with a shrill high-pitched voice, the physically un-impressive Stephens was nevertheless a rising young Whig leader and an elo-quent speaker.[26] In the house on June 16, he carefully examined the causes of the war before concentrating on what seemed to him the probable territorial objectives of the war. Denying that he was an "enemy to the extension of our domain," Stephens forcefully denounced the very idea of an American war of conquest. His idea of American destiny embraced a gradual, orderly, and peaceful expansion rather than the greedy, thoughtless, headlong rush to the Pacific advocated by rabid expansionists. He welcomed the day "when the whole continent will be ours, when our institutions shall be diffused and cher-ished, and republican government felt and enjoyed throughout . . . from the far south to the extreme north, and from ocean to ocean." But this "destiny" must be achieved, not by the sword, but by voluntary accession: "Fields of blood and carnage may make men brave and heroic, but seldom tend to make nations either good, virtuous, or great." Aggressive expansionism promised only to undermine the virtue of the republic through a kind of *"downward progress. It is a progress of party—of excitement—of lust of power—a spirit of war—aggression—violence and licentiousness. It is a progress which, if indulged in, would soon sweep over all law, all order, and the Constitution itself."*[27] Isolated as they might have been in June 1846, Stephens' arguments would subsequently be expanded, modified, and constantly reiterated by other Whigs throughout the war.

A more urgent concern to numerous Whigs than the yet remote question of Polk's war objectives was the immediate danger that war with Mexico would result in European intervention and threaten the pending Oregon set-tlement. Like Democratic Senator Calhoun, Whigs Willie Mangum, Webster, Clay, Stephens, and others expressed this fear.[28] "The dogs of war are now let loose, and I should not be surprised if a general war with England and France should ensue," confided Stephens to his brother. "The gates of Janus are open, and I fear they will be as the gates of hell."[29] To prevent this prospect, several leading senators supported John Crittenden's suggestion that a nonpar-tisan peace commission, composed of such prominent individuals as Clay,

---

26. Abraham Lincoln to William Herndon, 2 February 1848, in *The Collected Works of Abraham Lincoln,* ed. Roy P. Basler, 10 vols. (New Brunswick, N.J., 1953), 1: 448.

27. *Cong. Globe,* 29th Cong., 1st Sess., 1846, Appendix, 949–50.

28. See for example, Mangum to Charity A. Mangum, 11 May 1846, in *The Papers of Willie P. Mangum,* ed. Henry T. Shanks, 5 vols. (Raleigh, N.C., 1950), 4: 435; Web-ster to P. Harvey, c. 17 May 1846, in *The Writings and Speeches of Daniel Webster,* ed. Fletcher Webster, 18 vols. (Boston, 1903), 16: 453; Webster to Franklin Haven, 28 May 1846, ibid., 454–55; Clay to John J. Crittenden, 1 June 1846, Crittenden Papers, Wil-liam R. Perkins Library, Duke University, Durham, N.C.

29. Stephens to Linton Stephens, 13 May 1846, Stephens Papers.

Benton, and Calhoun, be dispatched promptly to Mexico to negotiate a "liberal, generous & magnanimous" treaty providing a "solid & enduring" foundation for lasting peace.[30] But the president, more concerned with his continental objectives than with an immediate end to the fighting, never entertained this proposal seriously.

The large majority of the Whig party, then, denounced the war as a blunder of the Polk administration while voting to support the conflict. During the early months of fighting, most Whigs contented themselves with a relentless verbal assault on the war and the president's responsibility for it but simultaneously granted the chief executive everything he needed to prosecute the conflict. Seeking a prompt and just settlement, the Whigs vowed to "hold the guilty authors to a strict account" for the outcome.[31] An important determinant of this divided Whig response was the lingering memory of the last war with England. During the War of 1812, a hostile Federalist minority had refused to support the war effort, a course which brought great discredit to the Federalists at the end of the conflict when news of the peace treaty and the American victory at New Orleans reached the eastern United States only weeks after the Hartford Convention had met. The Federalists, already a moribund minority by 1815, never freed themselves from the stigma of their dissent and soon disintegrated as an effective national political party. The Whigs, reluctant to repeat history, intended to discredit the Democratic administration for the war, while reaffirming their patriotism.

But a small minority of radical northern Whigs adopted a bolder and more direct strategy of dissent. These were the fourteen antislavery Whigs who had voted against the war bill in the House.[32] Unlike the politically oriented opposition of their conservative Whig colleagues, the dissent of the radical Whigs reflected their emphatic moral convictions and firm antislavery principles.[33] Because of their antislavery convictions and hatred of the southern-dominated Polk administration, the radical Whigs viewed the war as an immoral act perpetrated by the Slave Power to expand its political influence and peculiar institution. Most prominent of this Whig group was John

---

30. Mangum to Gales and Seaton, 29 June 1846, *Papers of Mangum,* 4: 453–54.

31. Corwin to Greene, 16 June 1846, "Greene Papers, I," 16; for a concise summary of the Whig position, see Webster to Fletcher Webster, 20 May, 1846, *Writings of Webster,* 16: 450.

32. In adddition to Adams and Giddings, the other House Whigs who voted against the war bill were George Ashmun, Joseph Grinnel, Charles Hudson, and D. P. King of Massachusetts; Henry Cranston of Rhode Island; Erastus Culver of New York; John Strohm of Pennsylvania; Luther Severance of Maine; and Columbus Delano, Joseph Root, David Tilden, and Joseph Vance of Ohio.

33. The radicals were known by several labels including "ultras," "Conscience" Whigs, and "Young Whigs." By 1847, they frequently referred to themselves as the "Young Whigs."

Quincy Adams, but because he was nearly seventy-nine years old and much less active than in previous years, the effective leader and spokesman of the radical Whigs was Joshua R. Giddings from Ohio. A large impressive man with a powerful personality, Giddings was a political abolitionist who well reflected the sentiments of his district in Ohio's Western Reserve. He was a politician of strong moral convictions and an individual of great courage. Since his entry into Congress in 1838, he had labored incessantly against what he believed to be the designs of the sinister Slave Power. A slashing speaker who loved to create tension and turmoil in Congress, Giddings had been un-yielding in his attacks on the "gag" rule, the slave trade, slavery in the District of Columbia, the annexation of Texas, and, now, the Mexican War. Com-bined with the Ohio firebrand's hatred of slavery and the Slave Power was his disgust at the moral cowardice and political subservience of timid northern politicians to the interests of the slave states at the expense of northern rights. "It is the curse of our Country and of our party that northern men are too Craven hearted to maintain their own rights," wrote Giddings upon receiving word of hostilities on the Rio Grande.[34]

The day after his futile vote against the war bill, and even before it be-came law, Giddings anticipated the imminent charges of treason and replied immediately. Undoubtedly Giddings, who had dauntlessly faced political ad-versity. physical threats, and even House censure in previous years, relished the moment as he worked himself into a "free perspiration" with a slashing indictment of the impending war.[35] Speaking as the leader of the antislavery radicals and expressing their sentiments well, Giddings depicted the present crisis as "one scene in the drama now being enacted by this Administration." The purpose was "to render slavery secure in Texas" while extending the slave domain. To this end, the president, *"for the purpose and with the full intention of bringing on a war with Mexico without consulting Congress,"* had ordered American troops across the Nueces into Mexican territory. To Giddings, Polk's war objective was clear; the "game" was to be played for the *"conquest of Mexico and California. . . ."*[36]

Like other war critics, Giddings claimed that the Nueces River, not the Rio Grande, was the legitimate border of Texas. The president's conflicting assertion was ridiculous. If the Rio Grande were the true border, then the town of Santa Fe, located to the east of the river near its headwaters, must by definition belong to Texas. But such an assertion was, of course, absurd since Santa Fe was the capital of the Mexican province of New Mexico. For Polk to

---

34. Giddings to Miss L. W. Giddings, 10 May 1846, Giddings Papers, Ohio Histori-cal Society, Columbus (microfilm).

35. Giddings to J. A. Giddings, 12 May 1846, Giddings Papers.

36. *Cong. Globe,* 29th Cong., 1st Sess., Appendix, 643, 642.

claim the Rio Grande was as preposterous as Mexico's claiming "Hudson's River" as her border and all territory to the south and west as her rightful possession.[37]

Giddings believed a quick peace treaty impossible and predicted grave consequences from an extended war of conquest. Beyond the needless loss of thousands of lives and the squandering of millions of dollars, thousands of new government offices would be created and filled at the president's partisan discretion with "fawning sycophants" eager to "fatten" on the very "lifeblood of the nation." But however great the tangible cost of war, Giddings was more concerned by the far-reaching moral effect which a "war of aggression and conquest" against a weak sister republic would have on the United States. "The virtue of our better days will yield and gradually disappear before the flood of vice and immorality now ready to rush in upon us."[38]

Condemning the chauvinistic maxim, "our country right or wrong," Giddings presented a definition of patriotic duty which contrasted sharply with that of conservative Whigs. He denied that a war once commenced had to be sustained. In "an aggressive, unholy, and unjust war," the true patriot must refuse to support his nation. Because justice remained "as unchangeable as its Author," those who acquiesced only shared the guilt of the crime. "In the murder of Mexicans upon their own soil, or in robbing them of their country," asserted Giddings, "I can take no part either now or hereafter. The guilt of these crimes must rest on others—I will not participate in them. . . ."[39]

These inflammatory remarks, preoccupied as they were with the slavery question and the immorality of the war, clearly manifested the views of the radical Whigs in Congress. Giddings himself was especially pleased with his effort. He had taken "vengeance on the whole slave holding crew" and happily reported that the speech was "perhaps . . . the most important one I ever made."[40] Emboldened by Giddings' harangue and angered by aspersions on their loyalty, other men who had voted against the war bill soon spoke out whenever they had the opportunity. Joseph Root and Columbus Delano of Ohio, Luther Severance of Maine, Charles Hudson and George Ashmun of Massachusetts, and Erastus Culver of New York assailed the president and justified their dissent. Like Giddings, these Whigs castigated the president's message, condemned the "false and snivelling preamble" to the war bill, and deplored the "precipitancy and rashness" with which the measure was passed.[41]

---

37. Ibid., 641.

38. Ibid., 643.

39. Ibid., 644.

40. Giddings to J. A. Giddings, 12 May 1846; Giddings to Wife, 17 May 1846, Giddings Papers.

41. *Cong. Globe,* 29th Cong., 2nd Sess., Appendix, 25 (speech was presented 13 May 1846); *Cong. Globe,* 29th Cong., 1st Sess., Appendix, 912.

On the purposes of the war, none of these men was so explicit as Giddings, but all agreed that it was to be a war of "plunder" and "conquest" waged to secure and extend the influence of the Slave Power.

But the most urgent consideration of these antislavery Whigs was the issue of patriotic responsibility in time of war. Like Giddings, they condemned blind allegiance to one's country, refused to sustain the country in its criminal course, and denied charges that they were apostates who could best be compared to the Federalists in the War of 1812.[42] These retorts established a precedent for their dissent for the duration of the war. Whenever the radicals spoke in ensuing months, they felt compelled to defend their loyalty and refute the incessant charges of their Democratic opponents.

Thus, while both the conservative and radical wings of the Whig party denounced the Mexican War in the months after its outbreak, their criticisms of the war contrasted sharply; conservative Whig opposition was politically oriented while the radicals scorned pure partisanship in their moral outrage. Conservative Whigs could vote to support a war already begun, but their radical Whig counterparts did not concur. While conservatives like Alexander Stephens of Georgia and Daniel Webster of Massachusetts argued that even an unjust war once begun had to be sustained to preserve the national honor, Joshua Giddings and his radical followers refused to implicate themselves in what they considered to be a national crime.

---

42. For these speeches, see *Cong. Globe,* 29th Cong., 1st Sess., 1846, 813, 814–15, 879; ibid., Appendix, 683–87, 763–67, 912–16, 934–35, 952–56.

3

★ *The Nation Responds and Reacts*

As NEWS OF WAR SPREAD across the nation, genuine enthusiasm quickly developed. Large prowar rallies in New York, Baltimore,
Indianapolis, Philadelphia, and dozens of other communities demonstrated
overwhelming support for the president's call to arms. "Mexico or Death"
and "Ho, for the 'Halls of Montezumas'!" became common cries as thousands rushed to answer recruiters' calls. "A military ardor pervades all
ranks," observed Herman Melville from Lansingburgh, New York, as he
described the "delirium" of the moment. "Militia Colonels wax red in their
coat facings—and 'prentice boys are running off to the war by scores. —
Nothing is talked of but the 'Halls of Montezumas.' . . ."[1] Similar scenes
occurred in countless towns across the country. Within days dozens of volunteer companies organized and prepared to march. Men who hesitated were
often too late to join rapidly filled volunteer units. Most Americans readily
agreed with President Polk that Mexico had long provoked the forbearance
of the United States. The attack on American troops on April 25 was merely
the last straw, the final proof that Mexico had to be quickly and decisively
chastised. Politicians might quibble over the precise border of Texas, but
geographic abstractions were quickly lost in the surge of patriotic emotion
demanding defeat for the invader. "Yes," wrote Walt Whitman, "Mexico
must be thoroughly chastised!"[2] Geographically, the war spirit was intense
not only in the southwestern and northwestern states closest to the fighting,
but also along the middle and southern Atlantic seaboard. Even in Ohio,
a center of western abolitionism and opposition to the annexation of Texas,
2,400 men were organized into volunteer companies within a month.

---

1. H. Melville to G. Melville, 29 May 1846, in *The Letters of Herman Melville,* ed.
Merrell R. Davis and William G. Gilman (New Haven, Conn., 1960), 29.
2. Walt Whitman, *The Gathering of the Forces,* ed. Cleveland Rodgers and John
Black, 2 vols. (New York, 1920), 1:240.

The immediate popularity of the war in May 1846 well reflected the adventuresome and aggressive mood of the nation. "Our people are like a young man of 18," wrote John Calhoun from Washington, "full of health and vigour and disposed for adventure of any discription [*sic*], but without wisdom or experience to guide him. . . ."[3] Proud of the impressive growth of their young republic, cognizant of their boundless energy, and confident of their burgeoning strength, Americans in 1846 beheld the future with buoyant optimism. As the nation looked expectantly toward Oregon, California, and the Pacific Ocean, the doctrine of Manifest Destiny flourished. This national emotion combined pride, confidence, and the long-standing sense of national mission with the doctrine of territorial expansion. But since neither the limits of this growth nor the means by which it was to be achieved had been defined, Manifest Destiny symbolized a national mood rather than a precise program.[4] An important tenet of this expansionism was the idea of cultural regeneration, the belief that the United States had a providential mission to uplift and civilize lesser races in order to prepare them to enter the "Temple of Freedom" and to share participation in republican institutions. Such a concept applied particularly well to the Southwest where Mexico stood in the path of America's drive to the Pacific. By arguing that the United States must uplift the inferior Mexicans, expansionists provided a convenient justification for expansion into areas traditionally subject to Mexican dominion. In fact, avid expansionists like John L. O'Sullivan contended that America's mission represented a claim superior to the traditional claims of discovery, exploration, settlement, and contiguity. Given this rationale and its widespread acceptance, many Americans and expansionist politicians, like President Polk, were unconcerned with the moral implications of an aggressive policy that was blind to the claims of other nations which stood in its westward path.

But combined with this confidence and sense of mission was a feeling of anxiety and insecurity which inflamed American expansionism in the mid-1840s. Although clear, the nation's ultimate destiny was yet unrealized. Half of the continent remained unsettled and without firm national allegiance. At the same time, the vast regions of Oregon, New Mexico, and California remained under foreign control or subject to the rival claims of other powers. England and France cast envious eyes on California, which remained under

3. Calhoun to Clemson, 28 May 1846, in *Correspondence of John C. Calhoun,* ed. J. Franklin Jameson, *Annual Report of the American Historical Association for the Year 1899,* vol. 2 (Washington, D.C., 1900), 2:692.

4. The best descriptions and analyses of Manifest Destiny are found in Norman Graebner, *Empire on the Pacific* (New York, 1955); Norman Graebner, ed., *Manifest Destiny* (New York, 1968), xv–lxx; and Frederick Merk, *Manifest Destiny and Mission in American History* (New York, 1963). For a perceptive description of the national mood of the United States in 1846, see Bernard DeVoto, *The Year of Decision, 1846* (Boston, 1943), 5–17.

the tenuous control of Mexico. To the north, England claimed a large portion of the Pacific coastline above the border of California. In short, with other nations competing for regions which the United States eagerly coveted, an element of urgency had been added to the expansionism of the mid-1840s. Thus the young American republic, confident, aggressive, and eager to expand its borders, marched enthusiastically to the drums of war in May 1846.

Enthusiasm lagged only in the northeastern states. In New York, the business and financial communities lamented the outbreak of war and its expected consequences.[5] Commercial publications, like the New York *Journal of Commerce* and *Hunt's Merchants' Magazine,* feared the worst. The outbreak of war with Mexico might well be followed by news of war with England, a prospect with frightening consequences for the business community. A blockade of American ports might result, Mexican privateers would surely prey on American shipping, the American export trade would be seriously deranged, and the vital extension of credit from England would be discontinued. Internally, war promised to depress the economy by creating uncertainty and instability; the cost of money would rise while the price of stocks dropped. Thus, according to the business community, did war with Mexico threaten to shatter the prosperity of the mid-1840s, a view echoed in Congress by conservative Whigs.

The sharpest and most outspoken dissent, however, centered in New England. Here Whig politicians, editors, clergymen, and social reformers joined in diatribes against the Polk administration's war. In Massachusetts, Whig Governor George Briggs was bitterly denounced when he issued a call for volunteers. Throughout the region, antiwar activity was varied and intense. Speeches, editorials, poems, petitions, and resolutions against the war abounded. Not surprisingly, enlistment lagged. Although hundreds of New England's sons served, they were but a tiny portion of the enlisted thousands from other sections of the nation.

A number of factors converged to explain New England's sharp dissent. The region was geographically remote from the field of battle and in no way endangered by military developments in the Southwest. New England was also strong in antislavery sentiment, hostile to what New Englanders thought was the disproportionate southern influence in the federal government, and unreconciled to continued southern expansion. New Englanders had bitterly opposed the annexation of Texas as a scheme designed to increase the power of the slave states, and these sentiments were easily translated into opposition to the Mexican War. Immediately, the war was interpreted as merely an extension of the whole annexation question.

---

5. Gurston Goldin, "Business Sentiment and the Mexican War with Particular Emphasis on the New York Businessman," *New York History* 33 (1952): 54–70.

The Whig party also enjoyed its greatest strength in New England, a fact which assured widespread opposition to the policies of any Democratic administration, but particularly for the southern-oriented programs of the Polk administration. A potent political force throughout New England, the Whigs were strongest in Massachusetts. Not one Democrat represented the Bay State in Congress during either the Twenty-ninth or the Thirtieth Congress. Serious divisions existed in the state party between the conservative and radical factions, or Cotton and Conscience wings as they were called, divisions which would tear the party asunder in 1848. But open partisan warfare had not yet erupted. Indeed, leaders and editors of both factions denounced the war with equal passion; in its early weeks, little difference of opinion existed on the war issue.

In addition, New England, especially the Boston area, was the center of the antebellum reform movement. Here a core of energetic reformers, clergymen, intellectuals, utopians, and genuine radicals constantly agitated for their favorite causes in an attempt to apply the precepts of democracy and Christianity to American society. Generally viewing war, slavery, and southern political power as impediments to the progress of American democracy and Christianity, these reformers interpreted the Mexican War in moral terms as an aggressive, unjust, and unholy war to extend the heinous institution of slavery.

But while the arguments of pacifists, abolitionists, and clergymen were similar and frequently overlapped, each was distinct. That is, the denouncements of these dissenting groups reflected their different frames of reference and the respective causes they espoused. Condemning the war as unnecessary, avoidable, and unjust, the American Peace Society respectfully petitioned the Polk administration to recall American troops from Mexico and to resolve the issue in dispute through either mediation or negotiation. In contrast, the abolitionists violently denounced the war. Interpreting the Mexican War within the context of their principles, the American Anti-Slavery Society maintained that the conflict was being "waged solely for the detestable and horrible purpose of extending and perpetuating American slavery throughout the vast territory of Mexico." The abolitionists charged that President Polk, in his transparent defense of war, could best be likened to the "fable of the wolf, who denounced and tore in pieces the lamb, that was drinking at the same stream below him, for muddying the water."[6] Accordingly, abolitionist leaders and editors promised to assail all who either openly or tacitly supported the military effort and urged all honest citizens to resist the government actively by refusing any "enlistment, aid and countenance to the War."[7]

---

6. *Liberator* (Boston), 22 May 1846.
7. Ibid., 5 June 1846.

However, it was the twenty-seven-year-old Boston poet, literary critic, and abolitionist, James Russell Lowell, who combined a variety of arguments into what became the most popular attack on the war. Lowell was particularly incensed by Massachusetts Whig Governor George Briggs's call for volunteers and by the part played by other prominent figures in the state, especially Daniel Webster's son Edward, who attempted to organize and lead one of the ten volunteer companies requested. Appearing anonymously on June 17, 1846, in the Boston *Courier,* a satirical poem of Lowell's, attacking the war, was so well received and widely read that he later wrote eight other satires in the same vein during and just after the war. They were collected and printed in 1848 as the *Biglow Papers.* In rustic New England dialect, a simple but shrewd Yankee farmer, Hosea Biglow, commented on the existing war and the excitement it had provoked. As a God-fearing Christian, Biglow evinced his hatred of all war in a typically direct manner:

> Ez fer war, I call it murder,—
>   There you hev it plain an' flat;
> I don't want to go no furder
>   Than my Testyment fer that;
> God hez sed so plump an' fairly,
>   It 's ez long ez it is broad,
> An' you 've gut to git up airly
>   If you want to take in God.[8]

Having condemned war as murder, Biglow curtly dismissed the inflated sentiments of Manifest Destiny and labeled the Mexican War a scheme of "them nigger-driven States" to extend their power and territory and make "wite slaves" of submissive northerners.

> They may talk o' Freedom's airy
>   Tell they 're pupple in the face,—
> It 's a grand gret cemetary
>   Fer the barthrights of our race;
> They jest want this Californy
>   So 's to lug new slave-states in
> To abuse ye, an' to scorn ye,
>   An' to plunder ye like sin.[9]

Hosea himself refused to support the war, while poking fun at the recruiters, chiding the "crowin' " editors who, despite their eagerness for battle, did not themselves enlist to fight, and lamenting that Massachusetts, the state which should cling "ferever in her grand old eagle-nest," was now "akneelin' with

---

8. James Russell Lowell, *The Biglow Papers* (Boston, 1848), 5.
9. Ibid., 6–7.

the rest. . . ." The Yankee poet even suggested the wisdom of separating from the slave states, so frustrated was he by the whole spectacle.[10]

Much to the dismay of some of the war's sharpest critics, the initial response of organized religion was both uneven and guarded. Generally, religious opinion paralleled regional response to the war. Throughout the South and West, where the war was popular, the pulpit openly supported the administration's Mexican policy, or at least withheld criticism. Initially, religious dissent was confined to various sections of Ohio, Pennsylvania, New York, New Jersey, and New England. In 1846, religious opposition was restricted to only a few denominations, although during the following year dissent became widespread within the churches, mainly because the war then seemed clearly to be one of conquest. With minor exceptions in the early months of fighting, the Baptists, Methodists, Presbyterians, Roman Catholics, as well as numerous minor sects, either supported, ignored, or offered only tepid opposition to the conflict. Only the Quakers, Unitarians, and Congregationalists openly condemned the war from its inception.[11] Particularly outspoken and forceful were Unitarians like Theodore Parker and Samuel J. May, who combined the principles of Christian pacifism with firm antislavery commitments.

In sharp contrast to various antiwar critics who sought a wider audience and attempted to mobilize public opposition to the war, Transcendentalist Henry David Thoreau was both unique and individualistic in his momentary dissent. Thoreau, who had not paid his Massachusetts poll tax for several years, denounced the Mexican War in his annual brush with Concord's tax collector and refused to pay again in July 1846. For this act, Thoreau spent one night in jail before his friends paid the tax, without his consent. Two years later he explained his actions in a lecture entitled "Resistance to Civil Government," which he presented to several audiences before its 1849 publication as an essay. Though he viewed the Mexican War as a conflict to extend slavery, Thoreau concentrated instead on what seemed to him a more fundamental issue: the duty of each honest citizen to resist his government when it condoned or perpetrated an evil such as slavery or a war to extend slavery. "When a sixth of the population of a nation which has undertaken to be the refuge of liberty are slaves, and a whole country unjustly overrun and conquered by a foreign army," Thoreau declared, "it is not too soon for honest men to rebel and revolutionize." Yet because he believed that he still had many lives to live, Thoreau's singular act of dissent terminated with his release from jail. "It is not a man's duty . . . to devote himself to the eradication

---

10. Ibid., 11.

11. For a well-researched survey of this topic see Charles Ellsworth, "The American Churches and the Mexican War," *American Historical Review* 45 (January 1940): 301–26.

of any, even the most enormous wrong; he may still properly have other concerns to engage him," explained Thoreau, "but it is his duty . . . to wash his hands of it, and, if he gives it no thought longer, not to give it practically his support."[12]

However isolated and inconspicuous his act, Thoreau was at the same time making himself an example to his fellow citizens of Massachusetts. He reminded them that their refusal to pay "their tax-bills" would not be as "violent and bloody" an act, "as it would be to pay them, and enable the State to commit violence and shed innocent blood." In fact, if only a few *"honest men"* were to "withdraw from this copartnership, and be locked up in the county jail . . . it would be the abolition of slavery in America. For it matters not how small the beginning may seem to be: what is once well done is done for ever." Unfortunately, New Englanders "love better to talk about it" than to do it: "Reform keeps many scores of newspapers in its service, but not one man. . . ."[13] Although the essay, later popularly known as "Civil Disobedience," has become justly famous as the eloquent manifesto of passive resistance, Thoreau's dissent and later explanation was meant primarily as a personal protest and attracted only local attention at the time.

Even though dissent was most intense in New England, it was not narrowly confined to this region of the nation. Reformers and some clergymen outside the New England states condemned the war. For example, abolitionists in Ohio and western New York assailed the conflict as violently as did the abolitionists of New England, and Unitarians and Quakers around the nation maintained a strong attack on the war. Nor was the nation's press unanimous in support of the Mexican conflict. Not only Whig editors but some Democratic editors also were disturbed by the administration's aggressive Mexican policy. Under the editorship of William Cullen Bryant, the *New York Evening Post* by early June was urging a quick end to the war to prevent a protracted war and an invasion of Mexico.[14] In South Carolina, the Democratic *Charleston Mercury* applauded Calhoun's independent course of opposition in the Senate and warned of the grave dangers inherent in an extended war with Mexico. Shuddering at the prospect of territorial conquest, the *Mercury* feared "the development of a love of conquest among our people. Such passion is the enemy of liberty and law. . . . Let us not cast away the priceless jewel of our freedom, for the lust of plunder and the pride of conquest." To those expansionists who advocated the acquisition of a vast amount of Mexican territory,

---

12. Henry David Thoreau, "Civil Disobedience," in *The Writings of Henry David Thoreau*, 10 vols. (Boston, 1894–95), 10:137, 142.

13. Ibid., 148–50.

14. Excerpts from the *New York Evening Post* as cited in the *National Intelligencer* (Washington, D.C.), 9 June, 13 June 1846.

the *Mercury* warned that the American republic could never exist in "copart-nery" with people "at war with us by race, by language, by religion, manners and laws. . . ."[15]

Although most Whig newspapers around the nation opposed the Polk administration's war, considerable diversity of opinion existed. A few Whig papers even lent their initial support. Papers like the Baltimore *American*, the *Nashville Republican Banner*, and the *Chicago Daily Journal* temporarily sus-pended judgment on the justice of the conflict and rallied to sustain the na-tional honor in a moment of crisis. Not yet fearing the consequences of war and urging vigorous prosecution of hostilities, they criticized the administra-tion only for not being prepared to conduct a more forceful and aggressive military effort.[16]

At the other end of the Whig spectrum were several papers which ex-pressed the views of the radical Whig faction in Congress. Horace Greeley's *New York Tribune*, Joshua Giddings' mouthpiece, the *Ashtabula Sentinel* of Ohio, and Charles Francis Adams' Boston *Daily Whig* concurred with leading Liberty party papers like the *Cincinnati Herald* and wrote their strong anti-slavery sentiment into their analyses of the war. Interpreting the Rio Grande border dispute as the transparent pretext of a southern president intent on provoking a war of conquest to extend southern power and institutions, edi-tors like Greeley and Adams predicted a war of invasion and conquest from the outset. Like the abolitionists, they never doubted the real purpose of Presi-dent Polk: "Our Government is bent on exacting California and several hun-dred miles in breadth of all Northern Mexico as the 'spoils of victory'. . . ."[17]

Between these poles of Whig opinion fell the majority of the nation's Whig journals. With frequent variations, most Whig editors reiterated the basic views of the conservative majority wing of the party. Led by the party's national organ, the *National Intelligencer* of Washington, D.C., the conserva-tive Whig press attacked President Polk in harsh partisan terms for provoking an unjust and unnecessary war, while affirming its loyalty by pledging support to the military effort. In May the *Intelligencer* set the tone which most Whig editors followed when it declared that "the first care is to meet the emergency . . . yet not to suffer it to absorb all our attention, so as to forget the account

---

15. *Charleston Mercury,* 19 May, 25 May 1846.

16. Baltimore *American,* 8 May, 27 May 1846; *Nashville Republican Banner* (Ten-nessee), 11 May, 22 May, 29 May 1846; *Chicago Daily Journal,* 14 May, 21 May 1846. For a survey of one state, see Billy H. Gilley, "Tennessee Opinion of the Mexican War as Reflected in the State Press," *East Tennessee Historical Society Publications* 26 (1954): 17–26.

17. *New York Tribune,* 22 June 1846; see also Boston *Daily Whig,* 5 June 1846; *Cincinnati Herald and Philanthropist,* 27 May 1846.

we have to settle with those who have wantonly brought it upon the country."[18]

The Whig press placed full responsibility on the president "alone." The attack on the Rio Grande represented a bloody monument to Polk's "rashness, incapacity and folly," wrote the *Augusta Daily Chronicle and Sentinel* of Georgia. In addition, arrogant administration forces in Congress had added to the crime by abetting the President. Democratic insistence on adding a preamble of "unsustained pretense" to a necessary supply bill had forced a loyal Whig opposition to choose between their consciences and their country. Never, railed the *Chronicle,* had a "party obtruded its sordid purposes into the arena of necessary legislation with a front more impudent, unjust, and unjustifiable. . . ."[19]

In addition to blaming the administration for the war, Whig editors consistently criticized Polk's inadequate conduct of the war and his treatment of his leading military commanders. After the initial American military victories in 1846, both Generals Winfield Scott and Zachary Taylor became potential Whig presidential candidates for 1848. At the same time, both men soon engaged in disputes with the administration and accused the president of maneuvering on their rear flank to undermine their prestige and authority. To their defense came the counterattacking Whig press with charges that Polk was playing partisan politics with loyal military commanders in a time of national emergency.

Across the nation, excitement over the war remained high throughout the summer of 1846. While opposition intensified among Whigs and in the New England states, so too did enthusiasm for the war continue to grow throughout the rest of the nation. News of General Taylor's initial victories at Palo Alto and Resaca de la Palma quickened the national pulse in anticipation of fresh victories and new glory. Meanwhile, after meeting the initial exigencies of the Mexican crisis in May and ratifying the Oregon treaty with England in June, Congress turned from foreign affairs to pressing domestic questions. With General Taylor out of immediate danger and the administration's undisclosed war goals not yet the center of controversy, all hoped that the war would end soon. Finally, after several hectic weeks of legislative activity and under the constant prodding of the ever-persistent president, Congress approved the creation of an independent treasury, a significant warehouse proposal, and a reduced tariff. Only a western sponsored measure to graduate land prices failed. This defeat disturbed western politicians, but they were more resentful over Polk's veto of their pet project, a rivers and harbors bill designed to improve water transportation throughout the Mississippi Valley.

---

18. *National Intelligencer,* 16 May 1846.
19. *Augusta Daily Chronicle and Sentinel* (Georgia), 18 May, 20 May 1846.

The main "achievements" of the Polk administration. *Yankee Doodle* 1 (1846–47): 84. *Courtesy of the Newberry Library, Chicago.*

THIS IS THE HOUSE THAT POLK BUILT.

During the congressional battles which raged over these domestic issues, the Whigs unsuccessfully used the existence of war as a convenient political lever by which they sought to strengthen opposition to a reduced tariff and the creation of an independent treasury. Calhoun had feared that this strategy might succeed in defeating these "reform" measures, but Polk's determination carried the day.[20] On the tariff question, the Whigs argued that because the war would require vast additional revenues, it was foolish to reduce custom duties at the very time when government expenses were soaring. The administration denied this and countered that reduced duties would encourage imports and actually increase government revenue.[21]

At the same time, to meet the additional demand for revenue, the admin-

20. See Calhoun to Clemson, 11 July 1846, *Calhoun Correspondence,* 2:701; Calhoun to Clemson, 30 July 1846, ibid., 703; Gideon Welles to Van Buren, 28 July 1846, Van Buren Papers, Manuscript Division, Library of Congress.

21. Secretary of the Treasury Robert J. Walker, however, did recommend higher duties for a limited number of items, including a 20 percent tax on tea and coffee, items previously on the free list. But the tea and coffee duty was defeated in 1846 after it was opposed by numerous Democrats as a class tax directed against the common man, to whom coffee and tea were necessities of life.

istration introduced a Treasury Note Bill in July which would authorize the president to issue up to $10 million in government treasury notes to circulate as currency. As an alternative, the administration was empowered to borrow up to $10 million at an interest rate not exceeding 6 percent per annum. But the bill limited the combined total of treasury notes and loans to $10 million. Whigs immediately objected to this proposal for two reasons. First, argued Daniel Webster, treasury notes were "perfectly inconsistent" with an independent treasury.[22] While the so-called subtreasury restricted all government receipts and disbursements to specie, the Treasury Note Bill proposed the issuance of a government paper currency. Second, the Treasury Note Bill represented an irresponsible means of meeting government financial obligations. Recognizing the need for immediate additional revenue, Garrett Davis pledged Whig readiness to "vote the Government all proper means of supply, but . . . [only] on safe principles."[23] Instead the administration proposal seemed an unsound evasion of the basic issue. "If the Government could not raise the money it needed from the tariff and public lands, let it say so," argued Davis, "and honestly and openly resort to a loan."[24] The Whigs, of course, did not want the cost of the war camouflaged. They stood to profit politically if the administration's fiscal policies resulted in additional taxes or the creation of a huge national debt. These were potent political weapons which Whigs could effectively utilize to reduce the popularity of the war and the Polk administration.

After what seemed endless days of activity in the oppressive heat of a Washington summer, Congress was nearing a welcome adjournment. Believing that the crucial issues of the session had been decided, some members of Congress had already departed for their home districts by Saturday, August 8, when President Polk unexpectedly revived the question of Mexican affairs with a brief message to Congress. The president now requested the House to appropriate $2 million to be used at the chief executive's discretion to facilitate the settlement of "all our difficulties with the Mexican Republic." In expressing his desire for a "peace just and honorable to both parties," President Polk emphasized that the chief obstacle was the unresolved border dispute. In the adjustment of the boundary, Polk now suggested that "we ought to pay a fair equivalent for any concession which may be made by Mexico."[25]

---

22. *Cong. Globe,* 29th Cong., 1st Sess., 1846, 1015.
23. Ibid., 1095.
24. Ibid.
25. James D. Richardson, ed., *A Compilation of the Messages and Papers of the Presidents, 1789–1902,* 10 vols. (Washington, D.C., 1903), 4: 459. Before presenting his request to the House, Polk had carefully sought the approval of members of the Senate Foreign Affairs Committee, as well as the views of his cabinet. On August 4, he had sub-

In private conversations, Polk had denied that this was to be a war of conquest, while at the same time he maintained that the purchase of additional Mexican territory represented both a legitimate and indispensable condition of any peace settlement. Although he did not publicly discuss his precise objectives, Polk intended to pay $2,000,000 to Mexico and have the United States assume the outstanding claims owed by Mexico to citizens of the United States as partial payment for the cession of "Upper California, New Mexico, and perhaps some territory South of these provinces."[26] To insure lasting acceptance of a satisfactory treaty by Mexico, Polk planned to forward the money to the weak Mexican regime immediately upon her ratification of a settlement, that is, before the treaty was officially ratified by the United States Senate, a process which could take months and might endanger the settlement.[27]

After the message had been read, the Democratic chairman of the House Ways and Means Committee, James McKay of North Carolina, translated the President's request into a bill granting $2 million "for the purpose of defraying any extraordinary expenses which may be incurred in the intercourse between the United States and foreign nations. . . ."[28] To this first public admission of territorial objectives, Whig reaction was sharp and immediate. Polk's statement did not mention either California or New Mexico, but its meaning was clear. "It looked very much," declared New York Representative Charles Carroll, "as if this money was wanted to purchase California, and a large portion of Mexico to boot."[29] Other Whigs quickly agreed with the obvious. The president intended to have Congress endorse his position *"that the main object of this war is California,"* asserted Kentucky's Garrett Davis. Then if Polk failed to obtain "it by a foul treaty, the war is to be prosecuted, persevered in, until Mexico is *whipped into its cession."*[30]

The Two Million Bill closely paralleled the original war bill because of the dilemma in which it again placed the Whig opposition. As they had in May, the Democrats had fused partisanship and national policy. Realizing the president's intended use for the $2 million, the Whig opposition was loathe to sanction the administration's scheme of territorial expansion by voting the ap-

---

mitted a brief message to the Senate, seeking its approval of his plan to make an appropriation request of the House. With Senate approval, he then forwarded his message to the House on August 8.

26. Milo M. Quaife, ed., *The Diary of James K. Polk, 1845–1849,* 4 vols. (Chicago, 1910), 2: 76–77.

27. Ibid.; Polk reasoned that immediate payment would help the Mexican government retain power and hence insure official recognition of the treaty. The money could be used by the bankrupt government to sustain its army in return for military support, thereby strengthening the regime, despite its unpopular cession of territory to the United States.

28. *Cong. Globe,* 29th Cong., 1st Sess., 1846, 1211.

29. Ibid.

30. Ibid., 1215.

propriation. Robert Winthrop of Massachusetts stated simply that the proposal asked a "vote of unlimited confidence in an Administration, in which . . . there was very little confidence to be placed."[31] But at the same time the bill was ostensibly a peace proposal. According to the president, the money was needed to conclude a peace settlement with Mexico, a goal in which all Whigs heartily concurred. Hence, the Whig dilemma was as unpalatable as it had been the previous May on the war bill. At that time, for Whigs to vote against the outrageous preamble to the war bill was to vote also against reinforcements for an embattled American army on the Rio Grande. Now in August, for the Whigs to deny the president the funds he needed to achieve his territorial objectives was also to run the risk of endangering a possible peace settlement. In May, the penalty Whigs faced for voting against the war bill was exposure to the politically fatal charges of disloyalty in a time of national crisis; now by voting against the Two Million Bill, Whigs might well have to answer charges that they, not the president, were responsible for prolonging the war. Obviously if the Two Million Bill were rejected and the war continued, Democrats could reasonably contend that the Whig opposition had denied the president the resources he sought to make an honorable peace.

The Whigs responded variously to this decision. Although they acknowledged "well-founded apprehensions" about the appropriation, some Whigs like Kentucky's Henry Grider, Pennsylvania's Joseph Ingersoll, and John Quincy Adams, were willing to support the bill.[32] Adams viewed the measure primarily as a peace proposal and emphasized his willingness to "vote for the bill in any form"; he did, however, suggest that it be amended "to specify expressly that the money is granted to the President . . . for negotiating peace with Mexico."[33] In response, McKay's bill, which, unlike Polk's own message, did not mention a word about Mexico, the Texas border, or even a peace settlement, was amended. In its altered form, the bill granted Polk an additional $30,000 to negotiate "for the restoration of peace with Mexico," and stipulated that the $2 million must be used "to conclude a treaty of peace with the Republic of Mexico. . . ."[34]

But most Whigs remained unmoved and demanded further revisions. Winthrop requested assurance that the funds would not be used to annex "another Texas, or even to the purchase of another Louisiana" and recommended that the appropriation be expressly restricted to the "settlement of those boundaries which have been the subject of dispute," namely the Rio Grande.[35]

31. Ibid., 1214.
32. Ibid.
33. Ibid., 1215.
34. Ibid., 1217.
35. Ibid., 1214.

A more serious apprehension of northern Whigs was that the area to be acquired would become slave territory. Thus Representative Hugh White of New York spoke for his northern colleagues when he emphasized that he could vote for the bill only if it "be so amended as to forever preclude the possibility of extending the limits of slavery."[36]

Although the Democratic House leadership ignored Whig requests to restrict Polk to the settlement of outstanding issues, David Wilmot promptly met Representative White's challenge. After a recess for dinner, the Pennsylvania Democrat introduced his famous amendment to the Two Million Bill: "Provided, That, as an express and fundamental condition to the acquisition of any territory from the Republic of Mexico by the United States . . . neither slavery nor involuntary servitude shall ever exist in any part of said territory. . . ."[37]

Wilmot's motion was not, of course, designed strictly to remove Whig objections to the Two Million Bill. Rather it reflected the discontent of northern Democrats with the Polk administration and represented an attempt by antislavery Democrats to preserve their political power, challenged as they were by growing antislavery sentiment in their home districts. In short, the proviso's purpose was to signify clearly to northern voters that the Van Burenites and other northern Democrats were not aiding slavery and that the existing war was not being waged to extend southern slave power. As far as the Van Burenites were concerned, this amendment represented a significant shift in their position on the war. Until August, the Van Burenites had swallowed their bitterness over the war and loyally supported the administration's Mexican policy, while privately seeking assurances from the president that he contemplated no war of conquest which might extend slavery. In July, New York's Senator John Dix received private confirmation from Polk that he entertained no territorial goals.[38] Now, several weeks later, after the president had presented his request for $2 million and thereby indicated his territorial intentions, the Van Buren Democrats felt compelled to reinforce their political position and to reassure their constituents. Because antislavery Democrats wanted to maintain their support of the administration's war policy, there was no other choice.[39]

The introduction of Wilmot's amendment immediately altered the nature

---

36. Ibid.

37. Ibid., 1217.

38. For a good discussion of whether Dix received any such assurance, see Chaplain Morrison, *Democratic Politics and Sectionalism; The Wilmot Proviso Controversy* (Chapel Hill, N.C., 1967), 176–77. Morrison believes that Dix did receive such assurance.

39. An excellent account of the origin and purpose of the proviso is found in Eric Foner, "The Wilmot Proviso Revisited," *Journal of American History* 56 (September 1969): 262–79.

of the proceedings on the Two Million Bill. Party lines quickly snapped as sections aligned. Individual votes were not recorded on the 87 to 64 margin by which the bill and attached proviso passed the House.[40] But on two earlier motions, one to table the bill and one to advance the measure to a third reading, the recorded division was largely sectional. For example, numerous antislavery, western Democrats deserted the administration and supported the proviso. Freshly bitter over the compromise Oregon settlement, the failure of the bill to graduate land prices, and Polk's veto of the rivers and harbors bill, these westerners felt betrayed by the southern orientation of the administration and the proviso offered an ideal chance to vent their anger.

For Whigs, the introduction of the proviso proved an event of unexpected good fortune by releasing them from their difficult dilemma on the Two Million Bill. With the interjection of the slavery question, debate on this war measure was broadened and more options were available to the opposition. Now Whigs did not have to choose between endorsing the president's territorial ambitions by supporting the Two Million Bill or running the risk of being blamed for the defeat of a presidential peace proposal. By voting for the bill and the attached proviso, northern Whigs could gain favor with their constituencies. Not only were they registering a popular vote against the extension of slavery, they were also affirming support for Polk's efforts to end the war. At the same time, by opposing the measure, southern Whigs also were assuming a popular political position with voters who were unlikely to fault their representatives for defending southern rights.

On August 10, the last day of the session, the bill, along with the attached proviso, reached the Senate floor shortly before Congress was to adjourn. There administration forces led by Alabama's Dixon Lewis attempted to strike the proviso from the appropriation and return the bill in that deleted form to the House only minutes before the lower chamber would adjourn, thereby forcing approval of the Two Million Bill minus the Wilmot amendment. But the issue never came to a vote. After being recognized, John Davis of Massachusetts refused to yield the floor until word had arrived that the House had adjourned. This brief but successful filibuster defeated the Two Million Bill.

An immediate response among Whigs was general relief. What conservative Whig observer, Philip Hone, called "the most corrupt, profligate, and disastrous" session ever was finally over.[41] In the weeks following adjournment, the great importance of the Wilmot Proviso, so obvious later, went unrecognized. Rather, editors and politicians of both parties concentrated upon

---

40. *Cong. Globe,* 29th Cong., 1st Sess., 1846, 1217–18.
41. Allan Nevins, ed., *The Diary of Philip Hone, 1828–1851,* 2 vols. (New York, 1927), 2: 769.

the significance of Polk's request for $2 million, not Wilmot's amendment. What later became a rallying principle for northern antislavery sentiment was generally considered in August 1846 to have been but a momentary political maneuver by a small group of Democrats. In both slave and free states, Wilmot's amendment evoked little attention and did not influence the outcome of various state and congressional elections during the fall of 1846. It was not until November, for example, that John C. Calhoun commented that "Wilmot's proposition will prove an apple of discord, that will do much to divide the party."[42] The *Charleston Mercury,* ever the guardian of southern rights, commented only that the proviso was "absurd," while other southern journals made little note of it.[43]

Northern politicians reacted similarly. Even the small band of antislavery Whigs, who had quickly read the designs of the Slave Power into the war, did not immediately embrace the antislavery potential of the proviso. Gleeful as they were in August 1846, these radical Whigs viewed the proviso, not as a broad principle, but as a maneuver which had clearly exposed the naked ambitions of the southern-controlled administration. "Does it not look," wrote A. R. McIlvaine of Pennsylvania to Joshua Giddings, "as if the south wished to acquire this new territory for the purpose of extending slavery? Oh Cracky."[44] Giddings, who had returned to Ohio before the session ended, received a similar appraisal from Columbus Delano; Polk's request for $2 million and its subsequent defeat because of the introduction of the *"freedom* proviso," observed Delano, had "opened the eyes of many who had been in political life more than *nine days,* but who hitherto seemed to require more *years,* than dogs do *days,* before they can see."[45]

The Whig press also made little note of the proviso, concentrating instead on the significance of the Two Million Bill as a war measure. The president's sudden desire for peace seemed to indicate his belated awareness of the "consequences of his own wicked war" and his realization that the war was "not likely to be a source of profit to Mr. Polk."[46] Observing that "gold" was to be tried if "steel shall fail," the Baltimore *American* chided Polk for attempting to buy a peace he previously had boasted he would conquer.[47] Critics

42. Calhoun to Lewis S. Coryell, 7 November 1846, *Calhoun Correspondence,* 2: 710.

43. *Charleston Mercury,* 14 August 1846.

44. A. R. McIlvaine to Giddings, 9 August 1846, Giddings Papers, Ohio Historical Society, Columbus (microfilm).

45. C. Delano to Giddings, 25 August 1846, Giddings Papers. Also, Joseph Root to Giddings, 29 August 1846, Giddings Papers.

46. *Ohio State Journal,* 18 August 1846; also, *Augusta Daily Chronicle and Sentinel,* 15 August 1846.

47. Baltimore *American,* 2 August, 15 August, 27 August 1846; *Augusta Daily Chronicle and Sentinel,* 15 August 1846; *National Intelligencer,* 15 August 1846; *Ohio State Journal,* 18 August 1846; *Chicago Daily Journal,* 20 August 1846.

also noted that the requested appropriation was not necessary for a peace settlement. The president already had full power to negotiate a settlement with "the entire assurance" that the Senate would ratify any treaty "not seriously objectionable in its terms. . . ."[48]

The potential of the proviso was, however, recognized by a handful of antislavery Whig journals like the *New York Tribune* and Boston *Daily Whig*. From the first, Horace Greeley interpreted the proviso as more than a political tactic of the moment and labeled the amendment *"a solemn declaration of the United North against the further extension of Slavery under the protection of our Flag."*[49] In the *Tribune,* Greeley urged northerners to unite on the "true ground" of "No more Slave Territory! . . . no more Slave States!" Furthermore, Greeley argued that the proviso offered an effective antiwar strategy. Because the war had originated in a scheme to add slave territory, passage of the proviso would end the war by destroying its purpose.[50] The principles embodied in the proviso also won favor among some western Whigs. The *Ohio State Journal* endorsed the principle as "just and righteous."[51] More emphatic was the *Chicago Daily Journal* which was incensed by Polk's sacrifice of western interests to southern goals. Abandoning its early endorsement of the war, the *Daily Journal* labeled the conflict an "unhallowed scheme" to extend slavery and asserted its opposition to the "annexation of FURTHER SLAVE TERRITORY to this Union in any shape or manner."[52]

In short, the president's request for $2 million to end the war and the subsequent introduction of the Wilmot Proviso changed the course of war debate, for before August, the administration's war objectives had remained unclear. In response, Whig opponents had directed their attacks at the blunders of the Democratic administration and had said little about the goals of war. The Two Million Bill, however, for the first time publicly signified that the president's objectives were territorial, even if their precise bounds remained undefined. Subsequently, an overriding concern of the opposition was the administration's war goals. In addition, the Wilmot Proviso added another element to the debate by formally connecting slavery with the Mexican War for the first time in Congress.[53] Although President Polk found it "difficult to conceive" what "connection slavery had with making peace with Mexico,"

---

48. *Richmond Whig* (Virginia), 11, 12 August 1846.

49. *New York Tribune,* 12 August 1846.

50. Ibid., 14, 18 August 1846; see also Boston *Daily Whig,* 15 August, 18 September 1846.

51. *Ohio State Journal* (Columbus), 20 August 1846.

52. *Chicago Daily Journal,* 7 August 1846.

53. The radical Whigs, of course, had since May alleged that slavery was the sole cause of the war, but their assertions had been temporarily ignored by most politicians.

slavery soon became an integral part of the question.[54] By the time Congress reconvened in December, it was difficult to separate the issues of war and slavery.

---

54. Quaife, *Polk Diary,* 2: 75.

4

★ *A War of Conquest*

WITHIN SEVERAL WEEKS of President Polk's request for $2,000,000, news from across the continent undeniably confirmed what the Two Million Bill had clearly suggested. This was indeed to be a war for Mexican territory. In June, Colonel Stephen Watts Kearny, in command of the small "Army of the West," had marched southwest from Fort Leavenworth, Kansas. More than a month later, Kearny advanced into the province of New Mexico and continued toward the capital, Santa Fe, which he entered on August 18 without encountering resistance. To New Mexico's inhabitants, Kearny issued a proclamation declaring that the province would be retained as "part of the United States, and under the name of the 'territory of New Mexico.'" As "citizens of the United States," all inhabitants of New Mexico were absolved "from any further allegiance to the republic of Mexico."[1] During the following month, Kearny proceeded to organize a civil government and to appoint officials to govern the territory. The American commander was operating under confidential instructions from the Secretary of War, orders directing Kearny to "establish temporary civil governments" in New Mexico and Upper California if he should take possession of either province.

Having executed his orders, Kearny with three hundred dragoons began a march to California, where similar events had already occurred. Commodore John Sloat had taken possession of Monterey on July 7, two weeks before he was replaced by Commodore Robert Stockton, who had been dispatched to take command. Acting with the colorful American explorer Captain John Charles Fremont, then on a "scientific" expedition in northern California, Stockton had moved south and taken possession of Santa Barbara and Los Angeles by August 13. Under instructions similar to those issued to Kearny, Stockton proclaimed California's annexation on August 17 and organized a

---

1. U.S. Senate, *Executive Documents*, No. 60, 30th Cong., 1st Sess., 169.

new government with himself as governor. When news of these events reached the east coast, the designs of the administration could no longer be denied: it was obvious that the cession of California and New Mexico would be demanded in any peace treaty.

At the same time, by the early autumn of 1846, it had become apparent to the administration, despite its hopes to the contrary, that territorial objectives were not to be gained easily or promptly. Originally Polk had hoped to attain his goals through a quick war and successful treaty. During the previous February, Polk's hopes had been raised after private conversations with Colonel A. J. Atocha, an engaging United States citizen of Spanish birth and a friend of the exiled Santa Anna. Through the person of Atocha, Santa Anna suggested that in return for $30 million he could arrange the cession of San Francisco Bay and the recognition of the Rio Grande as the border of Texas. After hostilities had commenced, the exiled Mexican leader advised United States Navy Commander Alexander MacKenzie that he would cooperate with the United States. Santa Anna was then permitted to pass through the naval blockade and return to Mexico. Arriving in Mexico on August 16, within days he had assumed command as the general in chief of the Mexican army. Several weeks later all hopes for an early peace ended; for after his return to power, Santa Anna's willingness to cooperate with the administration vanished.

On September 19, Polk received from M. C. Rejon, the new Mexican Secretary of Foreign Relations, a communiqué which stated that Mexico was not ready to negotiate. Polk then moved immediately to intensify the war, ordering that the towns in the northern province of Tamaulipas be occupied, the coast of Tampico be invaded, and supplies previously purchased by the American forces in northern Mexico henceforth be confiscated. At the same time, he urged his leading generals, particularly Winfield Scott, to hasten their preparations and proceed to the field of battle. In mid-October, after the American victory at Monterey and the ensuing armistice promised no change in the Mexican disposition, and with the prospects of negotiation dim, Polk decided to invade central Mexico. On October 12, the cabinet agreed unanimously with Polk and serious planning for the invasion began. It was plain that Mexico would not come to terms in the near future. "Mexico is an ugly enemy," Daniel Webster had observed. "She will not fight—and will not treat."[2]

These developments between August and October, 1846, defined the true nature of the war. In the initial three months of fighting, uncertainty had surrounded the war. Because Polk neither publicized nor betrayed his intentions, it was not yet possible to predict how long the war would last, how extensive

---

2. D. Webster to Fletcher Webster, 6 August 1846, in *The Writings and Speeches of Daniel Webster*, ed. Fletcher Webster, 18 vols. (Boston, 1903), 16: 465.

the fighting would be, or precisely what the goals of the administration were. Although rumors were numerous, it was unclear whether the president sought Mexican territory, or whether a full-scale invasion of Mexico would be necessary. But the introduction of the Two Million Bill, the proclamations of Kearny and Stockton in New Mexico and California, and the failure of Polk's peace initiative removed uncertainty. An extended war of conquest was under way.

In response to these events, the Whig opposition intensified its political attack on the president, and especially on the question of war objectives. This, of course, represented a distinct departure for the conservative wing of the party. Unlike the radical Whigs, who had maintained from the outset that this was to be war for the extension of slave territory, the conservative Whigs had concentrated, not on the possible result of the war, but rather on the causes and responsibility for its outbreak in an attempt to discredit the Polk administration politically. Responding to rumors and isolated events, such as the organization of a regiment of New York volunteers who were to serve and be discharged in California, only a few Whigs had seriously noted the distinct possibility that this might indeed become a war of conquest. Scattered politicians like Alexander Stephens of Georgia and several journals like the *Augusta Chronicle and Sentinel* and the *Richmond Whig* warned that a war of conquest would dangerously strengthen the executive power, demand extravagant public expenditures, endanger public morals, and threaten the very fabric of the republic. For example, the *Augusta Chronicle* cautioned that not only would America's true mission of peaceful, orderly expansion be perverted, but also the addition of thousands of acres of Mexican soil would endanger the Union itself. Although vast amounts of Mexican territory might be swallowed by advancing American armies "as easily as Jonah was by the whale," such a meal would not sit well on "the great republican stomach. . . . It would likely prove to be a sickening mixture, consisting of such a conglomeration of Negroes and Rancheros, Mestizoes, and Indians, with but a few Castilians."[3]

Now, in September and October, more and more Whigs began to reiterate and intensify these earlier warnings, with no lessening of their political assault on the president. They utilized each new development to remind the American public of Polk's treachery and to substantiate their lengthening indictment of the administration. But combined with this narrow partisan attack were more and more frequent warnings about the grave dangers inherent in a war for Mexican territory. Although the anti-imperialistic slant of Whig criticism was not yet fully developed, it grew steadily in volume and content throughout the last months of 1846.

---

3. *Augusta Chronicle and Sentinel* (Georgia), 31 July 1846; see also, *Richmond Whig* (Virginia), 10 June 1846; *Augusta Chronicle and Sentinel,* 11 June 1846.

Among the developments which fueled the fires were reports which leaked to the press of Polk's clandestine peace overtures to Santa Anna. Whigs professed horror when they learned that, armed with the proposed $2 million appropriation as partial compensation, Polk had planned, in effect, to bribe the infamous Mexican general to make a suitable peace treaty. What "infatuation," asked the *New York Express,* could have moved the president to allow a leader of Santa Anna's stature to return to Mexico and unify a previously weak and distracted enemy? "How many lives he [Polk] has thus to answer for!" At least, the nation had not paid the $2 million to Santa Anna. "But for 'Wilmot's proviso' we should have lost our money as well as our wits."[4]

In regard to New Mexico and California, Whigs conceded that military action in these Mexican provinces might well have been strategically desirable, but argued that the actions of Kearny and Stockton had far exceeded necessary or legitimate limits. Not only had the two Mexican provinces been occupied, they had been annexed, civil governments established, and civilian officials appointed. Furthermore, the inhabitants had been summarily declared to be citizens of the United States with full rights and privileges. "Annexation is now the greatest word in the American vocabulary," wrote New Yorker Philip Hone. " 'Veni—vidi—vici!' is inscribed on the banners of every Caesar who leads a straggling band of American adventurers . . . into the chaparral of a territory which an unprovoked war has given them the right to invade. . . ."[5] In "an open and flagrant violation of the constitution and laws," the president had delegated to military subordinates, "legislative, judicial, and executive" powers expressly reserved for civilian authorities.[6] Furthermore, the arbitrary annexation of these provinces represented a perversion of a basic precept of American democracy, the principle of consent of the governed. Regardless of their personal sentiments, the residents of New Mexico and California had been forcibly absolved of their allegiance to Mexico. In "a striking monument to the spirit of American freedom," declared the *Richmond Whig* of Virginia, American commanders had issued an ultimatum to these Mexican citizens: "You must have the same degree of freedom which we enjoy, whether you are fit for it or not. . . . If you refuse, we will ravage your fields, hang you up by the neck until you are dead . . . and leave your towns in smoking ruins. . . ."[7]

---

4. Excerpt from *New York Express* in *National Intelligencer* (Washington, D.C.), 24 October 1846; see also, Nashville *Republican Banner* (Tennessee), 2 October 1846; *Augusta Chronicle and Sentinel,* 25 November 1846; Baltimore *American,* 26 September 1846.

5. Allan Nevins, ed., *The Diary of Philip Hone, 1828–1851,* 2 vols. (New York, 1927), 2: 774.

6. *Richmond Whig* (Virginia), 9 October 1846; *National Intelligencer,* 17 October 1846.

7. *Richmond Whig,* 16 October 1846; see also, Boston *Daily Whig,* 15 November 1846; *National Intelligencer,* 17 October 1846.

Beyond the questions of legality and democratic principle, the addition of New Mexico and California interjected a racial issue into the debate. Whig journalists doubted that the "inferior" inhabitants of these provinces were fit to share the privileges and duties of full citizenship in a predominantly Anglo-Saxon republic. During the autumn of 1846, although these apprehensions were not yet fully developed, they were expressed in scattered Whig editorials. For example, the *Richmond Whig* found "far more to dread from the acquisition of the debased population who have been summarily manufactured into American citizens, than to hope from the extension of our territorial limits."[8]

The frightening prospect of a prolonged war of conquest prompted Whig journals of all shades to amplify their warnings. Noting that "conquest and oppression has never yet escaped the rebuke of the Supreme Power of Justice," the *Richmond Palladium* of Indiana cautioned that "the same volume that contains a record of the triumph of wrong and oppression, contains the history of its downfall."[9] Among those editors who were particularly distressed by the threat which military aggression posed for the nation's republican virtues was Horace Greeley. Because "war and its necessities" made their own laws, Greeley warned that "any amount of despotism and crime" would inevitably follow careers of "Invasion and Conquest. . . ." "Has the world ever known a Republic," he asked, "which extended its boundaries by the subjugation of diverse and hostile races without undermining thereby its own liberties?"[10]

By the autumn of 1846, previously restrained Whig journals in the free states began to sharpen their indictment of the war. Given recent events, more and more men now suspected that this might, indeed, be a war to extend slave territory. Scattered Democratic editorials tended to substantiate these fears. For example, in November the *National Intelligencer* decried as "atrocious" an editorial it reprinted from the *Federal Union* in Milledgeville, Georgia. This Democratic paper had asked how any true southerner could oppose the Mexican War when its results would "be to secure to the South the balance of power in the Confederacy, and, for all coming time, to give to her the control in the operations of the Government?"[11] In response to this kind of narrow, sectionally oriented, expansionist rhetoric, some northern Whig papers increased their denunciations of administration war policy and renewed their

8. *Richmond Whig,* 9 October 1846; see also, *Augusta Chronicle and Sentinel,* 14 October 1846; *Richmond Whig,* 6 October 1846; *Ohio State Journal,* 3 October 1846.

9. *Richmond Palladium* (Indiana), 27 October 1846; see also *Chicago Daily Journal,* 14 November 1846; *Richmond Whig* (Virginia), 27 November 1846.

10. *New York Tribune,* 27 November 1846.

11. *Federal Union* (Milledgeville, Ga.), 10 November 1846, as quoted in *National Intelligencer,* 21 November 1846.

call for adoption of the Wilmot Proviso. Its views reinforced by recent events, the *Chicago Daily Journal* in November reiterated its previous charge that the "conquest of Mexico" was the policy of an administration "goaded on as it was by a *Southern spur* to perpetuate a peculiar institution . . . blood flowed in streams that the brilliant achievements . . . might redound to the credit of a purely Southern policy. . . ."[12] During that same month the *New York Tribune* renewed its call for adoption of the proviso as the most effective strategy to insure a prompt and honorable termination of the war. Since the war had been motivated by a southern desire to increase slave territory, the most effective means of ending it was to destroy southern support for the conflict by prohibiting slavery from all conquered territory.[13]

At the same time, as sectional tension increased, moderate Whigs, who feared the threat posed by the war to the Union and to their party, decried both southern and northern extremism. With the preservation of national Whig unity ever in view, the *National Intelligencer* condemned both rabid antislavery Whigs and southern extremists as equally dangerous to the nation. Outraged by southern papers like the *Federal Union,* the *Intelligencer* warned that ideas of "Southern aggrandizement" could benefit neither southern interests nor the "permanent security of slave property. . . ." Fortunately, the Whig party was composed of a strong majority of "sober and just men" who stood unified "the instant you would attack the UNION. . . ."[14]

Friends of Whig harmony suggested a yet undetailed strategy designed to avoid a divisive debate on the explosive joint issues of territorial acquisition and slavery expansion. In its desire to preserve the "permanency of the Union," the *Richmond Whig* suggested that the present limits of the nation along the "Southwestern frontier" should not be extended as a result of the war. If no territory were acquired, bitter debate would be avoided, the stability of the Union preserved, and the unity of the Whig party insured. To achieve this end, the *Whig* proposed that the Army cease its invasion of Mexico and hold its position along a defensive line below the Rio Grande until Mexico agreed to make peace on honorable terms. If Mexico refused, the territory now held would, of necessity, be annexed and settled. In additon to confining the war and limiting its cost, a defensive-line strategy would virtually eliminate any possibility of adding substantial portions of Mexican soil. The *Whig* emphasized that, with the possible exception of California, because of its commercial importance, "We would not, if our will could decide the

---

12. *Chicago Daily Journal,* 14 November 1846; also, *Richmond Palladium* (Indiana), 3 November 1846.

13. *New York Tribune,* 16 November, 24 November 1846; for an earlier expression of this idea, see *Ohio State Journal* (Columbus), 20 June 1846.

14. *National Intelligencer,* 25 November 1846.

question, and if it could be had for the asking, ANNEX to this Union a foot of soil beyond the Rio Grande. . . ."[15] In late November, when the *Whig* spoke, the plan of taking no territory from Mexico was not yet widely endorsed by Whig politicians or editors. But by February 1847, under the pressure of congressional debate on slavery and the war, this strategy would become the accepted position of most Whigs.

For Whig opponents of the administration, 1846 was a year to test their views by the most important of all indicators, the popular ballot. During the late summer and autumn, local, state, and congressional elections were held across the Union. Contests for the Thirtieth Congress, which would not convene until December 1847, were held in sixteen states, involving more than 130, or about 60 percent, of the seats in the House. In these congressional elections, concentrated in the free states, the Whigs gained more than two dozen seats.[16] Holding their own in most states, they gained twenty-three seats in Pennsylvania, New York, and Ohio, and retained control of the entire Massachusetts delegation. If they were successful in the elections of 1847, which would select the remaining ninety representatives to the House, the Whigs might well overthrow the sixty-five vote majority held by the Democrats in the Twenty-ninth Congress.

Although the 1846 elections indicated widespread dissatisfaction with the Polk administration, they did not provide an accurate index to the war's popularity. Despite the prominence of the war issue, a profusion of national, state, and local questions existed. The Oregon settlement and Polk's veto of the Rivers and Harbors Bill were unpopular in the West; the Walker Tariff was widely denounced in protectionist areas; and the establishment of the independent treasury was attacked by conservative financial interests. In addition, factionalism and personal animosity weakened the Democrats.

Although it had been widely criticized, the Mexican War was only months old and embellished by several brilliant American victories. Reveling in this newly won glory, many Americans were not yet disillusioned by countless months of fighting and remained unconcerned with the justice of the conflict. In their campaign rhetoric, Whig critics themselves continued to vacillate on the war issue. Most were unwilling to stake their political futures on its popularity. As they had since May, the Whigs condemned the conflict as chargeable to the Polk administration and impeded by insufficient preparedness for battle. Yet they celebrated each American success with superlatives and urged contin-

---

15. *Richmond Whig* (Virginia), 21 November, 25 November, 29 November 1846.

16. In 1846, Congressmen were selected in Vermont, Massachusetts, New York, New Jersey, Pennsylvania, Delaware, Florida, South Carolina, Georgia, Ohio, Illinois, Missouri, Iowa, Texas, Michigan, and Wisconsin. Maine's representatives to the Thirtieth Congress were selected in both 1846 and 1847.

ued support for the military effort. According to the Whigs, Zachary Taylor and his men had achieved their remarkable victories almost without support. The failure to score a decisive victory and conclude a quick peace they attributed to the logistical incompetence of the administration.

Yet the opposition presented no viable alternative to the president's policies. They demanded that the conflict be promptly settled by honorable negotiation, and some suggested the withdrawal of American troops, but they recommended no options should the intransigent Mexicans refuse to negotiate. This vacillation indicated that most Whigs sought political capital from the war, not a forum for committed opposition. Although they were disturbed by the conflict and its possible consequences, Whig politicians still prized military commissions from the president's pocket. Thus, if the congressional elections of 1846 did not offer a simple mandate on the war, they indicated growing disfavor with the Polk administration.

In Ohio the Whigs gained three congressional seats and retained control of the state legislature and governorship. Of the five Ohio men who had voted against the war bill, Joshua Giddings and Joseph Root won reelection, while the other three dissidents did not stand for reelection. However, their places were filled by other Whigs. During the campaign, state issues, especially the currency and state banking questions, overshadowed national topics.[17] In Pennsylvania, where the Whigs gained six seats, the central issue was the Walker Tariff. In this state, a stronghold of protectionist sentiment, the reduction of duties was especially unpopular.[18] Whig gains were the most dramatic in New York, where the party added fourteen men to its delegation. Although the war was much debated and violently condemned by the opposition, the Democratic defeat was probably attributable to severe divisions within the party between the conservatives, or Hunkers, and the Van Burenites, or Barnburners.[19]

In Massachusetts, where the Democrats were already weak and the Polk administration unpopular because of the Walker Tariff and the war, the Whigs retained control of the state's ten congressional seats. But in Massachusetts' First Congressional District, the war was the crucial issue in an election which demonstrated increasing Whig division over the war and slavery. During 1846, the so-called Cotton and Conscience wings of the Massachusetts

---

17. Edgar Holt, *Party Politics in Ohio, 1840–1850* (Columbus, 1930), 145–47, 234–35, 244–47; Francis Weisenburger, *The Passing of the Frontier 1835–1850*, vol. 3 of *The History of the State of Ohio*, ed. Carl Wittke, 6 vols. (Columbus, 1941–44), 3: 427–31.

18. Charles M. Snyder, *The Jacksonian Heritage; Pennsylvania Politics, 1833–1848* (Harrisburg, Pa., 1948), 196–98; Henry R. Mueller, *The Whig Party in Pennsylvania* (New York, 1922), 130–33.

19. John A. Garraty, *Silas Wright* (New York, 1949), 334–39, 355–56, 362–63.

Whig party had become more and more antagonistic.[20] Headed by such prestigious figures as Daniel Webster, John Davis, Robert Winthrop, Abbott Lawrence, and Nathan Appleton, the Cotton or conservative wing was dominant. But a small group of young Whigs, motivated by their strong aversion to slavery, were girding to contest the established leaders. Charles Francis Adams, Charles Sumner, Stephen Phillips, and John Gorham Palfrey spearheaded the Conscience or radical wing which advocated unequivocal Whig reprobation of slavery, even at the price of alienating the southern Whigs. Contending that antislavery principles should transcend traditional party ties, the Conscience faction charged that their conservative Whig allies, motivated by economic ties to the cotton South, were determined to evade the slavery question in order to preserve the national unity of the party. Despite their criticism of the Cotton wing, however, the radicals pledged their devotion to the party and "true" Whig principles, which they believed should encompass a strong moral position on slavery.[21]

The split between the two factions had its origins in the Texas question. Although all elements of the Massachusetts Whig party had vigorously opposed annexation, the Conscience men believed that their conservative colleagues had acquiesced too readily. The antislavery Whigs supported resolutions threatening the secession of Massachusetts from the Union if Texas were annexed. They had maintained their stand until the fall of 1845, just prior to the entry of Texas into the Union as a state. When the Mexican War commenced later, both factions remonstrated against it and the president in sharp language, while praising those men who had voted against the war bill. However, an open breach appeared during the summer of 1846 when Sumner, Adams, and Palfrey attacked Abbot Lawrence, Nathan Appleton, and Robert Winthrop in a series of articles. Under the pseudonym "Sagitta," Adams charged that Lawrence valued sheep, cotton, and his economic ties with southern Whigs more than the true Whig principles of human freedom and moral right. In another series of essays, later printed as *Papers on the Slave Power* . . . , Palfrey traced the growth of slavery and the aggressions of the Slave Power from 1789 through the annexation of Texas. In an incredible assertion, Palfrey argued that, at a critical moment during the autumn of 1845, Appleton had withdrawn his support from Whig protests on the pending admission of

20. An excellent monograph on this subject is Kinley Brauer, *Cotton Versus Conscience; Massachusetts Whig Politics and Southwestern Expansion, 1843–1848* (Lexington, Ky., 1967); also David Donald, *Charles Sumner and the Coming of the Civil War* (New York, 1960), 130–69; Martin Duberman, *Charles Francis Adams, 1807–1886* (New York, 1961), 110–38.

21. To express their views, the Conscience men purchased the Boston *Daily Whig* in May 1846 and installed Charles Francis Adams as its editor.

Texas, and thereby had encouraged President Polk to provoke the Mexican War.[22]

But it was Robert Winthrop who was subjected to the most brutal abuse for his reluctant support of the war bill on May 11. On July 16 in a *Whig* editorial, Adams launched the Conscience barrage by asking Winthrop how he could "justify it to his own conscience to set his name in perpetual attestation to a falsehood?"[23] In an unsigned article in the Boston *Courier*, Sumner followed by assailing the moral bankruptcy, rather than the practical reality, of Winthrop's vote. In the future when they viewed Winthrop, the youth of Massachusetts could say only, " 'There goes a man who voted for the Mexican War, and a National Lie.' "[24] In early August in a personal letter to Winthrop, Sumner explained that he had authored the abusive articles, but emphasized that he was writing in the "spirit of friendship." Sumner declared that he was "grieved" that his friend Winthrop had "voted what seemed to us a Declaration of an unjust War, & a Falsehood, in the cause of Slavery." Undoubtedly, the war bill with its hateful preamble was the "wickedest act in our history."[25]

Winthrop himself was initially confused and then angered by these assaults on his integrity and moral judgment. In a letter to a friend, he conceded that his vote was certainly fair ground for criticism, but he objected to the abusive language of the charges. He had neither told the " 'Christian world a downright lie,' " nor had he voted a " 'falsehood.' " Almost every other Whig had taken the same path, and they were all "honest & trustworthy" men. Conceding that the preamble to the war measure was odious, Winthrop argued that it represented only a matter of appearance rather than of substance. Thus by his vote, he had sacrificed *"appearances,* & appearances only."[26]

When he received Sumner's personal letter in August, Winthrop's anger turned to rage. Within days, he replied in a letter of stinging rebuke. He informed Sumner that he would "allow no man to cast scandalous imputations on my motives & apply base epithets to my acts in public, & to call me his

---

22. John Palfrey, *Papers on the Slave Power First Published in the Boston Whig* (Boston, [1846]), 24–27.

23. Boston *Daily Whig,* 16 July 1846.

24. Boston *Courier,* 31 July 1846.

25. Sumner to Winthrop, 5 August 1846, Winthrop Family Papers, Massachusetts Historical Society, Boston; also, Sumner to N. Appleton, 11 August 1846, Nathan Appleton Papers, Massachusetts Historical Society, Boston.

26. Winthrop to J. C. Gray, 20 July 1846, Winthrop Family Papers. Earlier Winthrop had explained that an important consideration in his vote was his determination that the whole Masssachusetts delegation not be associated with a "little knot of ultraists," as he referred to the fourteen radicals who voted against the war bill. Winthrop to E. Everett, 7 June 1846, Edward Everett Papers, Massachusetts Historical Society, Boston.

friend in private." Sumner's attacks on his character abounded in the "coarsest personalities" and in the "grossest perversions," and Winthrop vehemently objected to being categorized as "a confessed, or convicted criminal." Clearly Sumner was confused, charged Winthrop. He had "confounded Geography with morals." "Sir, I am conscious of having done nothing inconsistent with the cause of Humanity, of Right, of Freedom, of Truth, or even of Peace," continued Winthrop; "my vote was given, honestly, conscientiously, & with a sincere beief that it was the best vote which an arbitrary & overbearing majority would permit us to give."[27] While Winthrop restricted his own rebuttal to private channels, the Cotton presses, the *Boston Atlas* and the *Boston Advertiser,* sprang to his defense in a heated round of charge and countercharge with the *Daily Whig.*

Sentiments were further exacerbated in September 1846, during the Massachusetts State Whig Convention. Through their unyielding control of the convention and their rejection of a series of resolutions drafted by Stephen Phillips, the conservatives whetted Conscience anger. Although they pledged their support to the Whig ticket selected by the convention, the radicals were determined to run an independent Whig candidate against Winthrop in the first district. Sumner and Adams believed that Winthrop's reelection would represent a vindication of his immoral vote on the war bill. The most obvious choice was the well-known Sumner, but he quickly declined, pleading that his tastes were "alien to official life."[28] In his stead, Samuel Gridley Howe was nominated on November 3. At a rally two days later at Boston's Tremont Temple, speaking in support of Howe, Sumner maintained his assault on Winthrop's failure to resist the encroachments of slavery by voting against the war: "The conclusion is irresistible, that Mr. Winthrop cannot fitly represent the feeling palpitating in Massachusetts bosoms . . . with regard to slavery." Although Winthrop had urged an "honorable peace," Sumner noted that he had failed to sound a call to "Duty." "Nowhere," said Sumner, "does he tell his country to begin by doing right. Nowhere does he give assurance of aid by calling for the instant stay of war."[29] Despite these cries of moral indignation, Howe did not seriously challenge Winthrop who was easily reelected in November.[30] Disappointed by their defeat, the radicals temporarily retrenched to reaffirm their party loyalty; chastened, they looked silently to the future.

---

27. Winthrop to Sumner, 17 August 1846, Charles Sumner Papers, Houghton Library, Harvard University, Cambridge, Mass.

28. "Letter of Sumner Declining to be a Candidate, 31 October 1846," in *Charles Sumner: His Complete Works,* 20 vols. (Boston, 1900), 1:332.

29. "Slavery and the Mexican War," ibid., 337, 339.

30. In the election, Winthrop received 5,980 votes; Howe, 1,334; the Democratic candidate, 1,688; and an Independent candidate, 331.

Although the congressional and state elections held in the autumn of 1846 resulted in substantial Democratic losses, they did not indicate strong public reproof of the administration's war policy. In the midst of frequent objections to the war, few political critics advocated measures which would effectively end the fighting. Even in strong antiwar areas, like the First Congressional District in Massachusetts, the voters overwhelmingly vindicated the moderate position of Robert Winthrop over the alternative of a radical Whig antiwar candidate. At the same time, then, that the popularity of the Polk administration waned during late 1846, general enthusiasm for the Mexican War remained high.

By December the military situation remained unsettled despite the succession of American victories during the first six months of the war. New Mexico and California were now securely under American control. In northern Mexico, General Taylor had occupied Saltillo, the capital of Coahuila, after the fall armistice had ended. Nearby waited the Mexican forces under the command of newly elected President Santa Anna. In Washington, President Polk, believing that a decisive invasion of Vera Cruz and a successful march on Mexico City were prerequisites to a satisfactory settlement, proceeded with preparations for a spring invasion under General Scott's command. At the same time, Polk instructed Taylor to maintain a defensive position in northern Mexico, and in January 1847 ordered 9,000 of Taylor's troops to join Scott's expedition. But Taylor suspected that the administration was only attempting to discredit him, and he resumed his advance toward the south in early February in an effort to strike a telling blow at Santa Anna's army. Throughout the winter of 1846–47, then, the military situation did not yet promise victory. Hard fighting lay ahead if Santa Anna's revitalized forces were to be defeated and Mexico brought to terms.

Precisely for this reason, the second session of the Twenty-ninth Congress was crucial to the outcome of the war. The previous session had not been in a position to deal decisively with the war, because it had adjourned in early August before the extent or goals of the conflict had become clear. Likewise, the Thirtieth Congress, to convene in December 1847, would not be in a position to affect the outcome of the war because the actual fighting would be concluded by that time. Thus, as Congress convened in December 1846, its support was vital to the administration. If a military victory and Polk's still undefined territorial goals were to be achieved, additional men, money, and supplies had to be approved.

5

★ *Politics and Opposition*

On December 8, 1846, Congress received the president's annual message. This important document presented a comprehensive and resolute defense of Polk's Mexican policy. Because of its partisan tone and debatable content, the message immediately renewed controversy on the war issue. While adamantly refusing to alter his previous view of the war, Polk now attacked critics of his policy. Referring to what he called "misapprehensions" regarding the "origin and true character" of the conflict, Polk denied that this was an "unjust and unnecessary" war of "aggression on our part upon a weak and injured enemy." In fact, the consequence of voicing such "erroneous views" was dangerous. Polk charged that a "more effectual means could not have been devised to encourage the enemy and protract the war than to advocate and adhere to their cause, and thus give them 'aid and comfort.' " Fortunately, the great majority of Americans had not embraced these mistaken sentiments; rather they had demonstrated their patriotic determination "to vindicate their country's honor and interest at any sacrifice."[1] By his insinuations, President Polk cast aspersions on the loyalty of anyone who dared question the justice of the war and clearly alleged such action to be treasonous. Previously such charges had been confined to the partisan hyperbole of Democratic editors and politicians; but now the official prestige of the nation's highest elective office had been lent to these political attacks.

Polk also ensured renewed debate on the causes of war by firmly repeating his questionable assertions of the previous May. By defaulting on legitimate claims, by arrogantly rejecting an American peace commissioner, and by ignoring the true border of the Rio Grande, Mexico had finally "consummated her long course of outrage against our country by commencing an offensive war and shedding the blood of our citizens on our own soil."[2] Polk then pro-

---

1. James D. Richardson, ed., *A Compilation of the Messages and Papers of the Presidents, 1789–1902,* 10 vols. (Washington, D.C., 1903), 4: 473.

2. Ibid., 487.

ceeded to defend recent controversial developments in the war. The decision to allow Santa Anna to return to Mexico from Cuban exile had been wise, the president averred, since it enhanced the prospect of an early peace. If the bellicose Paredes regime had remained in power, it was "morally certain" that a peaceful settlement would have been "hopeless." But as a true Mexican patriot, Santa Anna "must see the ruinous consequences of prolonged war," and although fighting even now proceeded under Santa Anna's command, Polk suggested that "it remains to be seen whether his return may not yet prove to be favorable to a pacific adjustment of the existing difficulties."[3]

The president also congratulated the nation on the signal success of American arms which had resulted in the occupation of "a territory larger in extent than that embraced in the original thirteen states of the Union. . . ." In New Mexico and California, where further resistance was not expected, "temporary governments" had necessarily been established in order to maintain "civil order and the rights of the inhabitants." Turning to the question of war goals, Polk conceded his territorial objectives without actually defining them. The war had "not been waged with a view to conquest," but Polk emphasized that any treaty of peace must include "ample indemnity for the expenses of war" as well as for the outstanding claims. Although Polk did not expressly admit the fact, it was widely understood that, since Mexico was bankrupt, compensation for the expenses of war would have to assume another form, namely the cession of Mexican territory.[4]

The forcefulness of Polk's assertions clearly indicated that his determination was undeterred by the war opponents. His resolve was further evinced by the legislative program he submitted to Congress for approval. Simply stated, the administration sought the men, money, and supplies necessary to intensify the war effort, as well as the funds and authority needed to increase the president's military and diplomatic authority. Specifically, the administration requested authorization for a $23 million loan to meet the rising public deficit, an additional duty on tea and coffee, specific military appropriations to sustain the war effort, and ten additional regiments of regular troops to compensate for the expiration of short-term enlistments. In addition, Polk asked that he be empowered to appoint a lieutenant general to "take command of all our military forces in the field" and that he be granted the special $2 million appropriation denied him the previous August.[5] This request was enlarged to $3 million by administration floor leaders and became known as the Three Million Bill.

Despite the president's determination and a Democratic majority in both

---

3. Ibid., 491, 492.
4. Ibid., 493, 494.
5. Ibid., 508.

Houses, serious obstacles did, however, threaten passage of the program. And if Polk failed to resolve these problems, opponents of war might well defeat his war measures and force him to reverse his war policy. Admittedly, most congressional critics of the war sought an American military victory, but they might hasten a peace settlement by limiting the extent of the conflict and preventing any territorial cessions to the United States. Although hopelessly outnumbered in the House, Whig opponents in the Senate could join dissident Democrats to block needed war measures and thereby handcuff Polk.

One annoying problem was the controversial nature of several of Polk's requests. While the great majority of Whigs and Democrats conceded the necessity of the loan bill, military appropriations, and troop reinforcements, the lieutenant general proposal and the Three Million Bill, along with the related question of the Wilmot Proviso, provoked heated debate. These were explosive measures which impaired the effectiveness of the Democratic majority by contributing to sectional tension, increasing Democratic factionalism, and intensifying Whig bitterness. In addition, the heated and prolonged debate provoked by consideration of the Three Million Bill and the lieutenant general proposal resulted in postponement and delay for necessary war measures. For example, the lieutenant general measure quickly became a political football. In requesting this new post, Polk's political motives were undeniable. He was aroused by the open hostility of Generals Scott and Taylor, their ever-growing popularity, and their apparent political ambitions. Polk desperately wanted to appoint a loyal Democrat to this supreme military field position. Here the president was motivated by his desire to retain the support of the Benton faction of the party in the face of Democratic splintering. When Senator Thomas Hart Benton suggested the measure, Polk agreed, and promised that Benton would be the appointee, even though Polk believed that the proposal would probably not pass.[6] Once under consideration, the bill met stiff resistance from dissident Democrats, as well as from Whigs. Especially antagonistic were the Calhounites, who were ever hostile to Benton, the acknowledged choice for lieutenant general. In the Senate, Whigs and Calhoun Democrats joined to defeat the measure, while Whigs, southern Democrats, and some western Democrats combined to do the job in the House.[7]

Another problem which frustrated the President throughout the session was continued Democratic factionalism which allowed Whigs to join with dissident Democrats to prevent prompt passage of war measures. "In truth," observed Polk, "faction rules the hour, while principle & patriotism are forgot-

6. Milo M. Quaife, ed., *The Diary of James K. Polk, 1845–1849*, 4 vols. (Chicago, 1910), 2: 286.

7. *Journal of the Senate of the United States . . . 1846–1848* (Washington, D.C., 1846–1848), 104.

TRIUMPH OF THE LETHEON.

A satirical view of Polk's intended use of the $3 million appropriated in 1847 to negotiate a peace with Mexico, this cartoon depicts Polk administering Letheon (an anesthetic) to one-legged Santa Anna, while Senator Thomas Hart Benton removes the other leg. *Yankee Doodle* 2 (1847–48): 5. *Courtesy of the Newberry Library, Chicago.*

ten." Adding to Democratic division was the coming presidential election of 1848. Throughout the session, Polk complained that already the "several cliques & sections of the Democratic party are manifestly more engaged in managing for their respective favourites in the next Presidential election, than they are in supporting the Government in prosecuting the war. . . ."[8] Although the followers of Benton and Lewis Cass actively supported the administration, the Calhoun and Van Buren wings acted in different ways to retard approval. Always unsympathetic to the southern-oriented Polk administration and already bitter over the outbreak of war, the Van Burenites were further angered by developments in New York state politics during the fall of 1846. In the state elections in November, the Democrats lost fourteen congressional seats and the Barnburners' presidential hopeful, Governor Silas Wright, failed in his bid for reelection. Adding to the anger of the Van Buren wing was the fact that during the fall campaign the conservative Hunker wing of the state Democratic party worked covertly to defeat Wright; the Barnburners charged presidential complicity, despite Polk's protestations to the contrary.

Yet circumstances continued to dictate that the embittered Van Burenites not break with the administration during the second session of the Twenty-ninth Congress. Although Wright's defeat represented a serious setback to his presidential potential, the Van Buren wing nevertheless hoped to win the Democratic nomination for him. They also continued to favor the acquisition of free territory through war with Mexico. When they returned to Congress in December, their strategy was to accommodate growing antislavery sentiment in their home districts by opposing the further extension of slavery and by demonstrating their independence of the Polk administration, which was dominated by southerners. Led by Representative Preston King, the Van Burenites attempted to attach the Wilmot Proviso to the three million appropriation to assure their constituents that this was not a war to extend slavery. In short, they maintained the strategy that they had hastily adopted in August 1846: they patriotically continued to vote support for the war while laboring constantly for congressional adoption of the Wilmot Proviso.

The effect of the Van Burenites' position was to postpone and endanger administration war measures by provoking a heated controversy over the slavery question which superseded debate on the war itself. Polk himself was both irritated and baffled by debate on the question. "Its [slavery's] introduction in connection with the Mexican War is not only mischievous but wicked," he wrote. "It is, moreover, practically an abstract question. There is no probability that any territory will ever be acquired from Mexico in which slavery would ever exist."[9] Some prominent southerners like Calhoun agreed with the

---

8. Quaife, *Polk Diary*, 2: 328; see also 330, 334, 340, 347–48, 366, 368, 392.
9. Ibid., 308; see also 305, 334, 340, 348.

president that "Slavery would probably never exist in these provinces."[10] But they were vehemently opposed to the principle embodied in the proviso and refused to accept any bill or treaty which violated southern rights by prohibiting slavery.[11]

But a more annoying problem for the president during this session of Congress was John C. Calhoun. Much to Polk's chagrin, Calhoun and his followers held the balance of power in the Senate.[12] With the Democrats holding only a four-vote majority over the Whigs in the Senate, Calhoun and a handful of southern senators loyal to him might join with a unified Whig opposition to defeat administration war measures. Although Calhoun had sustained the administration in Congress during the early weeks of the session, his hostility to Polk grew constantly. Finally, in February 1847, as a result of his personal ambition, concern over the course of the war, and position on the slavery issue, he broke openly with the president.

Calhoun had returned to Washington in December a confident and determined man. He had resolved to maintain his independent position, clearly aware that his stand on the war and his presidential aspirations were closely related. Thinking that time had justified the wisdom of his stand on the war's outbreak, Calhoun believed that his candidacy was steadily gaining momentum with reflective men around the country. Although he professed "little, or no interest" in the presidency, Calhoun's ambitions were then, as always, intense.[13] Once Congress convened, Calhoun maintained a temporary and ominous silence on the war calculated to enhance his national stature until new developments presented a propitious moment for him to publicize his views. Necessary war measures won his patriotic support, but politically expedient proposals such as the Lieutenant General Bill prompted his opposition. Near the beginning of 1847 Calhoun noted that his "inaction and silence" had made his position "more imposing" than ever. "My friends think I never stood higher, or stronger than I now do," reported a happy Calhoun, as he surveyed his prospects for 1848. "We hold the balance, and it is felt."[14]

10. Ibid., 283–84.

11. Calhoun to Mrs. T. G. Clemson, 27 December 1846, in *Correspondence of John C. Calhoun,* ed. J. Franklin Jameson, *Annual Report of the American Historical Association for the Year 1899,* vol. 2 (Washington, D.C., 1900), 2: 716; see also, Calhoun to H. W. Conner, 14 January 1847, Henry W. Conner Papers, Manuscript Division, Library of Congress, Washington, D.C.

12. Among Calhoun's Senate supporters during the session were Andrew Butler of South Carolina, as well as David Levy Yulee and James Westcott of Florida.

13. Calhoun to Mrs. T. G. Clemson, 21 November 1846, *Calhoun Correspondence,* 2: 713.

14. Calhoun to Mrs. T. G. Clemson, 27 December 1846, ibid., 716; Calhoun to Mrs. T. G. Clemson, 30 January 1847, ibid., 717.

Although he remained silent in December and January, Calhoun's hostility toward the Polk administration deepened and his despair over the Mexican War grew. "We never had a darker, or more uncertain future before us," he wrote on December 27, "and all from the rash step of rushing into war, when it could have been easily avoided. . . ." To his previous criticism of the war, Calhoun now added more urgent objections. A full-scale invasion of central Mexico would inevitably expand into an unlimited "war between races and creeds, which can only end in the complete subjugation of the weaker power." Furthermore, a war of conquest promised to incite a dangerous internal struggle in the United States over the slavery extension question.[15] Confronting this gloomy situation in early 1847, Calhoun formulated a plan to shorten and limit the war. In contrast to the Whigs who demanded that no Mexican territory be acquired and to the president who was pursuing an aggressive offensive strategy, Calhoun wanted the war changed from "an offensive to a defensive" conflict. The United States should propose to negotiate on the basis of a limited territorial indemnity by merely holding territory that it already occupied militarily. If Mexico refused to settle on such "just and liberal terms," then the United States would merely hold and defend what it already controlled.[16]

Calhoun selected early February to present his views on the war question. His speech, which was already scheduled for the Senate on February 9, assumed added significance when he, along with three of his supporters and Senator John Niles of Connecticut, voted the day before with the Whigs to defeat temporarily the administration's request for ten additional regiments of troops.[17] Basic to Calhoun's advocacy of a defensive strategy was his assumption that the planned invasion of Vera Cruz represented a dangerous escalation of military activity. A full-scale invasion of central Mexico threatened to transform the conflict from one of limited territorial objectives into an unlimited war of conquest, a threat to the existence of the Mexican nation itself. If such an invasion were successful, Mexico would be completely subjugated and fall under the dominion of the United States. Instead, Calhoun urged that the

---

15. Calhoun to Mrs. T. G. Clemson, 27 December 1846, ibid., 716; also, Calhoun to J. E. Calhoun, 12 December 1846, ibid., 714; Calhoun to T. G. Clemson, 17 February 1847, ibid., 718; Calhoun to Wilson Lumpkin, 13 December 1846, John C. Calhoun Papers, William R. Perkins Library, Duke University, Durham, N.C.

16. Calhoun to H. W. Conner, 14 January 1847, Conner Papers.

17. The vote was 22 to 18 against approval. The Democrats voting with Calhoun were Butler of South Carolina, Mason of Virginia, and Yulee of Florida, in addition to Niles (Cong. Globe, 29 Cong., 2nd Sess., 1847, 349). Calhoun based his opposition to the measure on the bill's first section, which granted the president broad power of appointment over what Calhoun termed "inferior" level officers. Once this section was deleted, the bill passed with Calhoun's vote and became law.

United States renounce the "mere principle" of conquest in formulating policy and in negotiating a peace settlement. The "true policy" of the nation was not to humiliate Mexico, but to preserve her honor and her strength. To those who would crush the enemy and exact a humiliating indemnity, Calhoun warned, "Mexico is to us the forbidden fruit; the penalty of eating it would be to subject our institutions to political death."[18]

Thus Calhoun presented an alternative which would allow the administration to secure the limited territorial indemnity it sought without a prolonged war of invasion. In his dramatic speech, Calhoun urged that the forces of the United States assume a stationary position running along the Rio Grande to the southern border of New Mexico, then due west along the thirty-second parallel to near the head of the Gulf of California, then south through the Gulf to the Pacific Ocean. By maintaining such a "defensive position," the United States would not only terminate the fighting but establish the Rio Grande as the permanent border of Texas and secure a limited territorial indemnity from the enemy. Calhoun claimed that the geographic line he had recommended was particularly good because if could be defended with little expense or difficulty. In addition, the area to the north was sparsely settled and of little value to Mexico, but of great potential to the United States. Thus, the line could provide the basis for a permanent and honorable peace. No longer threatened with complete subjugation and recognizing the extreme difficulty involved in dislodging the American forces, Mexico would be strongly induced to make peace. When Mexico was willing to negotiate and settle "fairly," the United States should then not hesitate to "pay liberally" for any territory ceded, beyond what constituted a just territorial indemnity.[19]

In contrast, Calhoun argued that Polk's offensive strategy would prove ruinous. Not only would it be costly in lives and resources, it also was militarily impractical. It promised not to shorten the war, but to prolong it. Even if Mexico City was conquered, peace was not assured. With their capital occupied, the notoriously stubborn Mexicans struggling for their very survival as a nation, might well refuse to negotiate and commence guerrilla warfare. On the other hand, if Mexico did surrender, new and insurmountable difficulties would be created. The rule of a conquered Mexico would be virtually impossible. Eight million Mexicans "so little qualified for free and popular government" could never be incorporated into the Union on an equal basis. At the same time, to hold Mexico as a "subject government" would destroy the very fabric of the Union by dangerously aggrandizing the power and the influence of the executive branch. Finally, there was the always present slavery question. With the free states determined to exclude slavery from the huge conquered

---

18. Ibid., Appendix, 323, 324.
19. Ibid., Appendix, 324, 325.

area of Mexico, and with the slave states just as adamant in their determination not to "be deprived of their rights," the Union itself would be endangered.[20]

Calhoun's speech criticizing administration policy and his vote against the Ten Regiment Bill quickly made him editor Thomas Ritchie's target of abuse in the administration newspaper, the *Washington Union*. Although he did not mention Calhoun by name in the February 9 issue, Ritchie directed his readers' attention to an article which declared that "the Mexicans [had] achieved another victory" with the Senate's temporary rejection of the Ten Regiment Bill.[21] In retaliation, Calhoun and his followers immediately joined with the Whigs to expel Ritchie from the Senate floor. Calhoun's ominous silence of December was now an open break with the administration, which seriously injured the South Carolinian's hopes of winning broad support among loyal Democrats for his presidential candidacy.[22] Particularly critical was the southern Democratic press. Furthermore, in Virginia, a state crucial to his ambitions and strong in Calhoun supporters, the Democratic state convention endorsed the administration's vigorous prosecution of the war and expressed regret that several Democrats had voted for Ritchie's expulsion from the Senate floor.[23]

In his speech of February 9, Calhoun had not discussed the status of slavery in the provinces to be ceded by Mexico as indemnity. But a few days later in a move which widened his breach with an administration already intent on avoiding the slavery question until the war could be ended, Calhoun made his position clear. On February 19, he introduced a series of resolutions in the Senate which declared that Congress had no constitutional power to make any law which would prohibit citizens of any state "from emigrating, with their property, into any of the territories of the United States. . . ."[24] Since early in the session, Calhoun had been disturbed by growing antislavery sentiment in the free states and the increasing determination of northern politicians of both parties to support the Wilmot Proviso. To Calhoun, the potential exclusion of slavery from the new territories threatened to deny the South equal rights and violate southern interests by erecting a cordon of free states around the slave South. Clearly, the North selfishly intended that southern "blood & treasure

20. Ibid., Appendix, 326, 327.

21. *Washington Union,* 9 February 1847, as cited in Charles M. Wiltse, *John C. Calhoun: Sectionalist, 1840–1850* (Indianapolis, Ind., 1951), 299.

22. For descriptions of the Ritchie affair and Calhoun's break with the Administration see Charles Ambler, *Thomas Ritchie: A Study in Virginia Politics* (Richmond, Va., 1913), 265–69; Morrison, *Democratic Politics and Sectionalism; The Wilmot Proviso Controversy* (Chapel Hill, N.C., 1967), 42–43; Wiltse, *Calhoun: Sectionalist,* 299–302.

23. Morrison, *Democratic Politics,* 43.

24. *Cong. Globe,* 29th Cong., 2nd Sess., 1847, 455.

shall be expended freely in the war to acquire territory, not for the common good, but as a means of . . . ruling us. We are to be made to dig our own grave."[25] In response to the prospect of a North united on the slavery question, Calhoun resolved to lead a southern-rights movement on the question. While unifying the South on the issue, Calhoun also hoped to reaffirm his stature as the leading spokesman of southern interests and thereby to further his presidential ambition with southerners of both parties.

Adding to the president's problems was an embittered Whig opposition, always eager to harass him. Polk complained frequently during the session that the "Federalists," as he referred to the Whigs, "manifestly enjoy the divisions within the Democratic ranks, and make it a rule of party action always to unite with the minority of the Democratic party, because in that way they hope and expect to make party capital for themselves." By February 1847, after two months of delay and inaction on Capitol Hill, Polk was so frustrated that he seriously considered appealing "boldly" to the nation for action in the form of a dramatic message to Congress.[26] Throughout the session, the Whigs did, of course, contribute to the president's exasperation. Some joined antislavery Democrats to agitate the troublesome slavery issue, while most voted with dissident Democrats to postpone, delay, and amend the administration's war program. At times, the opposition was even able to defeat such controversial measures as the special duty on tea and coffee and the Lieutenant General Bill. And in February, a much-needed Ten Regiment Bill was temporarily voted down by a Whig-Calhounite Senate coalition.

But eventually the president received the legislation he needed to continue his war policy. The Senate vote on the Ten Regiment Bill was reversed several days after its initial defeat when the measure was altered to limit the president's power to appoint officers.[27] After long delays, the loan and military appropriation bills passed with large bipartisan majorities.[28] Near the end of the session Congress also approved the president's request for $3 million. After long debate and bitter strife, the House finally acquiesced in the Senate

---

25. Calhoun to H. W. Conner, 14 January 1847, Conner Papers; also, Quaife, *Polk Diary*, 2: 283–84; Calhoun to Mrs. T. G. Clemson, 27 December 1846, *Calhoun Correspondence*, 2: 716.

26. Quaife, *Polk Diary*, 2: 348, 368–69.

27. *Cong. Globe*, 29th Cong., 2nd Sess., 1847, 349, 375–77.

28. The loan bill passed the House 165 to 22 and the Senate 43 to 2. (*Journal of the House of Representatives*, 29th Cong., 2nd Sess., 1847, 202; *Journal of the Senate*, 29th Cong., 2nd Sess., 1847, 137). The military appropriation bill passed the House 152 to 28; and the Senate without a roll call (*H. R. Journal*, 29th Cong., 2nd Sess., 1847, 406; *Sen. Journal*, 29th Cong., 2nd Sess., 1847, 247).

version of the Three Million Bill and approved the measure without the Wilmot Proviso.[29]

In spite of Polk's frequent complaints, then, the Whigs did not mount a serious challenge to administration war policy during the second session of the Twenty-ninth Congress. This Whig failure resulted from the party's inability to resolve a number of formidable problems which had existed since the outbreak of war the previous spring. In opposing a war supported by most Americans, the Whigs remained extremely sensitive to charges that their dissent offered "aid and comfort" to the enemy. Most dared not vote against the necessary men, money, and supplies. Another basic Whig problem was continued Democratic control of Congress, where the Democrats still held almost a two-to-one majority in the House and a less comfortable, but workable, four vote edge in the Senate. Although the Whigs had won dramatic victories in the congressional elections of 1846, these gains would not be realized until the Thirtieth Congress convened in December 1847. With a large numerical disadvantage in Congress, the Whigs' only possible hope for effective opposition was a temporary coalition with the Calhounites in the Senate to obstruct necessary war measures until the president altered his war policy.

In reality, however, such a coalition was never realized for several reasons. Both Calhoun and the great majority of Whigs were always unwilling to vote against needed supply bills. In addition, the South Carolina Democrat and the Whig party distrusted each other and their basic partisan differences remained. For example, just as the Whigs hoped to use the war as an issue with which to win the presidency in 1848, Calhoun predicted that one of the "evil consequences" of the war would be the "elevation of the Whigs to power. . . ."[30] More important was the fact that Calhoun and the Whigs disagreed on such crucial questions as the proper conduct and legitimate goals of the war, as well as the slavery question. While Calhoun spoke of accepting a

---

29. In the House, the proviso was added to the Three Million Bill by a 115 to 106 margin; the bill then passed 115 to 106 (*H. R. Journal,* 29th Cong., 2nd Sess., 1847, 346–50). In the Senate, the proviso was deleted by a 32 to 21 count and the Senate version then passed without a roll call (*Sen. Journal,* 29th Cong., 2nd Sess., 1847, 252–53). Once returned to the lower chamber, the bill minus the proviso eventually passed 115 to 82 (*H. R. Journal,* 29th Cong., 2nd Sess., 1847, 505).

30. Calhoun to James Edward Calhoun, 12 December 1846, *Calhoun Correspondence,* 2: 714. Intense partisanship remained an important feature of proceedings during this Congress with the exception of action on a few measures like the Wilmot Proviso and the Lieutenant General Bill. At one point in the House, for example, a seemingly innocuous resolution expressing appreciation to General Taylor and his troops for their victory at Monterey was amended by Democrats to include an open criticism of Taylor's agreement to a temporary armistice after the battle. The vote was a strongly partisan 110 to 69 with only 7 Democrats opposed, *H. R. Journal,* 29th Cong., 2nd Sess., 1847, 275.

"limited" territorial indemnity from Mexico, most Whigs firmly opposed any acquisition.

In addition, the Whigs confronted the specter of rising dissension within their own ranks. Differences between the conservative and radical wings of the party, which had been exacerbated by the outbreak of war, continued to grow during the winter of 1846–47. While the conservative majority of Whigs attempted to strengthen their political position by offering an equivocal opposition to the war and to preserve party unity by sidestepping the slavery issue, a small group of antislavery radicals struck an unqualified antiwar posture and agitated for their antislavery principles ever more anxiously. To the so-called "ultras," moral convictions on slavery increasingly superseded such expedient political considerations as party unity.

Whig factionalism, however, was not yet so serious as the divisions within the Democratic party. Unlike the Democrats, the Whigs did not suffer from intense personal rivalries in Congress. The Whigs naturally had their share of proud, jealous men and numerous presidential aspirants, but they were temporarily free from the bitter personal antagonisms which characterized Democrats Calhoun, Benton, and Cass. More important, the Whigs were the opposition party in Congress. As a clear minority, their divisions could be readily concealed. Constructive legislative proposals which might be offensive to one faction did not have to be presented as the Whigs united in a multi-faceted verbal assault on the Democratic administration.

If the Whigs failed to restrict administration war policy, they did succeed, however, in maintaining their bitter assault on Polk, the war, and its ramifications. And while antislavery and conservative Whigs disagreed sharply on antiwar strategy and differed in the general tone of their attacks, Whigs of all shades repeatedly used similar arguments to assail Polk's policies. Their main target throughout the session was, of course, President Polk's December congressional message which renewed controversy on a wide range of topics. Tirelessly, Whigs of all factions replied to its every objectional phrase. More often directing their efforts toward the voters at home than toward their bored colleagues, a constant procession of Whigs dissected, censured, and, to their own satisfaction, refuted the abundant falsehoods and distortions of the message.

As they had since the previous May, the Whigs completely rejected the president's own account of the coming of war and placed full blame on Polk. He had provoked hostilities by ordering American troops into Mexican territory. Such questions as the claims issue and the diplomatic rejection of Slidell represented mere subterfuges of a president bent on war. Compounding this reckless act was the president's subsequent conduct of the war. Whigs repeatedly observed that Polk had strengthened the enemy by allowing Santa Anna to return from exile, while at the same time he had weakened the American military effort by actively undermining Generals Scott and Taylor. In addition, the Administration had not made "a single serious effort" to increase government revenue in the face of soaring expenses. The tariff had been reduced, additional taxes had not been levied, and the restrictive subtreasury remained in operation as the administration resorted to an evasive and ruinous system of issuing treasury notes and negotiating loans.[31]

A constant preoccupation of the Whigs was the issue of their loyalty. They reacted furiously to Polk's insinuations that they were disloyal and offered valuable "aid and comfort" to the enemy with their criticism of the war. "Because we will not crouch, with spaniel-like humility, at his feet, and whine an approval of *all his acts,* we are met . . . with the grateful compliment from the President that we are traitors to our country," declared Representative Meredith Gentry of Tennessee.[32] According to the "new and strange doctrine" embodied in this "Executive ukase," Congress was to do nothing during a war but vote men and supplies as the president's "folly and caprice may dictate."[33] The acceptance of such a doctrine could only represent "a long stride on the road to tyranny."[34] To Whig partisans, Polk's efforts to discredit his leading Whig field commanders and his attack on the loyalty of the opposition indicated that "instead of waging this war with vigor against Mexico, the President and his party are more intent on waging war on a certain political party within the United States. . . ." To the administration, the Whigs charged, "political victory" seemed more important than a military triumph over a foreign enemy.[35]

Along with this unceasing partisan attack went a growing emphasis on two related issues which dominated the content of congressional debate and Whig rhetoric. Central during the session were administration territorial objectives and slavery extension. The Whigs understood that the invasion of northern Mexico, the subjugation and establishment of civil governments in the remote provinces of New Mexico and California, and the president's admission that any treaty must include "ample indemnity for the expenses" of war represented a virtual declaration that this was indeed a war of conquest. Particularly disturbing about a war waged to dismember a weaker sister republic were its moral and practical implications. " 'As a city set upon a hill,' " the United States traditionally stood before the world as a virtuous and peaceful republic, "devoid of an eager thirst for conquest," a propagandist of only the peaceful doctrine of "true republicanism." To this young republic, the people

---

31. *Cong. Globe,* 29th Cong., 2nd Sess., 1847, Appendix, 197.
32. Ibid., Appendix, 57.
33. Ibid., Appendix, 351.
34. Ibid., Appendix, 205.
35. Ibid., 226.

and nations of the world looked "as a beacon light . . . first in the lead of the great principles of liberty and justice. . . . We are the great *exemplar*," asserted Tennessee's E. H. Ewing.[36] Mexico herself was "guided by our example," declared Senator John Berrien of Georgia, "and striving to imitate it." Such an exalted stature demanded that the American people renounce any aggressive spirit of conquest, while demonstrating their understanding, charity, and forbearance.[37]

For the United States to subjugate Mexican provinces and virtually compel Mexican citizens to renounce their national allegiance and join the Union represented a violation of "the great principle of consent, which is the foundation of this republic." Even by conquering and annexing under the guise of a treaty, "the seeming consent is but the acquiescence of *compulsion,* not of *volition,*" argued Columbus Delano of Ohio.[38] The Whigs stressed that they objected not to the acquisition of territory, but to the means being employed. Although frontage on the Pacific was valuable, this goal could and must be achieved by legitimate purchase or by the voluntary annexation of an area rather than by the force of arms. "Our national character, and the purity of our political system," pleaded Henry Hilliard of Alabama, "are of far more consequence to us than any amount of territory which we can acquire."[39]

If the present war of conquest promised to pervert republican principles, it also posed a dire threat to the future existence of the Union itself. Once the unquenchable spirit of conquest had been aroused, future presidents, bent solely on personal glory and sustained by an eager populace, might well involve the nation in similar wars of aggression. Once excited, the passion would be hard to quell. But the prospect of future wars aside, the immediate consequences of adding Mexican provinces to the Union were ominous. Neither northern nor southern Whigs wanted the "amalgamation" of these "mongrel races" into the Union.[40] To the antislavery Whig Delano, these people were racially inferior: "they embrace all shades of color. . . . They are a sad compound of Spanish, English, Indian, and negro bloods . . . and resulting, it is said in the production of a slothful, indolent, ignorant race of beings."[41] Such a "medley of mixed races," Washington Hunt of New York warned, was fit "neither to enjoy nor to administer our free institutions. . . ."[42]

Distressed as they were by the incorporation of an alien people, most

36. Ibid., Appendix, 268.
37. Ibid., Appendix, 301.
38. Ibid., Appendix, 280; see also 232, 357.
39. Ibid., Appendix, 228.
40. Ibid., Appendix, 301.
41. Ibid., Appendix, 281.
42. Ibid., Appendix, 363.

Whigs were more frightened by the specter of slavery. And with the increasing likelihood of expansion into the Southwest and the reintroduction of the Wilmot Proviso during the session, the issue was hotly debated. Although the viability of slavery as an institution in the new territories was doubtful, the question was now widely interpreted as one of political power and sectional rights. Neither northerners nor southerners were prepared to give ground, though the Union be sundered. Recognizing the resolve of each section, most Whigs sought to avoid the explosive issue. They realized that the heated exchanges of 1847 were but a mild prologue to the struggle which would ensue if Mexican territory were ceded. "You are rushing headlong and blindfold upon appalling dangers, before which the stout heart shrinks, and brave men turn pale," declared Solomon Foot of Vermont. "You are rekindling the slumbering fires of a volcano, which, whenever they shall burst forth, will consume all the plain."[43] Whigs of all persuasions agreed that what might be a fatal victory must be prevented; the fighting must be stopped and indemnity forsworn. Northerners, like the antislavery representative from Indiana, Caleb Smith, cautioned that "the only ground of safety—the only ground which will secure the peace and harmony of the country—the welfare and prosperity of the Union, is to keep the territory, with all the distracting questions connected with it, out of the Union."[44] Georgia's John Berrien spoke for his section when he implored his colleagues to exclude "this demon of discord" from the "national councils" by forbidding the acquisition of territory.[45]

Although almost every Whig agreed on the misdeeds of the Polk administration and the tragedy of the war, the Whigs continued to disagree sharply on antiwar strategy. And as the session progressed, existing tensions and divisions between the radicals and the conservatives were sharpened rather than allayed. In contrast to the great majority of Whigs were a few party members in Congress who suspended judgment on the justice of the war and urged intensive military activity as the best means of restoring peace. These few men assailed the president only because he had been ill prepared for the crisis and had not been able to crush Mexico militarily. For example, Illinois Whig Edward Baker resigned his House seat in December 1846 to join the volunteers in Mexico. In his departing remarks before the House, Baker urged bipartisan support for the military effort as he alluded in chauvinistic terms to "new conquests" and "fresh triumphs."[46] In the Senate, Reverdy Johnson of Maryland emphasized that he "cared not under what circumstances it [the war]

---

43. Ibid., Appendix, 339.
44. Ibid., Appendix, 233; see also 225.
45. Ibid., Appendix, 301; see also 354.
46. Ibid., 92, 93; see also Appendix, 242.

was declared," but only how the enemy was to be crushed. He opposed the Ten Regiment Bill then under consideration only because "it did not go far enough." Congress should "raise twenty or thirty thousand men," and fully support them with a comprehensive revenue system.[47]

At the other end of the spectrum was the tiny "ultra" or radical wing of the party. Including most of the "immortal fourteen" who had voted against the original war bill, these "Young Whigs," as they often referred to themselves, were joined during the second session of the Twenty-ninth Congress by other sympathetic Whigs on the war issue. Almost all represented strong antislavery, antiwar, northern congressional districts. This situation allowed them great freedom to speak and act with bold convictions on the slavery and war questions without fear of alienating voters at home.

Lacking an active Senate spokesman and without real support for their views in the upper chamber, these radicals found their strength in the House where they could usually count on about two dozen votes on the war, some of which came from Whigs not sharing their antislavery opinions. With seventy-nine-year-old John Quincy Adams slowly recovering from a stroke, Joshua Giddings remained the "ultras' " most prominent, most radical, and most active spokesman. None of the radical Whigs was nearly so rabid on the slavery question as Giddings, but several men like Daniel Tilden and J. M. Root of Ohio sympathized with his abolitionist views. In addition, a number of other Whigs such as Daniel King and Charles Hudson of Massachusetts, Columbus Delano of Ohio, and Abraham McIlvaine of Pennsylvania, who were not political abolitionists, nevertheless viewed the Mexican War as proslavery in intent and refused to vote for some supply bills. Finally, a number of other northern Whigs, like Robert Winthrop of Massachusetts, who did not share the antislavery orientation of the "ultra" Whigs, voted with the radicals against several important supply measures because of their determination to prevent the addition of Mexican territory and to avoid a bitter struggle over the slavery extension question.

Like other Whigs, the radicals constantly condemned the president and discussed the causes, conduct, and objectives of the war. But unlike the conservative Whigs, who viewed the war as little more than another partisan issue, the radicals continued to interpret the conflict as part of an ongoing moral struggle. To them the war represented a criminal attempt by the Slave Power to extend its power and institutions. Such a moral outrage, asserted the antislavery Whigs, demanded unyielding opposition. Infuriating to these Whigs were attempts to impugn their loyalty and patriotism. Men like Representative Daniel King met such charges with proud defiance: "If an earnest desire to

---

47. Ibid., Appendix, 119–20.

save my country from ruin and disgrace be treason, then I am a traitor: if the fear to do wrong makes a man a coward, then I am a coward."[48] Just as a mariner, who saw his ship "plunging madly upon the breakers through the wickedness or unskillfulness of the pilot," would warn of the danger, declared Caleb Smith, so too should the true patriot now speak out in this hour of national crisis.[49]

Denying that any war, especially an unjust war, once commenced must be sustained by Congress, the radicals vowed to refuse their support. Those conservative Whigs who verbally condemned the war while voting men and money to sustain the killing only implicated themselves in the crime. Admittedly, this vacillating course might yield political rewards, but it also placed political expediency above moral right. For such a course, the radicals held only contempt. "I cannot sacrifice twenty thousand of our citizens annually, for the purpose of bringing more odium upon the present occupant of the Presidential chair," said Representative Charles Hudson. "I never will consent to play at a game where the lives of my countrymen are the stakes."[50] As an alternative to continued fighting, the radicals demanded its immediate end. A summary American withdrawal would insure prompt settlement and the renunciation of all territorial indemnity. Abraham McIlvaine summarized the antislavery position well when he said, "withdraw your troops within your acknowledged territory. Propose to Mexico terms of peace just and honorable, and she will not, she dare not, refuse them."[51]

While calling for troop withdrawal, the radicals pledged their support for the Wilmot Proviso should the war continue and result in the cession of Mexican soil. By early 1847, these men embraced the proviso as a broad antislavery principle on which all northerners could unite effectively to resist the Slave Power. But as Horace Greeley of the *New York Tribune* had earlier, Giddings now began to view the proviso as a viable antiwar tactic, as well as an antislavery principle. Passage of the proviso would end the war simply by destroying its motive. Realizing that slavery and southern power were not to be aggrandized by war, southerners would refuse to support it, thus forcing the withdrawal of troops and an honorable peace settlement.[52] But Giddings' views at this time were more advanced than those of his antislavery colleagues.

---

48. Ibid., Appendix, 294.
49. Ibid., Appendix, 230.
50. Ibid., Appendix, 370; see also 295.
51. Ibid., Appendix, 157. In the Senate, Joseph Cilley introduced a resolution for a temporary withdrawal which was defeated 44 to 0; in the House, Robert Schenck of Ohio attempted to introduce a resolution for withdrawal. The House did not allow Schenck's resolution to be introduced, the vote being 153 to 22 against when a two-thirds majority was required to suspend the rules and introduce the proposal. Ibid., 267, 273–74.
52. Ibid., Appendix, 404, 405.

They did not yet recognize the proviso as a direct antiwar tactic; instead, they continued to clamor for American troop withdrawal.

For most of the session, the radical Whigs in the House lacked a bold and persistent ally in the Senate. Their hopes were suddenly raised, however, late in the session by Thomas Corwin's famous speech of February 11, 1847. Witty and eloquent, the popular "wagon boy" of Ohio was an influential and nationally prominent Whig leader. But as a conservative Whig who felt strong devotion to his party and its principles, Corwin feared rather than sympathized with the antislavery principles of the Whig radicals. He wanted to avoid the whole slavery question by ending the war without territorial acquisition because of the great stress the controversy would place on the Union and his beloved Whig party. Thus, it was moral aversion to the war rather than antislavery conviction which finally compelled Corwin to speak out in such bold and extreme language.[53]

Speaking on the Three Million Bill, Corwin boldly labeled the president's explanation for the war "an egregious, palpable misrepresentation of fact" and his message of December 8 a "feculent mass of misrepresentation." Although Corwin had supported the war in its early months because he "hoped" that Polk "did sincerely desire a peace," Corwin now denounced the president for invading Mexico and demanding indemnity for war expenses. Repulsed by this spectacle of conquest, Corwin assailed the expansionists who supported the policy; their justifications were but a "hypocritical pretense, under which we sought to conceal the avarice which prompted us to covet and to seize by force, *that* which was not ours." For example, the argument that the nation needed more space for its future growth had "been the plea of every robber chief from Nimrod to the present hour," railed Corwin. "If I were a Mexican I would tell you 'Have you not room in your own country to bury your dead men? If you come into mine, we will greet you with bloody hands, and welcome you to hospitable graves.'" And to those who argued that the United States must have San Francisco Bay because it was the best harbor on the Pacific coast, the Ohioan responded with a bitter sneer: "I have never yet heard a thief, arraigned for stealing a horse, plead that it was the best horse that he could find in the country!"[54]

As an alternative to the present policy of fighting for indemnity, Corwin demanded immediate troop withdrawal. If the president refused, Corwin had

53. Corwin later explained his motives for the speech in Corwin to the editor of the Lafayette (Indiana) *Journal,* 4 April 1847, as cited in Boston *Daily Whig,* 19 May 1847; also, excerpts from Speech of Thomas Corwin on 28 August 1847 as cited in Daryl Pendergraft, "The Public Career of Thomas Corwin" (Ph.D. diss., State University of Iowa, 1943), Appendix H, 793–96.

54. *Cong. Globe,* 29th Cong., 2nd Sess., 1847, Appendix, 214, 215, 216, 217.

no option but to refuse to support the war: "Call home your army—I will feed and clothe it no longer—you have whipped Mexico in three pitched battles—this is revenge enough—this is punishment enough." It was time for the nation to reverse its insane and immoral course: "Let us here, in this temple consecrated to the Union, perform a solemn lustration; let us wash Mexican blood from our hands, and . . . swear to preserve honorable peace with all the world, and eternal brotherhood with each other."[55]

Predictably, Corwin's harangue evoked a spirited national response. This was not an antislavery firebrand who had spoken, but a thoughtful and highly respected Senator. The Democratic press rushed immediately to vilify "Black Tom" Corwin. One Ohio paper suggested a fitting inscription for Corwin's grave: "Thomas Corwin—A Traitor to His Country." In Washington, the *Union* charged that Corwin's speech belonged to the "nightmare school of literature."[56] Reportedly, when news of the speech reached the American army in Mexico just after the bloody Battle of Buena Vista, infuriated soldiers burned an effigy of Corwin dressed in a Mexican uniform and composed a bitter epitaph:

> Old Tom Corwin is dead and here he lies;
> Nobody's sorry and nobody cries;
> Where he's gone and how he fares;
> Nobody knows and nobody cares.[57]

Some Whig editors joined the Democratic chorus. In New York, James Webb's *Courier and Enquirer* declared the speech "anti-American."[58] But generally Whigs united in his defense. The Louisville *Journal* stated that "posterity would honor Mr. Corwin for his course," the Cleveland *Herald* praised the Senator for exposing the "miserable, wicked, and unholy" acts of the administration, and Horace Greeley in the *Tribune* lauded Corwin as "An Apostle of Truth."[59]

Especially happy were Giddings and his Conscience Whig allies in Massa-

---

55. Ibid., Appendix, 215, 218.

56. Easton *Argus* (Ohio), quoted in *Cincinnati Daily Enquirer*, 29 January 1848; Washington *Daily Union*, 18 February 1847, both as cited in Pendergraft, "Corwin," 421, 423. A detailed discussion of the impact of and reaction to Corwin's speech is presented in Pendergraft, "Corwin," 415–27.

57. Cited in Justin H. Smith, *The War With Mexico*, 2 vols. (New York, 1919), 2: 278.

58. New York *Courier and Enquirer* quoted in Washington *Daily Union*, 18 February 1847, as cited in Pendergraft, "Corwin," 423.

59. Louisville *Journal* as cited in *Ohio State Journal* (Columbus), 25 August 1847; Cleveland *Herald* as cited in *Ohio State Journal*, 3 March 1847; *New York Tribune*, 19 February 1847.

chusetts. Having mistaken Corwin's intense moral views for antislavery convictions, they believed that they now had found a fitting leader for the cause and a popular candidate for 1848. From Congress, Giddings reported to Charles Sumner that "Corwin has spoken, and retires this night in the proudest attitude of any man in the nation. . . . He maintains every position the Young Whigs occupy."[60] From the Bay State, Henry Wilson commented happily that Corwin's speech had "touched the popular heart" and because its "boldness and high morral [*sic*] tone" matched the sentiment in New England, people there readily responded to it and "tens of thousands want to hear more from him."[61]

However, the conservative majority of the Whigs, consisting of both northerners and southerners, were unwilling to follow the bold course charted by Corwin in the Senate or by the radicals in the House. In fact, Corwin's presidential stock dropped sharply with his fellow conservative Whigs who spurned his bold antiwar sentiments. The most prominent leaders of this wing continued to be men like Daniel Webster of Massachusetts, John Berrien of Georgia, John Crittenden of Kentucky, John Clayton of Delaware, and Willie Mangum of North Carolina in the Senate; and Georgia's Alexander Stephens and Robert Toombs, Tennessee's Meredith Gentry, Kentucky's Garrett Davis, and Massachusetts' Robert Winthrop in the House.

The speeches and remarks of these Whigs continued to stress the mendacity, deviousness, and blunders of Polk's war policy, as well as their genuine concern with the war's larger moral implications. While eschewing the moral outrage of radical Whig rhetoric, the conservatives forcefully warned of the practical and moral dangers inherent in a policy of aggressive expansionism. In practice, however, the conservative majority of Whigs still refused to translate their dissidence into a position of wholehearted opposition. They continued to speak peace while voting war. As Congress convened, Robert Winthrop, fresh from his overwhelming election victory in November, spoke for his wing of the party when he agreed with his friend Edward Everett, that the "true policy of the Whigs" during the session should be "to protest against the War in its causes or rather pretexts," while saying to the administration that "it is necessary to get creditably out of it:—take as many men and ships and as

---

60. Giddings to Sumner, 11 February 1847, in George Julian, *Life of Joshua Reed Giddings* (Chicago, 1892), 199.

61. Henry Wilson to Giddings, 24 February 1847, Joshua Reed Giddings Papers, Ohio Historical Society, Columbus (microfilm); see also, C. F. Adams to J. G. Palfrey, 14 February 1847, Adams Family Papers, Massachusetts Historical Society, Boston (microfilm copy in Alderman Library, University of Virginia). C. F. Adams to J. R. Giddings, 22 February 1847, Giddings Papers; Giddings to C. F. Adams, 15 March 1847, Adams Family Papers.

POLKING IT INTO HIM.

"HIT HIM AGAIN, JIM; HE HAINT GOT NO FRIENDS."

This cartoon chides the conservative Whigs in Congress for their contradictory position on the war. As Polk beats Mexico, in the background a Whig, declaring the war "wrong" and "unholy," at the same time urges the president to fight vigorously. *Yankee Doodle* 1 (1846–47): 179. *Courtesy of the Newberry Library, Chicago.*

much money as you please."[62] Although Winthrop denied that Polk should have a carte blanche, he reluctantly admitted that, except in special instances, he did "not see any way quite clear to refusing everything now."[63]

This conservative Whig position on the war resulted from the circumstances they confronted and their partisan political orientation. Although they wanted to end the fighting quickly and without Mexican territory, they were more determined to turn the war to their political advantage. They intended to use the war as a means of discrediting and defeating the Democrats and President Polk at the polls. Because their dual goals of ending the war and defeating the president were not always compatible, the conservative Whigs necessarily had to compromise their opposition. Basic to their ambivalent position was the knowledge that they could not realistically refuse to vote supplies. For a minority opposition to refuse to support the military effort would be both futile and politically destructive. Unable to defeat essential war measures with their votes, the conservatives would be confirming Democratic allegations that they were self-seeking, unpatriotic, and even treasonous politicians. "Those who oppose the prosecution of the War *now*," wrote Representative James Graham of North Carolina in January 1847, "will take the responsibility from the shoulders of the Administration and *shoulder* it themselves." The Whigs must then vote "all *proper* supplies" to continue the war.[64]

In charting their course, the conservative Whigs renounced the outlook, rhetoric, and extreme position of the "ultras." As party-oriented men dealing with a political issue, the conservatives remained unmoved by moral outrage. Furthermore, they believed that the radicals' refusal to vote supplies and their demands for immediate and unconditional troop withdrawal offered neither an effective nor an honorable solution to the war. "We are involved in a war: that is a 'fixed fact,' " declared Representative Alexander Harper of Ohio, "it [the army] must be supported, by both men and money, until it 'conquers a peace.' . . ."[65] Because they had pledged their loyal support to the military effort and refuted antiwar extremism, the conservative Whigs were infuriated by administration charges which lumped both conservative and radical Whig dissenters together as unpatriotic politicians giving encouragement to Mexico.

62. Everett to Winthrop, 5 December 1846, Winthrop Family Papers, Massachusetts Historical Society; and Winthrop to Everett, 12 December 1846, Edward Everett Papers, Massachusetts Historical Society. For an excellent public expression of the Whig position, see Daniel Webster's address "The Polk Administration," on 2 December 1846, in *The Writings and Speeches of Daniel Webster,* ed. Fletcher Webster, 18 vols. (Boston, 1903), 4: 1–66.

63. Winthrop to My Dear Sir, Christmas Eve, 1846, Winthrop Papers.

64. James Graham to William A. Graham, 10 January 1847, J. G. de Roulhac Hamilton, ed., *The Papers of William Alexander Graham,* 4 vols. (Raleigh, N.C., 1960), 3: 171.

65. *Cong. Globe,* 29th Cong., 2nd Sess., 1847, Appendix, 204; see also, 197.

In response, the conservatives vehemently asserted their right and their patriotic duty to question and criticize the causes, conduct, and goals of the conflict before voting needed supplies. In this regard, New Jersey Senator Jacob W. Miller's sentiments were typical. "Called upon, day after day, to vote men and money . . . to sustain a war, for the origin of which I thank God I am in no way responsible," Miller affirmed his duty to speak out. "I feel it due to myself, and to those who have honored me with a seat on this floor . . . to express plainly, but fearlessly, my views and feelings upon all the subjects connected with the Mexican war."[66]

Although both northern and southern Whigs denounced the war with equal vigor, Whigs from the slave states were more willing to support the war and less reluctant to acquiesce in the probable acquisition of Mexican territory than were their conservative colleagues from the North. In fact, as the second session of the Twenty-ninth Congress progressed, as the war continued to escalate, and as tension over the slavery question grew in early 1847, a few conservative northerners like Robert Winthrop felt compelled to modify their earlier positions. Always cautious, prudent, and proper and never as extreme on the war issue as Thomas Corwin, the Boston Cotton Whig continued to denounce what he believed to be the irrational antislavery agitation of the Conscience Whig extremists in Massachusetts. Nevertheless, the ever-sensitive Winthrop observed the increasing antislavery militancy of his home state and watched the growing public conviction in the North that this was a war to extend slavery. Sensing the trend of northern public opinion, Winthrop moved to accommodate it, even if he did not sympathize with it.

In Congress, Winthrop now moderated his earlier willingness to vote almost complete support of the war and endeavored to place himself between the radicals' uncompromising resistance and the conservatives' almost indiscriminate support.[67] Assuming that he wanted to refuse all support, which he did not, Winthrop believed that Mexican intransigence made such a stance impossible: "when she persists in breathing nothing but threatenings & slaughter, & has an army of 30,000 men in martial array, it is rather a delicate matter to take ground for disbanding our own armies or bankrupting the Treasury."[68] But Winthrop "would limit the supplies to some reasonable scale

---

66. Ibid., Appendix, 274; see also, 143–44.

67. Winthrop to Appleton, 5 February 1847, Winthrop Papers.

68. Winthrop to Mrs. Gardiner, 2 February 1847, Winthrop Papers. Other conservative Whigs also believed that continued Mexican belligerence made either the rejection of supplies or the withdrawal of American troops an unrealistic course. But while Winthrop voted against several important war measures, most conservatives supported virtually every war bill. See, for example, Graham to William Graham, 10 January 1847, *Papers of William Graham*, 3: 171.

of defense, rather than withhold them altogether . . . pay for all services of regulars or volunteers already contracted for . . . provide ample means to prevent our army from suffering, whether from the foe or from famine. . . ."[69] In translating his ideas into action, Winthrop actually voted against the major army appropriation bill, the Ten Regiment Bill, and the Three Million Bill, but supported the loan bill as "necessary whether we have peace or War measures."[70] In short, while condemning the "ultra" Whigs, Winthrop and several other northern Whigs voted much as they did.

Although Winthrop and the other conservative Whigs did not agree on precisely how they should vote, they did concur on their suggested alternative war strategy. Uncertain at the beginning of the session, the Whigs had finally settled on their so-called "No Territory" strategy by early February under the pressure of political necessity. Here the slavery issue was paramount. The conservatives feared that the addition of any Mexican territory would threaten the national unity of the Whig party and ultimately endanger the Union itself by raising the explosive slavery question. For this reason, Calhoun's defensive strategy offered no solution to them. Since Calhoun accepted the principle of "limited" Mexican territorial indemnity for war expenses and favored the acquisition of New Mexico and California, the slavery issue would have to be resolved.

Instead, the Whigs proposed an alternative on which both northern and southern Whigs could safely unite. The United States should immediately renounce all intentions of dismembering Mexico or of demanding any territorial indemnity. Under the leadership of Georgia's Representative Alexander Stephens and Senator John Berrien, the Whigs attempted to amend war measures to define explicitly the intent of Congress in sustaining the prosecution of the war, "provided, always, and it is hereby declared to be the true intent and meaning of Congress in making this appropriation, that the war with Mexico ought not be prosecuted by this Government with any view to the dismemberment of that republic, or to the acquisition, by conquest, of any portion of her territory. . . ."[71] In addition to avoiding the slavery question and thus preserving the Union as well as the Whig party, conservative Whigs argued that "No Territory" was a viable principle which would end the war. Once Mexico realized that her territory was not to be wrested from her and that she faced continued military humiliation, she would willingly negotiate the outstanding

---

69. *Cong. Globe,* 29th Cong., 2nd Sess., Appendix, 1847, 407.

70. Winthrop to Appleton, 21 January 1847; Winthrop to Appleton, 5 February 1847, Winthrop Papers.

71. *Cong. Globe,* 29th Cong., 2nd Sess., Appendix, 1847, 297. In the House the resolution was defeated several times. See *H. R. Journal,* 29th Cong., 2nd Sess., 347, 403–4. The resolutions were also easily defeated in the Senate; see *Sen. Journal,* 29th Cong., 2nd Sess., 252.

differences between the two countries, namely the border dispute and the claims issue. If this plan failed, argued the Whigs, the nation could then unite and raise a "force so overwhelming, as would promptly terminate the strife."[72] However, once introduced, these resolutions met defeat in both chambers of Congress. The expansionistic Democratic majority would not accept such a self-defeating restriction.

"No Territory," however, was primarily a political strategy designed to protect the Whig party rather than a means of ending the war. With the administration's territorial objectives clear, it was logically inconsistent for the Whigs to continue to vote supplies while demanding that no territory be taken from Mexico. If allowed to continue its vigorous and aggressive prosecution of the war, the administration would obviously demand that territorial indemnity be a necessary part of any peace settlement. At the same time, if the war was to be ended without the acquisition of Mexican territory, American troops had to be withdrawn and a total Mexican military defeat prevented. But the conservative Whigs never favored troop withdrawal and denounced the radical Whigs for suggesting just that idea.

Hence the conservative Whig position was fraught with contradiction. Demanding that the war be terminated, the conservative Whigs declared that it must be successfully prosecuted; denouncing an aggressive war of conquest, the Whigs fully supported American soldiers in Mexico. In their demands that the war cease and in their belief that the "No Territory" strategy would bring a quick settlement, the opposition placed full blame on President Polk for continued fighting. But if Polk was responsible for provoking the conflict and waging a war of conquest, it did not necessarily follow that an honorable settlement could be reached at his wish. Although the Whigs recognized that Mexico was a persistent enemy and used this as a rationalization for continuing to vote supplies, they deliberately distorted the nature of Polk's diplomatic problem. While arguing that radical demands to withdraw American troops would not end the war because Mexico would belligerently continue to fight, the conservatives contended that if the administration would only renounce its territorial ambitions, Mexico would readily conclude an honorable peace. The opposition even suggested that if the war were settled without indemnity, Mexico might well be willing to sell California and New Mexico. As the war intensified, the opposition increasingly attributed Mexico's notorious stubbornness to the fact that the enemy realized she was fighting to preserve her territorial integrity and quite possibly her very existence as a nation. But such arguments misrepresented the situation; Mexico was a willing, if outclassed, belligerent. Mexican hatred of the United States ran deep. Clearly she preferred fighting to negotiating. Even if the enemy agreed to talk, it was highly

---

72. *Cong. Globe*, 29th Cong., 2nd Sess., Appendix, 1847, 297; see also 277.

unlikely that Mexico would be willing to recognize the Rio Grande as the border of Texas; nor would Mexico be willing to cede a large portion of New Mexico or California to her hated northern neighbor.

When Congress adjourned in early March, the military situation remained unsettled. Scott's invasion of Vera Cruz was yet forthcoming, and word of Taylor's stunning victory over Santa Anna at Buena Vista in late February had not reached the eastern seaboard. It was, however, clear that congressional opponents of the war had failed to alter the course of the conflict or to deter the resolute president. The opposition of dissident Democrats and partisan Whigs had contributed to considerable delay, doubt, and frustration for the administration; but by March Polk had won approval for his needed war measures and could pursue his territorial objectives with renewed persistence and without congressional interference for the next nine months.

But if the second session of the Twenty-ninth Congress did not alter administration war policy, it increased the existing factionalism already revealed by the outbreak of war in May 1846. While constant debate on the war and slavery extension contributed to full understanding of the nature and consequences of the war, it also heightened the pressure which threatened weakening party loyalties. By March, Calhoun had openly broken with the administration, and the determination of the Van Burenites on the slavery issue was equally ominous. Likewise, the boldness and resolve of the radical Whigs on the war and slavery promised similar problems for that party.

6

★ *Nonpolitical Dissent*
Pacifist and Abolitionist

FOR AMERICANS, 1847 was a year of both excitement and
frustration. From early March to October news arriving along the eastern
seaboard reported an unbroken string of military victories. First came word
of General Taylor's stunning and unexpected victory at Buena Vista in late
February. Since this decisive battle virtually terminated the war in northern
Mexico, attention then shifted to General Scott's invasion of central Mexico
and his advance on Mexico City. Beginning with the American landing and
capture of Vera Cruz in March, Scott's forces defeated the Mexicans in a
series of engagements before finally occupying Mexico City on September
14. Because they had been achieved in the face of great obstacles and difficult odds, the decisive American victories inflated national pride and excited
expansionist zeal. But at the same time, the failure to force a complete Mexican surrender or to bring an end to the war contributed to public disillusionment with President Polk's conduct of the war. During 1847, the overwhelming enthusiasm which had marked the initial months of battle dissolved in the face of a conflict that began to appear interminable. With each
new American victory came news of more casualties, along with word of
continued Mexican obstinance. The anticipated brief war which had seemed
to promise only easy glory in May 1846 now deteriorated into the harsh
reality of a costly, bloody, and prolonged struggle with an intransigent enemy.

By the fall of 1847, Americans of every political persuasion wanted the
war concluded. The desire for peace did not, however, translate into an overwhelming mandate against the war. While criticism grew in volume and intensity and the Polk administration continued to lose popularity, most Americans saw no real alternative to supporting the president. Pointing out that the
United States confronted an unreasonable enemy and that no viable alternatives were available, his Democratic supporters argued effectively that Polk's
war policy promised the only sure way to a "just" and "honorable" settlement. In addition, more-rabid Democrats and visionary expansionists contended that the war should be escalated. Pointing to Mexican stubbornness,

these men argued that only Mexico's total defeat and her complete absorption by the United States would effectively end the war.

At the same time, the opposition intensified its criticism, though it still disagreed as to how the war might best be ended. Extreme dissenters continued to demand immediate and unconditional withdrawal, just as more moderate critics argued that an honorable peace would follow promptly once the United States assured Mexico that she was not to be dismembered. Meanwhile, other critics, like the *New Englander,* assumed an ambivalent position. Edited by Edward Royall Tyler, this New Haven, Connecticut, quarterly generally espoused a Congregationalist view of the world. On political issues, the prominent regional journal was antislavery, antiexpansionist, and, although ostensibly nonpartisan, Whiggish in outlook. When war broke in 1846, the *New Englander* quickly decried the event as a southern phenomenon and renewed its sectional opposition to the expansionist scheme, warning that "nations, like other huge fabrics, drop to pieces by their own weight. . . ."[1]

But then in early 1847, this same journal shifted its position. It now conceded that considerable benefit might result from this "unchristian" but not "necessarily impolitic" war and endorsed the impending acquisition of California as commercially invaluable to the nation.[2] But having supported the addition of new territory, the *New Englander* continued to condemn this war of conquest, its cost in blood and treasure, its impact on declining public morals, and its "demoralizing and degrading" effects on the individual soldier.[3]

In short, a clear consensus either for or against the war failed to materialize during 1847. While continued fighting stimulated expansionist demands for larger and larger cessions of Mexican soil, it also inflamed antiwar sentiment and contributed to antiwar activity.[4] The war remained most popular in the West and Southwest, and most unpopular along the upper Atlantic seaboard, especially in New England. Critics of the war, however few, did exist in the West and Southwest, just as a few men in the intensely antiwar state of Massachusetts endorsed the war. Of the dozens of antiwar petitions presented to Congress, the great majority were from citizens above the Mason-Dixon line and east of Indiana, but a few did trickle in from the West and Southwest.[5] This division of opinion is largely explained by the fact that the war

---

1. *New Englander* 4 (July 1846): 432–33.

2. Ibid., 5 (January 1847): 141, 142.

3. Ibid. (October 1847): 604–13 passim.

4. While antiwar meetings and rallies were held in New England, in upstate New York, and in cities like New York, Philadelphia, Cincinnati, and Trenton, New Jersey, the American Peace Society's *Advocate of Peace* continued to lament the persistence of the war spirit.

5. A list of petitions addressed to Congress is available in the indices to the House and Senate Journals for the Twenty-ninth and Thirtieth Congresses.

remained primarily a partisan issue to most Whigs and Democrats. Thus New England Democrats, like Caleb Cushing and George Bancroft, defended their president's policies, just as western and southwestern Whigs condemned them. Of the state legislatures which officially criticized the war, all were under Whig control.[6]

Although numerous state and congressional elections were held during 1847, they, like the elections of 1846, did not accurately gauge the war's popularity for several reasons.[7] First, as usual in such elections, a variety of issues, personalities, and local circumstances affected the outcome of individual contests. For example, the Whigs gained three places on the North Carolina congressional delegation largely because a Whig majority in the state legislature had redistricted the state in 1847. In New York, the Whigs emerged victorious in the state elections mainly as a result of a serious division within the Democratic party between the Barnburner and Hunker factions. Second, although the war was the central issue in numerous congressional elections, the Whig position on the war and expansion remained purposely ambiguous. Relying on the declining popularity of the Polk administration, the Whigs were consistent only in their constant denunciations of the president. Damning the war itself, the Whigs nevertheless gloried in each military victory and attempted to outdo their opponents in eulogizing American soldiers and their Whig commanders. In the southern states, conservative Whigs simultaneously sought to fortify their antiwar, antiexpansionist attack and to identify themselves with American military success by eagerly trumpeting the name of Zachary Taylor for the presidency. They thus protected themselves against the most vulnerable point in their position, their dubious loyalty and patriotism, and countered Democratic charges that the Whigs had offered "aid and comfort" to the enemy. Finally, the elections were inconclusive; in state and congressional elections neither the Democrats nor the Whigs were able to score a decisive victory. On the state level, Connecticut and Polk's home state, Ten-

---

6. In Massachusetts, the Whig legislature not only adopted a comprehensive and strong antiwar report, but it also refused to appropriate funds to support a volunteer regiment. See Charles Sumner, *Report on the War With Mexico,* Commonwealth of Massachusetts, House Bill No. 187, April 1847. Although written by Sumner, this report was actually presented in the legislature by Edward L. Keyes.

7. An excellent analysis of the 1847 congressional elections is contained in Brian G. Walton, "Elections for the Thirtieth Congress and the Presidential Candidacy of Zachary Taylor," *Journal of Southern History* 25 (May 1969): 186–202. See also, for example, Charles M. Snyder's *The Jacksonian Heritage: Pennsylvania Politics, 1833–1848* (Harrisburg, Pa., 1958), 201. Snyder claims that the war remained popular in Pennsylvania during 1847. The 1847 elections were concentrated in the slave states, with contests being held in Virginia, Kentucky, Tennessee, Alabama, North Carolina, Maryland, Mississippi, Louisiana, as well as the free states of New Hampshire, Rhode Island, Connecticut, Indiana, and Maine.

nessee, elected Whig governors, but Maryland, Georgia, Pennsylvania, and New Jersey, all states important to the Whigs, chose Democratic governors. In the congressional contests, although the Whigs gained fourteen seats and a slight majority in the House, their victory was hardly overwhelming. In Rhode Island and Clay's Kentucky, the Democrats who willingly stood behind the achievements of the Polk administration and believed the war to be popular actually gained three seats.

Throughout the war the center of opposition continued to be the New England states, particularly the Boston area. Here Whig politicians, clergymen, pacifists, and abolitionists intensified their relentless attack. From this antiwar activity emerged a variety of often overlapping but distinct critical opinions of the war, which were to be fully developed during 1847. Nonpolitical dissenters agreed in interpreting the Mexican War primarily as a moral question rather than a partisan political issue. Confronting a horrible crime, they employed the language of moral outrage. Unlike the arguments of antiwar politicians, those of the pacifists, abolitionists, and clergy did not evolve markedly during the war. Because they never were in doubt as to the real purposes of the war, it made little difference that the administration's objectives, obscure at first in May 1846, were undeniable by 1847, or that by 1848 the war seemed to threaten Mexico's very national existence. To pacifists, the war always remained a flagrant violation of their principles of Christian pacifism; to abolitionists, it was an unholy war for slave territory in February 1848 just as it had been in May 1846; and to most antiwar ministers, it was an immoral and unholy crusade, whether the final objective be San Francisco Bay or Mexico City.

In addition to the proliferation of impassioned editorials, speeches, sermons, and resolutions, an effective though less frequently used literary form was antiwar satire. Most popular, of course, were the abolitionist oriented *Biglow Papers* of James Russell Lowell, but the Major Jack Downing letters of Maine humorist Seba Smith were also well received and frequently cited. The nonpartisan Smith had satirized politicians of both parties during the 1830s through the literary figure of Major Jack Downing, an unpretentious "Downeaster" from Maine. As a personal advisor and friend of "old Gineral" Jackson, Major Downing had depicted politics of his day in a style which combined understated and homespun monologues with incisive criticism. Now, a decade later, during the Mexican War, Smith had Major Downing reappear on the Washington scene as an advisor to Jackson's Tennessee protege "Young Hickory,"as Polk was sometimes known. While eschewing the slavery question, Smith now lampooned the president, his war, and the concept of aggressive expansionism. Although Smith was still nonpartisan in politics, the new series of twelve Downing letters was prominently printed in the Whig *National Intelligencer.*

In the role of Polk's trusted counselor, Major Downing commented knowingly on the president's personal feelings and political motives. For example, he reported a conversation in which Polk admitted that this "war is the concern of my getting up—for my own use; and I shall manage it just as I please. . . ." In this instance, Polk had become indignant after General Scott had requested more troops to accelerate the war effort. "I don't want them Mexicans whipped too fast," confided Polk to the Major, "especially when them upstart generals get all the glory of it."[8] During the summer of 1847, Smith had the Major leave Washington as Polk's secret peace commissioner. From Mexico City, Downing noted the amazing success of American arms and predicted that within a few years the Americans might well reach "clear to Cape Horn." Then if the government ever got into insoluble difficulty in North America, they "would have a horn in South America that they might hold on to."[9]

By presenting an enthusiastic and unqualified endorsement of the policy of aggressive expansionism through the person of Major Downing, Smith succeeded in ridiculing the whole concept. Major Downing's naive defense of an unrestrained program of "annexin' " clearly exposed the absurdity and danger inherent in such rampant expansionism. Once in Mexico, Major Downing was fully captivated by the exuberance of the moment and urged Polk to rush reinforcements to the area because what had been annexed "so far, isn't but a mere circumstance to what we've got to do." Numerous civilian settlers were also needed to consolidate the triumph by taking up the "slack themselves" and leaving "the army free to go ahead, and keep on annexin'." Because of his enthusiasm, the Major could not understand those thick-skulled Americans who thought such a policy unwise or unprofitable. In fact, reported Downing, "we get ten to one for our outlay. . . ." Mexico City "cost us only two or three thousand men to annex" and in return "we get at least one hundred and fifty thousand" Mexicans. Nor could the Major agree with those who questioned the "*quality*" of the people being annexed. "They ought to remember that in a Government like ours, where the people is used for voting, and where every nose counts one, it is the *number* that we are to stan' about in annexin', and not the quality. . . ." Indeed, the United States was doing a "grand business" in people.[10]

Downing also had special praise for the president's astute, if devious, policy of maneuvering to acquire all of Mexico while persistently denying that he was fighting a war of conquest. Once Mexico was safely annexed, the presi-

---

8. [Seba Smith] Major Jack Downing, *My Thirty Years Out of the Senate* (New York, 1859), 258, 251.

9. Ibid., 284.

10. Ibid., 275–76.

dent could step forward and announce to the nation that he had made "the greatest bargain that anybody ever made on this airth. . . ." If Polk succeeded, his place in history would be secure. Even if the annexation of Mexico later proved disastrous and resulted in the destruction of the Union, Polk "would still stand above Washington, and be remembered longer . . . in this grand annexin' business of yourn, if you should set fire to the great temple that Washington built, and burn it down, don't fear but your name will live on the page of history full as long as Washington."[11]

In their dissent, members of the American Peace Society were both mild and innocuous. More militant and extreme pacifists did, of course, exist. For example, one of the Society's own critics was the New England Non-Resistance Society. As early as 1838, its membership, composed of numerous Garrisonian abolitionists, as well as extreme nonresistant pacifists like Adin Ballou, had criticized the moderation and timidity of the American Peace Society. But the Non-Resistance Society was tiny in size and did not play an important role in opposing the Mexican War. In addition, the dissent of its Garrisonian members was primarily antislavery in content, rather than pacifist. Numerous antiwar clergymen, who were not members of a peace society, also used pacifistic arguments to condemn the war. But it remained for the members of the American Peace Society to present the most detailed and sustained pacifistic criticism of the Mexican conflict.

Basing their opposition on the principles of Christian pacifism, members of the Society emphasized that a "higher" law, the "Christian law of love, forbearance, long suffering, [and] forgiveness . . . ," undeniably forbade war.[12] Anyone engaged in war necessarily violated "every Christian principle, and every Christian institution."[13] Merchant Joshua P. Blanchard spoke for other pacifists when he argued that because of its "unprincipled depravity" and "unmitigated sin," the Mexican War could not be condoned even on the "cowardly and faithless" rationale of political necessity, national security, self-defense, or international law. Furthermore, what ultimate judgment, asked Blanchard, could the "war-maker and the war-supporter" alike expect from the Almighty for their participation in such a horrible war of murder and rapine.[14]

In their criticisms, the American Peace Society warned of the pervasive dangers inherent in the Mexican War. By creating a massive public debt and diverting the nation's resources from peaceful to bellicose purposes, the economic growth and prosperity of the United States would be forfeited to a

---

11. Ibid., 284–85, 289.
12. *The Advocate of Peace* 7 (February 1847): 16.
13. Ibid. (August 1847): 88.
14. Ibid., n. s. 1 (July 1846): 168, 169, 170, 171.

career of killing and invasion. In addition, the nation's republican form of government would be threatened by vastly increasing executive patronage power, giving a "dangerous ascendency" to military heroes, and rendering veteran soldiers unfit "to discharge the duties of a free and enlightened" citizenry. For example, the arbitrary annexations of New Mexico and California represented acts of "sheer despotism" and dangerous precedent. A future American Caesar or Napoleon, "at the head of a hundred thousand obsequious troops, [might] change at will the present form of our government, and, by the aid of their bayonets, impose himself upon the country as PERPETUAL PRESIDENT."[15] Meanwhile at home, the pacifists cautioned, the nation's moral sense and republican character were being perverted by the growth of a poisonous war spirit. Such "false and pernicious principles" as *"our country, right or wrong,"* were "subversive of God's authority . . . and likely, if not discarded by our people, to undermine, their moral character. . . ."[16]

While the members of the American Peace Society had no difficulty concurring on the "wickedness and folly" of the Mexican War, they did disagree sharply on the crucial questions of the Society's basic objectives and its antiwar tactics. Although its membership and following had been strengthened in the 1840s by the growth of reform sentiment and the absence of major wars, the American Peace Society nevertheless remained a small New England–centered organization always more earnest and articulate than it was effective. But by 1846, even the Society's limited influence was threatened by factionalism. One wing of so-called moderates, led by the corresponding secretary, the Reverend George Beckwith, encouraged and favored accepting all sorts of pacifists into the organization, including individuals who condoned the concept of defensive war. Beckwith, whose followers comprised a majority of the Society's membership, also believed that the organization should confine its activities solely to the objective of abolishing international war, while refraining from such "extraneous" issues as antigovernment action and the abolition of capital punishment.

Opposed to the moderate group was a more extreme or "reform" wing led by the increasingly prominent "Learned Blacksmith," Elihu Burritt. This unpretentious man, who at this time was editor of the Society's *Advocate of Peace and Universal Brotherhood* and also a member of the executive committee, had won the support of a majority of the Society's officers and its most fervent members. The "reform" wing, basing its views on a strict reading of the Society's 1837 constitution which declared that "all war is contrary to the spirit of the Gospel," believed that the Society should remain true to the letter

---

15. Ibid., 7 (February 1847): 19.
16. Ibid. (July 1847): 85.

of its constitution.[17] All war, defensive or offensive, should be condemned, antigovernment activity to achieve this end should be endorsed, and the abolition of capital punishment should be sought.

The basic differences of opinion finally came to a head during the American Peace Society's convention in May 1846. Because of the aggressive nature of the newly declared Mexican War, both the moderate and reform factions condemned the conflict but clashed on how the Society should oppose it. After a tense and high-spirited meeting, the convention adopted resolutions favorable to the moderates whereby the Society pledged itself to the single, innocuous, and vague objective of ending international war. Antigovernment activity and capital punishment were ignored. In addition, the convention approved a temperate report blaming the war on the United States, and the Society invited all friends of peace, whatever their views on defensive war, to join the organization.[18]

The adoption of these resolutions bitterly antagonized the reformers, since they had favored resolutions in strict accord with the letter of the 1837 constitution. Accordingly, at an executive meeting in June, Burritt, along with President Samuel E. Coues, Walter Channing, Amasa Walker, Joshua P. Blanchard, and several other committee members, withdrew from the Society, a break which was not made public until December. Explaining that he could not remain in the Society "for a moment after one jot or tittle" of the 1837 constitution had been "abated," Burritt denounced the new lenient standards of the Society. Now even Mexican and American soldiers "with the points of their bayonets newly dipped in human blood," might "subscribe to the highest article of faith remaining in the Society's creed. . . ."[19]

By previous arrangement, Burritt continued to edit the *Advocate* for several months, thus giving the reformers an effective voice in this journal until December 1846. Unlike the moderates, members of the reform wing, such as Boston merchant Joshua P. Blanchard, counseled active noncooperation with the government war effort. The "true course" for friends of peace was to withhold all support from the government. Blanchard argued that to do otherwise in a criminal war of invasion for Mexican territory was complicity. "It matters not that the war has commenced," argued Blanchard, "all human laws as well as common sense condemn, in a crime, an 'accessory after the fact,' as well as an 'accessory before the fact.' "[20] While a Christian pacifist could not

17. Elwin Whitney, *The American Peace Society, A Centennial History* (Washington, D.C., 1928), 40. For more detail on this schism, see Peter Brock, *Pacifism in the United States: From the Colonial Era to the First World War* (Princeton, N.J., 1968), 639–52.

18. *Advocate of Peace,* n. s. 1 (June 1846): 139–40.

19. Ibid. (December 1846): 275–76.

20. Ibid. (July 1846): 168, 169, 170.

condone "forcible resistance" to his government, he could certainly withhold all "support and cooperation" and give "every moral obstruction" to the war. Only by bearing firm and constant testimony against his government and its unjust course could the "Christian patriot" hasten the end of fighting while simultaneously affirming his own fidelity to the precepts of God.[21]

His principles having been rejected by the followers of Beckwith, Burritt traveled to England in the summer of 1846 while he was still editor of the *Advocate*. It was in England that Burritt founded the international League of Universal Brotherhood. The basis of this pacifist association was a pledge sworn by each member that he would never "yield any voluntary support or sanction to the preparation or prosecution of any war, by whomsoever, for whatsoever proposed, declared or waged."[22] Although it was most successful in the British Isles, an American branch of the League was founded in Boston during the Mexican War in May 1847 under the leadership of members of the old reform wing of the American Peace Society. Receiving its most enthusiastic support in the northeastern and some northwestern states, the League won the support of prominent clergymen and reformers, as well as the signatures of several thousand Americans. But because the League was primarily an Anglo-American association, it did not concentrate its activities on opposing the Mexican conflict.[23]

In contrast to the reform pacifists, the moderate pacifists refused to sanction or counsel antigovernment activity. In control of the American Peace Society by June 1846 and of the *Advocate of Peace* by the beginning of 1847, the moderates under George Beckwith's leadership directed the Society's activities in close accord with their lenient principles.[24] For example, the Society unsuccessfully petitioned the Polk administration to end the war. Beckwith, acting in behalf of the Society as its corresponding secretary, first appealed to President Polk in July, "earnestly" entreating the chief executive to end the war immediately *"by recalling our troops from Mexico"* and resolving the dispute by negotiation or "by reference to umpires mutually chosen." Beckwith argued that since American troops had invaded Mexican territory, the first initiative must come in the form of troop withdrawal. Furthermore, the United States would lose nothing by such a "magnanimous" act because nego-

---

21. Ibid., 170, 171.

22. Merle Curti, *The American Peace Crusade, 1815–1860* (Durham, N.C., 1929), 145.

23. For a detailed discussion of the League, see Brock, *Pacifism in the United States,* 652–66.

24. After Beckwith assumed control of the *Advocate* it was significantly renamed by dropping "Universal Brotherhood" from the title which the journal had carried under Burritt's editorship. Symbolically, this deletion demonstrated the society's concern for the sole objective of abolishing international war.

tiation would uphold the just claims of the country. If Polk sought additional territory, purchase would be both cheaper and more honorable than war.[25] Beckwith addressed another appeal to the president a week later and urged Polk to accept an alleged "generous" offer of mediation from the British, and recommended that he meanwhile suspend "all hostile operation against Mexico to give a fair trial to this overture. . . ." Mediation represented a more effective means of attaining a "speedy, equitable peace" than a continued "blind and brutal arbitrament of the sword. . . ."[26]

Not gaining the president's ear in the early months of fighting, the Society attempted to undermine the national "war spirit." To this end, the *Advocate of Peace* continued to issue a spate of antiwar propaganda—sermons, speeches, poems, and petitions. It also regularly printed eyewitness accounts depicting the pervasive corruption, mismanagement, and immorality of army life, as well as the horror and atrocity of battle. The Society also distributed more than 2,500 appeals for peace to clergymen and editors, petitioned both the Twenty-ninth and Thirtieth Congress to end the war, and urged local peace groups, religious congregations, and private individuals to address similar appeals to Congress. In their activities, the pacifists consistently argued that, because the United States was both the aggressor and the stronger party, it must initiate negotiations by withdrawing its troops from Mexican soil and agreeing to treat on honorable terms.

In an effort to encourage opposition, the Society offered a prize of $500 for the best book on the war. The winning manuscript, selected and published after the war, was *The Mexican War Reviewed* by the Reverend A. A. Livermore of Keene, New Hampshire. In his comprehensive review, Livermore described the war as one to extend slavery, detailed how the conflict might have been avoided, and catalogued its manifest evils. The only possible benefit of such a war, he concluded, might be the lesson of peace it could teach.[27] Another notable entry was a *Review of the Causes and Consequences of the Mexican War* by William Jay, the son of former Chief Justice John Jay. Also a broad indictment of the war, the book was printed and distributed by the Society in 1849.[28]

All these activities were directed toward the futile goal of mobilizing the full force of public opinion to demand that the government terminate the war. "This war might be terminated very soon," declared the *Advocate* in early 1847, "if the mass of people in each or either country would call aloud for

---

25. *Advocate of Peace,* 7 (February 1847): 16.
26. Ibid., 17.
27. Abiel A. Livermore, *The War With Mexico Reviewed* (Boston, 1850).
28. William Jay, *A Review of the Causes and Consequences of the Mexican War* (Boston, 1849).

peace. . . ."[29] The rise of a large, undeniable antiwar spirit, contended the pacifists, would be far more effective than any attempt to resist the government. If such a powerful sentiment were expressed in the form of thousands of petitions pouring in to Congress "from every party at the East and the West, at the North and the South," asked the *Advocate,* "would not their wishes be heeded, and the war be brought at once to a close?"[30]

Markedly more extreme and vehement in their opposition were the abolitionists. Although many abolitionists were avowed pacifists of varying degrees and advanced pacifist arguments to condemn the Mexican War, their attack on the conflict was always overwhelmingly antislavery in content and tone. Quick to register their violent protests when war commenced were the Garrisonians acting through the American Anti-Slavery Society which they controlled. When the Society held its annual meeting in May 1846, in attendance were William Lloyd Garrison, Wendell Phillips, Parker Pillsbury, Edmund Quincy, and W. H. Channing, as well as many other prominent radical abolitionists. In addition to dealing with the usual variety of antislavery matters, the Society adopted an "appeal," drafted by Garrison, which well summarized the radical abolitionist position in connecting the issues of slavery and the war. The resolution labeled the conflict one "of aggression, of invasion, of conquest, and rapine—marked by ruffianism, perfidy, and every other feature of national depravity—and waged solely for the detestable and horrible purpose of extending and perpetuating American slavery throughout the vast territory of Mexico." The United States, not Mexico, was to be blamed for the conflict. Previously Texas had been stolen from Mexico, and now territory "far beyond the limits ever known or recognized as Texas proper" had been occcupied. The appeal called on the friends of "JUSTICE, HUMANITY, PEACE, AND LIBERTY" to bring the war to an immediate end by paralyzing the government. Meetings, remonstrances, and testimonies must thunder forth demanding that the war cease. "No pains" should be spared to "discourage and prevent any fresh enlistment in the army. . . . Your motto is 'God and Liberty!' . . . give no support to this piratical war upon injured Mexico."[31]

Within days the abolitionists had given form to their protest by circulating petitions and enlisting dozens of signatures for an antiwar pledge. Again the familiar names of Garrison, Phillips, Pillsbury, Quincy, and Channing headed the list. Signers promised not to "aid, support, or countenance the Government in the War with Mexico, but at all hazards, and at every sacrifice to refuse enlistment, contribution, aid and countenance to the War."[32] This

29. *Advocate of Peace,* 7 (February 1847): 20.
30. Ibid. On the pacifists and the peace treaty, see Merle Curti, "Pacifist Propaganda and the Treaty of Guadalupe Hidalgo," *American Historical Review* 33 (1928): 596–98.
31. *Liberator* (Boston), 22 May 1846.
32. Ibid., 5 June 1846.

doctrine of active noncooperation represented the accepted antiwar strategy of the radical abolitionists during the Mexican War. For example, the Massachusetts Anti-Slavery Society in June 1847 labeled all who participated in or countenanced the war as "enemies to the country, and traitors to liberty and the rights of man. . . ." The Society also resolved "that no request or order of the Executive for aid in its prosecution, either by voting supplies, or enlisting in the military service ought to be complied with by Congress or the people. . . ."[33]

In the wake of this initial response came constant abolitionist antiwar activity. Although they differed sharply on the value of political activity and the idea of noncooperation with the government, the extreme Garrisonians and the more moderate abolitionists nevertheless concurred that the war was being waged by the Slave Power. Meetings of local and state abolitionist societies in New York, Ohio, and throughout New England became forums for antiwar speeches and resolutions. The pages of antislavery journals abounded with accounts of these meetings and with a steady stream of articles, editorials, atrocity stories, letters, and labored verse.

Because of the extreme tone of their dissent, the abolitionists, as well as other extreme dissenters in the eastern states, evoked both violent response and public indifference. Angry reactions to antiwar activity were most common in the initial weeks of the conflict when enthusiasm for the war was greatest and volunteer regiments, in the process of being organized, had not yet left for the battlefront. For example, in June 1846, prowar "rowdies" and "mobbites" forced a scheduled Syracuse antiwar meeting, with the Reverend Samuel J. May as chairman, to adjourn from the Empire House and reconvene at a nearby Congregational church. Here speeches were heard and resolutions condemning the war as an immoral scheme to extend slavery were adopted. But again the large prowar mob appeared, set up a large cannon by the rear of the church, and fired it three times, causing the meeting to be abruptly adjourned amidst the confusion of deafening noise and shattering windows.[34] But these incidents did not deter abolitionists or other dissenters from expressing their disapproval. In fact, a more serious problem for the abolitionists was public indifference to their appeals. Even in New England, where antiwar meetings were the most numerous, generally they were poorly attended except by hard-core reform leaders and their sympathizers. During the war, both abolitionists and pacifists complained about their inability to sap the war spirit.

An unexpected shock for the abolitionists came early in the war when

---

33. "Resolution of the Massachusetts Anti-Slavery Society" of 27 January 1847, in the *Liberator,* 5 February 1847.

34. *National Anti-Slavery Standard* (New York), 2 July 1846.

Cassius M. Clay annnounced in June that he had volunteered for service in the militia. As the outspoken antislavery editor of the *True American* in Lexington, Kentucky, Clay had previously won the praise of abolitionists for his bold attacks on slavery. Now, despite the fact that he had denounced the war as unnecessary, unjust, and motivated by greed for Mexican territory, Clay nevertheless affirmed his duty as a citizen to sustain his government. To do less, he said, would be treason. "Our opinion is, that the war, so unjustly and wickedly begun, should be pressed with vigor. It is the only alternative left. Clouds and darkness, in consequence rest upon our path in the future; but it has to be trod."[35] Northern abolitionists, both stunned and unconvinced by Clay's course of action and his logic, quickly charged him with treason to the cause of humanity, if not to his slavery-dominated government. Refusing to believe initial reports, the *National Anti-Slavery Standard* eventually labeled Clay's position "ridiculous and impossible!" "He has bartered away a glorious destiny for an ephemeral intoxication, and for the praises of men who despise him while they praise."[36]

The abolitionists, of course, never doubted the war's ultimate purpose. To them, debates over the true border of Texas, the rejection of a United States diplomatic envoy, and the outstanding claims issues were but the irrelevant sophistry of the politician, whatever his political stripe. Because the circumstances and immediate events preceding the outbreak of war explained how it had begun, rather than why, these factors were not central to an accurate understanding of the conflict. Instead, the abolitionists always asserted that the war had been motivated, provoked, and waged by a southern president and his willful cohorts for the sole purpose of extending slavery and the dominion of the Slave Power over the wide expanse of Mexican territory. Even during the early weeks of fighting, when Polk's territorial objectives were unclear, the abolitionists maintained this advanced position. Thus the Mexican War provided the abolitionists with a specific issue on which to attack war in general, the Slave Power, and slavery itself. Garrison in 1846 urged that all enemies of slavery now "consider it to be the chief anti-slavery work . . . to endeavor to paralyze the power of the government, that Mexico may be saved, and the overthrow of the Slave Power hastened."[37]

In this context, the abolitionists always viewed the war as a part of the larger slavery question rather than as an independent issue or an end in itself. Whatever the outcome of the war, the greed of the Slave Power for more territory would not end. Even if the war did not result in the acquisition of

---

35. *True American* (Lexington, Ky.), 17 June 1846.
36. *National Anti-Slavery Standard*, 9 July 1846, 13 August 1846.
37. Garrison to My Dear [George] Whipple, 19 June 1846, in the *Liberator*, 21 August 1846.

New Mexico and California, and abolitionists realized this possibility was remote, proslavery politicians would devise some other scheme to add those
areas. Thus, it was not enough for antislavery men to end the war; they must
be prepared to meet the next challenge of the avaricious Slave Power.[38] De-
pressed as they were by the war and realizing that it would most probably end
in the addition of slave territory, the radical abolitionists found cause for faint
hope. The spectacle of a costly war for slavery might finally serve as a moral
catalyst by awakening public opinion in the free states and alerting northerners to the magnitude of the threat posed by the southern Slave Power.[39]

To popularize and dramatize their indictment, abolitionists frequently utilized antiwar poetry, sarcasm, and satire. Among the most prominent antislavery literary contributions were those of John Greenleaf Whittier and James
Russell Lowell. In addition to his antislavery poems, Whittier wrote "The
Angels of Buena Vista" after that bloody 1847 battle. Printed in the *National
Era,* for which he wrote regularly, this poem depicted the battle and its poig-
nant aftermath, during which a Mexican woman reportedly ministered to the
wounded of both armies.

> "A bitter curse upon them, poor boy, who
> led thee forth,
> From some gentle, sad-eyed mother, weeping,
> lonely, in the North!"
> Spake the mournful Mexic woman, as she
> laid him with her dead,
> And turned to soothe the living, and bind
> the wounds which bled.[40]

Whittier also commented with devastating irony in the *National Era* on the
piety of the American army in Mexico. For example, after the shelling of
Vera Cruz, General Scott was observed in a Roman Catholic cathedral which
his army's shells had just shattered: "Verily, if the Catholics of Mexico, after
such a signal manifestation as this of the piety of their country's invaders,
harden their hearts against them [the Americans], and refuse to recognize
them as their true friends and benefactors, there is no longer any virtue in
Paixhans guns, and wax candles, [or] Bowie knives and Bibles. . . ."[41]

As in 1846, biting satire continued to be the weapon of abolitionist James
Russell Lowell. After publication of the first Biglow Paper in June 1846,
more than a year passed before the second number appeared in August 1847.

---

38. *National Anti-Slavery Standard,* 13 August 1846.

39. Ibid., 21 May 1846.

40. Horace Scudder, ed., *The Complete Poetical Works of John Greenleaf Whittier*
(Cambridge Edition, Boston, 1894), 35–36.

41. *National Era* (Washington, D.C.), 3 June 1847.

The subsequent seven numbers printed between November 1847 and September 1848 would treat events in Congress, slavery, and presidential politics, as well as the war. The second and third Biglow Papers, in particular, ridiculed both the war and its supporters. The second paper assumed the form of an account from Mexico by Birdofredum Sawin, a disillusioned Massachusetts recruit who, like hundreds of other naive volunteers, realized too late that his dreams of valor and fame were but a cruel delusion. As Sawin related, the army recruiters' descriptions of easy military glory quickly dissolved before the realities of an oppressive climate, wretched food, yellow fever, scorpions, and death. But in this letter, Lowell directed his most caustic jibes against the popular notion of an Anglo-Saxon superiority which justified aggression against and subjugation of lesser races.

> Afore I come away from hum I had a strong persuasion
> Thet Mexicans worn't human beans,—an ourang outang
>   nation,
> A sort o'folks a chap could kill an' never dream
>   on 't arter
>
>   .   .   .
>
> But wen I jined I worn't so wise ez that air queen
>   o' Sheby,
> Fer, come to look at 'em, they aint much diff'rent
>   from wut we be,
> An' here we air ascrougin' 'em out o' their own
>   dominions,
> Ashelterin' 'em, ez Caleb sez, under our eagle's
>   pinions,
> Wich means to take a feller up just by the slack
>   o' 's trowsis
> An' walk him Spanish clean right out o' all his
>   homes an' houses;
>
>   .   .   .
>
> It must be right, fer Caleb sez it's reg'lar
>   Anglo-saxon.
>
>   .   .   .
>
> Thet our nation's bigger 'n theirn an' so its
>   rights air bigger,
> An' thet it's all to make 'em free that we air
>   pullin' trigger,
> Thet Anglo Saxondom's idee 's abreakin' 'em to
>   pieces;
> An' thet idee 's that every man doos just wut he
>   damn pleases; . . .[42]

---

42. James Russell Lowell, *The Biglow Papers* (Cambridge, Mass., 1848), 23–25. In

While hoping that their persistent, violent, verbal assault would provoke hatred of the war and galvanize the morally quiescent North, the radical abolitionists urged their sympathizers to resist the war effort by withholding all cooperation from the government. Moreover, as they had throughout the 1840s, they refused to participate in politics and agitated for the dissolution of the Union under their phrase "No Union With Slaveholders." Because they viewed the Constitution as a proslavery document and believed the federal government to be morally bankrupt and dominated by the Slave Power, the abolitionists argued that neither traditional political activity nor existing political organizations offered any hope in the fight against the war and slavery. Speaking against the war in January 1847, Wendell Phillips declared simply that "In politics, there is no root which reaches deep enough to grapple with slavery. The anchorage is not firm enough."[43] A virtual revolution would have to occur before the Slave Power could be overthrown.

For politicians, political parties, and the political process itself, the Garrisonians continued to profess contempt. Only courageous and committed radicals like John Quincy Adams and Joshua Giddings received accolades for their antislavery struggles in Congress. At the same time, Massachusetts Whig Governor George Briggs received the special abuse of the abolitionists. Viewing him as a treacherous hypocrite, the *Liberator* charged that Briggs's hollow antislavery "cant" was as " 'empty as the whistling wind.' "[44] A critic of slavery who had denounced the annexation of Texas and warned of the threat of war with Mexico, Briggs drew abolitionist fire after he had issued a call for troop volunteers when the war began. Men like Frederick Douglass and James Russell Lowell were particularly upset that Massachusetts had lent its support to the war. Writing from London in August 1846, Douglass deplored the innocent blood being shed in the cause of slavery and bemoaned the Bay State's support of such a spectacle: "Massachusetts, with all New England, follows in the crusade like hungry sharks in the bloody wake of a Brazilian slave ship."[45]

The abolitionists held both the Democrats and Whigs accountable for the war. Although the Democrats had demonstrated "unparalleled audacity and untruthfullness" in defending the war as "just and righteous," the Whigs merited "far greater condemnation and guilt" for meekly denouncing the conflict while continuing to vote supplies with "energy and success."[46] Abolitionist

---

this passage, "Caleb" refers to Caleb Cushing, a prowar Democratic politician from Massachusetts. Cushing organized a regiment of volunteers during the war, and he rose to the rank of brigadier general. In 1847, he was also the unsuccessful Democratic candidate for governor in Massachusetts.

43. *Liberator*, 8 January 1847.
44. Ibid., 22 January 1847.
45. Frederick Douglass to Lynn Anti-Slavery Sewing Circle, 18 August 1846 in *National Anti-Slavery Standard*, 15 October 1846; Lowell, *Biglow Papers*, 11.
46. *Liberator*, 21 May 1847.

disgust with the Whig party reached a high point in January 1848 when only forty-one Whigs of the Whig majority that controlled the House of Representatives voted in favor of a resolution proposing the immediate withdrawal of all American forces from Mexico. In response, the *National Anti-Slavery Standard* observed that "the Whigs are no more opposed to the War, than the guerillas of Mexico are to sacking the baggage wagon. The wonder is, that they believe they can deceive anybody; but that is eclipsed by the still greater wonder, that anybody should be deceived."[47]

In similar fashion, the Garrisonians continued to denounce the views and very existence of politically oriented abolitionists and the Liberty party as "needless, corruptive and perilous" to genuine antislavery activity.[48] Though the Liberty party press might criticize the war, some Liberty papers, the abolitionists observed, still affirmed loyalty to their government. Particularly obnoxious to them was an article which appeared in June 1846 in Gamaliel Bailey's *Cincinnati Herald and Philanthropist*. In it, Bailey, prominent political abolitionist, announced that he would immediately postpone antiwar articles he was then printing if he thought for one moment that General Taylor and his soldiers were in danger: "Heaven forbid that word or act of ours should have the remotest tendency to jeopardize the safety of that noble officer and his brave army."[49] For Garrisonians, this and similar sentiments served to confirm what the radical abolitionists had been saying since 1840 about the irresolute and fraudulent nature of the Liberty party.[50]

In their denunciation of the war, the abolitionists openly wished the Mexican defenders well. During the fall of 1847, moved by what it considered to be the horror of the pending American occupation of Mexico City, the *Liberator* declared, "Every lover of Freedom and humanity, throughout the world, must wish them [the Mexicans] the most triumphant success." As word reached Boston that General Scott's troops had begun their final assault on the Mexican capital, the *Liberator* made its sentiments clear: "We only hope that, if blood has had to flow, that it has been that of the American, and that the next news we shall hear will be that General Scott and his army are in the hands of the Mexicans. . . . We wish him and his troops no bodily harm, but the most utter defeat and disgrace."[51]

The verbal extremism of the abolitionists was not, however, substantiated by action. Although they urged resistance to the government by the withholding of all support, they made no active attempt to obstruct government policy. Nor did they take the symbolic step of refusing to pay their state tax, as Tho-

---

47. *National Anti-Slavery Standard,* 13 January 1848.
48. *Liberator,* 12 March 1847.
49. *Cincinnati Herald* and *Philanthropist,* 3 June 1846.
50. *National Anti-Slavery Standard,* 4 February 1847.
51. *Liberator,* 15 October, 8 October 1847.

reau had done in 1846. As Emerson had noted sarcastically at that time, "Abolitionists denounce the war and give much time to it, but they pay the tax."[52] Instead, they merely eschewed all political participation and agitated abstractly for the Union's dissolution. To them, the choice was clear: "either withdraw from the government, or . . . become the advocates of war."[53]

A frustrating problem, of course, for the radical abolitionists and other would-be militant dissenters was the very nature of the Mexican War. Several distinctive characteristics of the conflict virtually prohibited any effective nonviolent dissent outside the realm of traditional political action. First, regular army enlistees and volunteer regiments did the fighting. Since conscription was not necessary, men in the armed forces were there by choice. Second, government loans, as well as the regular revenue sources of tariff duties and land sales, not direct compulsory federal taxes, financed the war effort. Thus, without compulsory military service or direct federal taxation, it was difficult for dissenters to strike directly, or even symbolically, at the war machine. In 1846, Emerson had shrewdly observed that even Thoreau's symbolic refusal to pay his state tax did not actually strike at the war. "The state tax does not pay the Mexican War," chided Emerson privately. "Your coat, your sugar, your Latin and French and German book, your watch does. Yet these you do not stick at buying."[54] Finally, while critics obviously refused to enlist and counseled others to follow their example, thousands of young men, including hundreds from New England, eagerly filled the ranks.

Nor could dissenters decry any loss of traditional civil liberties. Although they were occasionally heckled and harassed, even the most radical abolitionists spoke their minds freely and did not suffer from censorship of their publications. Largely because of the ease with which American troops triumphed and the absence of any real Mexican threat, the basic freedoms of speech, assembly, and the press remained unimpaired. Dissent was vocal and President Polk frequently complained of his antagonists in Congress, but he did not take steps to suppress dissent either in Congress or across the nation.

Thus abolitionists and pacifists failed to bring down a curtain on the maddening spectacle of what was to them an unjust and immoral war willingly sustained by a majority of Americans. None of the different methods of opposing war which were espoused succeeded in obstructing government policy or the war effort. The pacifists could not persuade their fellow citizens of the war's horror. Nor did the abolitionists arouse the American public to withhold from its government both direct and indirect support. These tactics, pacifists and abolitionists had argued, would hasten peace.

---

52. Edward Waldo Emerson and Waldo Emerson Forbes, eds., *The Journals of Ralph Waldo Emerson,* 10 vols. (Boston, 1909–1914), 7: 219.

53. *Liberator,* 18 December 1846.

54. Emerson, *Journals,* 7: 223.

7

★ *Nonpolitical Dissent*
Religious and Literary

N APRIL 1847, the *National Anti-Slavery Standard* asked, "What has the so-called Church of this country been about, during the period that the war of invasion and conquest has been waging against Mexico?" In answer to its own rhetorical question, this abolitionist journal noted that, although the conflict was now almost one year old and with only "here and there a solitary exception, the Church has had nothing to say! Alas! no, for that war, waged at Slavery's bidding, and therefore doubly execrable, the Church has had no thunders."[1] More pointed in his assessment was John Greenleaf Whittier. Writing in the *National Era*, Whittier ridiculed the spectacle of clergymen who would condemn such "sins" as dancing and Sabbath breaking, while looking with "complacency upon the sin and horror of slavery, and upon the unutterable horrors of war."[2] These sentiments well expressed the disillusionment of many dedicated dissenters with organized religion's response to the Mexican War.

Although numerous ministers and some outstanding clergymen like Samuel J. May and Theodore Parker did play a prominent role in opposing the war, religious opposition was neither overwhelming nor unanimous. Only the Unitarians, Congregationalists, and Friends wholeheartedly expressed outrage from the war's beginning to its end. In fact, more denominations supported or countenanced the war effort than actively opposed it; among these were the Roman Catholics, Methodists, Southern Baptists, and Old School Presbyterians. Other denominations were either divided or noncommital on the issue. Opinion among the Northern Baptists and New School Presbyterians was split; some ministers and religious journals abhorred the war while others defended it. Finally, the Episcopalians, the Lutherans, and some minor sects like the German Reform Church, the Disciples of Christ, and the Dutch Evangelical Reform Church refused comment.[3]

---

1. *National Anti-Slavery Standard* (New York, N.Y.), 22 April 1847.
2. *National Era* (Washington, D.C.), 20 May 1847.
3. For a more detailed treatment of the response of organized religion to the war,

Religious opinion generally followed a regional pattern and reflected the composition of individual congregations. In the northeastern states and in Ohio, where the war was remote, the reform impulse strong, antislavery sentiment growing, and the war unpopular, most churches attacked it vigorously. In New England, two strongly antiwar denominations, the Unitarians and the Congregationalists, had their greatest concentration of membership. In the South and the West, where enthusiasm for the war ran high, ministers of the Gospel found ample reason to support and even glorify a conflict which was supported by their congregations. Such denominations as the Methodists, Southern Baptists, and Roman Catholics had numerous members in the South and the Southwest and were also strong supporters of the conflict. Clergymen who took a stand contrary to that of their church also followed the regional pattern. For example, although the Methodists vigorously supported the war, the denomination's New England Conference twice passed general resolutions against the loss of life, cost, and irreligious features of the war.[4]

But internal factors, as well as regional composition, played an important role in determining the response of various denominations. The firm opposition of the Unitarians and Congregationalists resulted from their predominantly New England concentration, but long-standing antislavery and pacifist convictions prefigured the response of the Friends, who were strongest in the Middle Atlantic states. Even in Louisiana, where the war fever was high, the Society of Friends petitioned the Thirtieth Congress to move decisively to end the war without further fighting. Again, the Roman Catholics remained loyal war supporters because of their traditional obedience to authority, their eagerness to demonstrate their patriotism during a war against a Catholic enemy, their sensitivity to strong anti-Catholic feeling in the United States, and their awareness that any Mexican territory gained by the war would probably increase their number and strength.

A combination of internal factors, independent of regional composition, also induced other prowar denominations, namely the Methodists, the Old School Presbyterians, and the Southern Baptists, to support the war actively. Among these factors were the anti-Catholic feeling of these denominations, their evangelism, and their belief that the war offered a providential opportunity for a Protestant Christian republic to realize its destiny. Without compunction Southern Baptists and Methodists declared the war to be a crusade

---

see Charles S. Ellsworth, "American Churches and the Mexican War," *American Historical Review* 45 (January 1940): 301–26; also, John Bodo, *The Protestant Clergy and Public Issues, 1812–1848* (Princeton, N.J., 1954), 213–32.

4. *Zion's Herald and Wesleyan Journal* (Boston), 10 May 1847, as quoted in Ellsworth, "American Churches and the Mexican War," 304. In Ohio, another group of Methodists, the Wesleyan Methodists, also denounced the war.

against the Roman Catholic faith on the continent. Moved by evangelistic zeal, these denominations eagerly awaited the hour when vast new areas would be opened to the true Gospel of the Protestant missionary. Although at times they might concede the injustice of the conflict and acknowledge its great evils, the missionary fervor of these prowar denominations stifled whatever objections their consciences might have raised. Like their secular counterparts, religious supporters of the conflict spoke enthusiastically of extending the "area of freedom" and realizing the true destiny of the godly republic. Old School Presbyterians and Methodists argued that God was using the war to extend the "Redeemer's kingdom."

This variety of factors and responses precluded any unanimous condemnation of the war by the religious community. Though important, the geographic distribution and strength of a denomination were either reinforced or modified by other influences. The desire to win broad public approval, anti-Catholic sentiment, missionary zeal, the religious potential of adjacent Mexican territory, as well as a belief in the injustice of the conflict, antislavery feeling, and pacifistic convictions all affected the response of organized religion in the United States.

Although unanimous opposition was confined to three denominations, critics from other sects did criticize the war with commitment and force. If the Friends, Congregationalists, and Unitarians were the most active, sustained, and outspoken in their dissent, they were not alone. A prominent Roman Catholic spokesman, as well as a small minority of Methodists, Old and New School Presbyterians, Lutherans, and Northern Baptists, concentrated largely in the Northeast and Ohio, denounced the war. In sharp and singular contrast to the position of his fellow Catholics was that of Orestes Brownson. The ever independent and always outspoken Brownson was a searching thinker, editor, and prominent New England publicist who had converted to Catholicism in 1844 after a varied and active career as a social reformer and Unitarian clergyman. Writing in his own *Quarterly Review* in October 1846, Brownson stressed the duty of each citizen to remain loyal to his government, especially in the critical time of war. He also reminded misguided critics that war existed with the "divine permission" of the "sovereign Arbiter of Nations." "Mexico has offended God," wrote Brownson. "Almighty God is angry with her, and uses us as his instrument of her chastisement." Not only had Mexico overthrown her legitimate sovereign, she had neglected her religion and sought greatness in "infidelity and licentiousness. . . ."[5] But by July 1847, Brownson had substantially revised his position. The value of unquestioning loyalty was now outweighed by political reality. The United States had

---

5. [Orestes Brownson], "Fletcher Webster on War and Loyalty," *Brownson's Quarterly Review* 3 (October 1846): 493–518; see esp. 517, 518.

achieved its legitimate objectives and should now end the war without weakening Mexico. Brownson argued that it was in the national interest not to dismember or absorb Mexico, but rather to preserve her nationality and strength. A nation with weak neighbors would be "constantly tempted to the practice of injustice," and one with no neighbors would be torn by internal struggle and "sink into anarchy or despotism." But a more important consideration was Brownson's apprehension that a fierce domestic struggle over slavery would ensue if the nation added Mexican territory. This controversy could be prevented only if both the North and South united to end the war without the cession of new territory.[6]

The position of various antiwar Presbyterian, Lutheran, and Northern Baptist clergymen was dictated by either their moral repugnance of the war or their belief that the war was a slavery-inspired undertaking. Lutheran Samuel Schmucker condemned the spectacle as one which could never be vindicated "at the tribunal of true Christianity . . . ," and Northern Baptist William R. Williams objected to the war on moral grounds in demanding that the same standards of conduct apply to nations as to individuals.[7] Thomas E. Thomas of Ohio, an Old School Presbyterian, Samuel Burchard of New York, a New School Presbyterian, and Baptist Dr. Daniel Sharp of Boston agreed that the war was, in Sharp's words, "a war for southern territory, waged against justice, against humanity, and against the voice of God."[8]

A more prominent Baptist, the Reverend Francis Wayland, President of Brown University, also expressed his deep dismay in a series of three sermons delivered in the Brown University chapel during 1847 and entitled "The Duty of Obedience to the Civil Magistrate. . . ." Although he did not focus extensively on the war at hand and never developed a detailed indictment of it, Wayland did argue that war was justifiable only when utilized to defend the nation and its citizens "against wrong." Force should be employed only for "the protection of rights," and once that narrow objective was achieved, *"the reason for the employment of force ceases."* Under no circumstances

---

6. [Orestes Brownson], "Slavery and the Mexican War," ibid., n.s. 1 (July 1847): 334–67; see esp. 366.

7. Samuel Schmucker, *The Christian Pulpit the Rightful Guardian of Morals in Political No Less Than in Private Life* (Gettysburg, Pa., 1848), 30; William R. Williams, "The Prayer of the Church Against Those Who Delight in War," (1847), *Miscellanies* (New York, 1850), 386; both as quoted in Bodo, *Protestant Clergy*, 220–21.

8. Daniel Sharp, "Discourse on Peace," *Christian Reflector* 4 (June 1846), as quoted in Ellsworth, "American Churches and the Mexican War," 312; also, Thomas E. Thomas, *Covenant Breaking and Its Consequences: or the Present Posture of Our National Affairs, in Connection with the Mexican War . . .* (Rossville, Ohio, 1847); and Samuel D. Burchard, *Causes of National Solicitude. A Sermon Preached in the Thirteenth Street Presbyterian Church, New York, on Thanksgiving Day, November 25, 1847* (New York, 1848).

were a republic's civil magistrates ever to wage war "for purposes of conquest," to extend the area of freedom "by enlarging the domain of slavery," or in the name of the nation's "irresistible destiny."[9]

Having summarized his opposition to the Mexican War, Wayland turned to a related question of broad implications: To what extent was each citizen obligated to obey his civil magistrates? In a republic, because each individual was "morally responsible for all the wrongs committed by that society, unless he has used all the innocent means in his power to prevent them," Wayland argued that the paramount duty of each citizen was to evaluate personally the justice of his government's every act. Once convinced that the policy of his government was wrong, as in the case of an unjust war, the individual was then morally obligated to resist that wrong and "fearlessly *express*" his determination that his rulers adhere strictly to moral principle, lest he share the guilt of his rulers. But unlike the abolitionists who refused to participate in the political process, Wayland emphasized that the individual must actively engage in politics in an attempt to elect officials who would reverse the "wrong-doing." Yet even while the "wrong-doing" was in progress he must withhold his direct and indirect support from the government: "the fact that our country has commenced a course of wrong-doing, in no manner whatever alters the moral character of the action." Not only must military service be refused, the true Christian must "loan no money to government, no matter how advantageous the terms of investment" and he must "undertake no contracts by which he may become rich out of the wages of unrighteousness. . . ." If "moral principle" be superior to "gold," this was the occasion for the moral individual "to show his faith by his works."[10]

While such a course of action, if followed by all Christians, might well endanger existing political party organizations, it would create a new party of virtuous men "acting in the fear of God, and sustained by the arm of omnipotence." Then, "all parties would, from necessity, submit to their authority, and the acts of the nation would become a true exponent of the moral character of our people."[11]

Political activity, Wayland believed, could effectively reverse the government's immoral course, a faith not shared by abolitionists and extreme individualists like Thoreau. Yet Wayland's appeal was much akin to Thoreau's call for Americans to resist actively, not to witness passively, the moral wrong of their nation: "Cast your whole vote, not a strip of paper merely, but your whole influence. A minority is powerless while it conforms to the majority; it

---

9. Francis Wayland, *Sermons Delivered in the Chapel of Brown University,* 3d ed. (Boston, 1854), 274, 275–76.

10. Ibid., 288, 289, 290.

11. Ibid., 291, 292.

is not even a minority then; but it is irresistible when it clogs by its whole weight."[12]

But the sporadic objections of other denominations paled in comparison with the vigorous dissent of the Quakers, Congregationalists, and Unitarians. Through their official organizations, their press, and their clergy, these denominations intensified the attacks as the administration's goals broadened. Military events served to reinforce their original dissent by demonstrating that this was a war engineered for territory and slavery.

The Friends were doubly offended by the war: their traditional pacifism affronted by armed hostilities, and their antislavery convictions assaulted by the aggressive war's apparent relationship with the extension of slavery. The leading Quaker journals, the *Friend* and the *Friend's Review,* took a vigorous antiwar stand and filled their pages with accounts of antiwar activities, speeches, and appeals.[13] The Quakers also distributed widely a number of antiwar pamphlets, including reprints of *An Inquiry into the Accordance of War with the Principles of Christianity* by Jonathan Dymond, an English Quaker. This essay was forwarded to each member of Congress, to state legislators, to newspaper editors, and to clergymen of other denominations. In addition, a series of peace petitions were addressed to Congress during the conflict. The Quakers also urged the faithful antiwar testimony of all Friends in thought as well as action, and cautioned against supporting the war indirectly by financially profiting from it.[14]

In similar fashion, the Congregationalists and Unitarians voiced their objections through the resolutions of their official bodies and in their numerous publications. But they relied also on the eloquence of their clergy, who developed comprehensive moral criticisms of the war. It was, indeed, an ignominious spectacle: a supposedly Christian republic using the pretext of a border dispute to justify an imperialistic march to extend slavery. Congregationalist ministers realized that further expansion into the Southwest would strengthen the slave states while diminishing the already waning influence of the northeastern states in national affairs. But even more repugnant was the war's immorality.[15] The clergymen ridiculed arguments that the war was necessary to

12. Thoreau, "Civil Disobedience," in *The Writings of Henry David Thoreau,* 10 vols. (Boston, 1894), 10: 149–50.

13. For a thorough discussion of the pacifism of the Quakers during this general period, as well as during the Mexican War, see Peter Brock, *Pacifism in the United States: From the Colonial Era to the First World War* (Princeton, N.J., 1968), 333–88.

14. *Friend's Review,* 29 January 1848, 301–2.

15. Some of the more prominent Congregationalist clergymen were Horace Bushnell, Rufus Clark, Milton Braman, T. N. Lord, Richard Tolman, Burdett Hart, Henry Ward Beecher, and John Weiss (Ellsworth, "American Churches and the Mexican War," 315). See also, for example, Horace Bushnell, "Barbarism the First Danger," *National*

preserve the national honor or that it was a national act of Divine Providence. Burdett Hart of Connecticut pointed out that there was a "higher honor" demanding that a mighty nation treat a weak neighbor with "long suffering and great forbearance" rather than arbitrary highhandedness.[16] To expansionist assertions that the United States was predestined to extend "its possessions from one limit to another, till it acknowledges no boundaries but the ocean," Milton Braman countered with a question: "how do they know what the divine decree is with respect to the ultimate extent of the Union?"[17] Not honor and glory, but only wide-ranging damage and eventual retribution could result from such an attempt.

The stand of the Unitarians was similar as they frequently exhorted all true Christians to rise up and with one voice demand an end to the fighting. The most forceful and eloquent of Unitarian dissenters was the brilliant Theodore Parker. Thirty-five years old when the war began, Parker was an erudite theologian, a social reformer, and an impressive speaker. In his antiwar speeches, Parker defied the occasional disruptions of prowar hecklers and presented a forceful and sweeping indictment of war in general and the conflict at hand.[18] Combining biblical theology with detailed statistics, Christian precepts with hard logic, and uplifted vision with vitriolic denunciations, Parker charged that the Mexican War was at once unchristian, inhumane, unwise, unjust, and unprofitable.

Although he did concede that some wars, like the American Revolution, were justifiable because they involved a "self-protecting" struggle between a "falsehood and a great truth," Parker labeled the general practice of war an "utter violation of Christianity." If "war be right then Christianity is wrong, false, a lie. But if Christianity be true . . . then war is the wrong, the falsehood, the lie." In this context, the Mexican War was completely indefensible and, like all unjust wars of aggression, pregnant with manifest evils for the nation. Because he addressed an audience in Boston, a city "whose most popular idol is Mammon, the god of gold; whose trinity is a trinity of coin," Parker emphasized in June 1846 that the war with Mexico would be both unprof-

---

Preacher 21 (1847): 196–219; and Richard Tolman, *Evil Tendencies of the Present Crisis. A Discourse Delivered July 4, 1847* (Danvers, Mass., 1847).

16. Burdett Hart, *The Mexican War* (New Haven, Conn., 1847), 7, as quoted in Bodo, *Protestant Clergy,* 217.

17. Milton Braman, *The Mexican War. A Discourse Delivered on the Annual Fast, 1847* (Danvers, Mass., 1847), 10.

18. For a brief description of one of these disruptions, see John Weiss, *Life and Correspondence of Theodore Parker,* 2 vols. (1864; reprint ed., New York, 1969), 2: 78. For an excellent article on Samuel J. May, another outstanding Unitarian clergyman, see William H. and Jane H. Pease, "Freedom and Peace: A Nineteenth Century Dilemma," *Midwest Quarterly* 9 (1967): 23–42.

itable and expensive. It would disrupt the economy and misdirect productive industry despite the fact that it was a small war thousands of miles removed. Markets would be affected, stock prices would fall, and insurance rates for the shipper would soar. In addition, the inevitable creation of an enormous national debt would eventually result in oppressive excise taxes and custom duties which would be borne by all. Both businessman and worker would suffer. "In war," argued Parker, "the capitalist is uncertain and slow to venture, so the laborer's hand will be still, and his child ill clad and hungry."[19]

Beyond calculation, however, was war's cost in human lives and social corruption. Thousands of precious lives would be sacrificed in combat and thousands of other individuals would be maimed for life. In addition, because the whole system of warfare was "unchristian and sinful," sustained by "evil passions," and defended by what is "low, selfish, and animal," the contamination of public virtue would result. A soldier was a "costly . . . though useless" creature who "makes no railroads; clears no land; raises no corn." His return was in the worthless intangibles of "valor, glory, and—talk. . . ." Soldiers were instructed only "to lie, to steal, to kill." Every army camp was one of "profanity, violence, licentiousness, and crimes too foul to name." Thus the glory of war was but murder and plunder wherein the lowest of men, taught to kill as a trade, suffered further debasement. Such individuals were ruined for life and unlikely to make any positive contribution to their republic when they returned from battle.[20]

Because he believed the Mexican War to be a part of a larger proslavery conspiracy, Parker charged that the Constitution had been "violated by slavery," the nation's honor "betrayed by slavery," and her children "murdered by slavery. . . ."[21] At the same time, Parker displayed near contempt for the Mexican enemy. A "wretched people; wretched in their origin, history, and character," Parker conceded that at least they had abolished slavery and did not covet the territory of their neighbors. Evident here was Parker's belief in the innate superiority of the Anglo-Saxon race. Eventually Mexico must fall before the sweep of this "terrible Anglo-Saxon race . . . as the Indians before the white man." But this mission must be achieved by "the steady advance of a superior race, with superior ideas and a better civilization; by commerce, trade, arts, by being better than Mexico, wiser, humaner, more free and manly." Never doubting that the United States would one day control the entire continent, Parker asked if it was "not better to acquire it by the school-

19. Theodore Parker, "War," in *Sins and Safeguards of Society,* ed. Samuel Steward (Boston, 1904–5), 310, 291, 292, 293.

20. Ibid., 308, 296, 297, 308.

21. Theodore Parker, "The Mexican War," *Massachusetts Quarterly Review* 1 (December 1847): 24, 54.

master than the cannon? by peddling cloth, tin, anything rather than bullets?" On the general issue dividing the two nations, Parker argued, the United States was correct, but on the particular issue of the present war, the United States was dreadfully wrong.[22]

Confronting this criminal war, Parker appealed to the people of Massachusetts for active resistance to their government. "Let us remonstrate; let us petition; let us command," asked Parker. "If men love their country better than their party or their purse, now let them show it." The state's congressional delegation should be instructed to refuse all war supplies and to ask for the army's withdrawal. In addition, the general court must be asked to "cancel every commission" granted to volunteer officers, and the volunteers themselves must be encouraged to disband. The time for grass roots action had come and must not be allowed to pass, warned Parker in 1847. "Let it be infamous for a New England man to enlist; for a New England merchant to loan his dollars, or to let his ships in aid of this wicked war; let it be infamous for a manufacturer to make a cannon, a sword, or a kernel of powder to kill our brothers. . . ."[23]

More than most antiwar clergymen, Parker put his own dissent into a broader context in which the Mexican War represented only one aspect of a pervasive disorder infecting American life. Despite its horrors, Parker thought the war "the smallest part of our misfortune." Although the war might soon be ended, the larger "calamity" could not be. For the American people had lost "all reverence for right, for truth, all respect for man and God." Unfortunately they cared "more for the freedom of trade than the freedom of men; more for a tariff than millions of souls." The once virtuous republic had forgotten "any good besides dollars; any God but majorities and force." Abroad the United States was viewed as a "nation of swindlers and men-stealers!"—a nation which had chained the Negro slave and besmeared its own character with the blood of Indians and Mexicans. Parker lamented that the dissipated American republic now stood as a traitor to its own greatest principle: the idea "that all men are born equal—each with the same inalienable rights."[24]

Several leading literary figures shared this general diagnosis. Like Parker, these individuals were concerned about the course of American society in the 1840s. They were distressed that the democratic virtue and idealism of an earlier age had now been swept aside by a tide of pervasive materialism, grasping expansionism, and proslavery politics. But disgusting as it alone was, the Mexican War was only symptomatic of much deeper and more destructive

---

22. Parker, *Sins and Safeguards of Society,* 316, 317.

23. Theodore Parker, "The Mexican War," in *The Slave Power,* ed. James K. Hosmer (Boston, 1916), 28, 29, 30.

24. Parker, *Sins and Safeguards of Society,* 322, 323.

currents which threatened American society. Thus the dissent of Margaret Fuller, Henry David Thoreau, Ralph Waldo Emerson, and Herman Melville is notable not because these individuals were outspoken or effective public critics, because they were not. Rather their responses to the Mexican War are significant because they represent an eloquent expression of the deeper fears about the American republic which troubled these perceptive observers in the late 1840s.

Because she was then in Europe, Margaret Fuller was unable to oppose the war actively. She did, however, record her antiwar sentiments in several letters to the *New York Tribune*. Viewing the war as a proslavery project, she wrote that the American republic had "forsworn" its "high calling": "no champion of the rights of men, but a robber and a jailer; the scourge hid behind her banner; her eyes fixed not on the stars, but on the possessions of other men."[25] She lamented the present state of her country, once imbued with a noble spirit of "brotherhood," "pure faith and love." America "is not dead but in my time she sleepeth, and the spirit of our fathers flames no more, but lies hid beneath the ashes."[26] Similarly, Henry David Thoreau did not commit himself to a course of sustained public dissent. His act of protest was a personal and symbolic blow at the war machine. After spending his night in the Concord jail in July 1846, Thoreau returned to Walden Pond to live, uninterrupted by the war. Not until after the war ended in 1848 did he fully explain his dissent in "Civil Disobedience."

Another literary figure who opposed the war but did not speak out was Ralph Waldo Emerson. Forty-three years old when the war began, the nationally known Transcendentalist spokesman and public lecturer shunned participation in politics. "Is it not better," Emerson reflected in 1847, "not to mix or meddle at all, than to do so ineffectually? Better mind your lamp and pen as [a] man of letters, interfering not with Politics, but knowing and naming them justly, than to inculpate yourself in the Federal crime without power to redress the State, and to debilitate yourself by the miscellany and distraction from your proper task." Eschewing an activist role, he privately assessed political developments such as the Mexican War in his journal. He, like Parker, viewed the war, not as an isolated problem, but as a manifestation of the national character. The American people, wrote Emerson, were "eager, solicitous, hungry, rabid, busy-bodied . . . vain, [and] ambitious." Lacking in them was any reverence for justice, virtue, or true morality. Anxious to accom-

---

25. Margaret Fuller, Letter XVIII to the *New York Tribune* ([November, December] 1847), in *The Writings of Margaret Fuller,* ed. Mason Wade (New York, 1941), 427.

26. Margaret Fuller, Letter XXIV to the *New York Tribune* (April 19, 1848), ibid., 470.

plish much and convince the world of their talents, Americans hungered for material achievement and worshipped the dollar as a god. Understandably, their government, politicians, and national policies personified this aggressive materialism. The government stood as the responsive tool of "unscrupulous and energetic" politicians able to manipulate readily the emotions of the ruling majority. In Washington, a Democratic administration, distinguished by its "genius of bold and manly cast, though Satanic," initiated aggressive projects of territorial expansion. In so doing, it cleverly pandered to Americans' ambitions under the false guise of national mission and greatness. "The people," wrote Emerson, "are no worse since they invaded Mexico than they were before only they have given their will a deed. The United States will conquer Mexico, but it will be as the man swallows the arsenic, which brings him down in turn. Mexico will poison us."[27]

In undertaking the war, Emerson argued, the administration had nicely calculated "how much a little well-directed effrontery can achieve, how much crime the people will bear, and they proceed from step to step. . . ." But while accurately gauging the timidity of the political opposition, the administration had not counted on the simple, direct dissent of Thoreau. At least he was more consistent than Daniel Webster, "who told them how much the war cost, that was his protest, but voted the war, and sends his son to it." For his friend Thoreau's bold protest, Emerson expressed both admiration and skepticism. Thoreau's admirable act was wrongheaded and futile. First, because of his objections to the general state of society, Thoreau would not be any more content if a few specific grievances like the war and slavery were removed: "No government short of monarchy, consisting of one king and one subject, will appease you." Incisively, Emerson observed that Thoreau's true quarrel was not with the "State of Massachusetts" but rather "with the state of Man." Second, Thoreau's refusal to pay his state tax in no way inhibited the government's war effort. To strike at the government and end such evils as the war and slavery, one had to attack, not the government, but the powerful economic structure and ties which united and bound the states. "Cotton thread holds the Union together," Emerson noted in 1846; it "unites John C. Calhoun and Abbott Lawrence." These deep economic bonds explained why the North, although vocally objecting to the present war, readily continued to tolerate the insolence of the haughty southerner: "Yes, gentlemen . . . do you know why Massachusetts and New York are so tame?—it is because we own you, and are very tender of our mortgages which cover all your property."[28]

Because to oppose the war actively or commit himself to politics advanced

---

27. Edward Waldo Emerson and Waldo Emerson Forbes, eds., *Journals of Ralph Waldo Emerson,* 10 vols. (Boston, 1909–14), 7: 267, 286, 205, 219, 206.

28. Ibid., 219, 222, 201, 206.

nothing, the "scholar" Emerson remained in his study. During 1847, along with Theodore Parker, J. E. Cabot, Dr. Samuel Gridley Howe, and others, Emerson did, however, engage in the planning of a new literary journal, the *Massachusetts Quarterly Review*. Though he refused to serve as the associate editor, Emerson did finally consent to write the editor's address which appeared in the first edition in December 1847. Here Emerson briefly expressed sentiments that he had previously confided to his journal. Lamenting the absence of "any profound voice" in the country to speak out and revitalize the tainted "moral influence of the intellect," Emerson urged that the nation's direction be reversed: "We have a bad war, many victories—each of which converts the country into an immense chanticleer;—and a very insincere political opposition. The country needs to be extricated from its delirium at once."[29]

Like Emerson, Herman Melville viewed the war with alarm but refrained from public dissent. For Melville, the war years were a busy time of literary apprenticeship. In addition to his marriage in 1847 at age twenty-eight, Melville published *Typee* in 1846, *Omoo* in 1847, and finished *Mardi* for publication in early 1849. He also published a light satirical series in the humorous periodical *Yankee Doodle* during 1847. Entitled "Authentic Anecdotes of 'Old Zack,' " these seven articles poked fun not only at General Taylor, but also at the thousands of Americans who, blindly worshiping him as a military idol, thirsted to know of his every act and personal habit.[30] Absent from the articles, however, was not only the quality of skilled satire, but also the incisive political and antiwar commentary of a James Russell Lowell or a Seba Smith. But the Mexican War did disturb Melville. As early as May 1846, he wrote of the war's unsettling prospects: "The Mexican War . . . is nothing of itself—but 'a little spark kindleth a great fire' . . . and who knows what all this may lead to—Will it breed a rupture with England? Or any other great powers?—Prithe are there any notable battles in store—any Yankee Waterloos? . . . Lord, the day is at hand when we will be able to talk of our killed & wounded like some of the old Eastern conquerors reckoning up by the thousands. . . ."[31] Beyond his immediate concern over its military results, Melville was apprehensive about the meaning of an aggressive war which he feared was betraying the nation's best interests and most basic ideals. Melville best expressed these thoughts in his novel *Mardi,* written during 1847 and 1848, but not published until 1849. "Your nation," observed Melville refer-

29. Ralph Waldo Emerson, "Editor's Address," *Massachusetts Quarterly Review* 1 (December 1847): 1–5.

30. Luther Stearns Mansfield, "Melville's Comic Articles on Zachary Taylor," *American Literature* 9 (1937–38): 411–18.

31. H. Melville to G. Melville, 29 May 1846, in *Letters of Herman Melville,* ed. Merrell R. Davis and William H. Gilman (New Haven, Conn., 1960), 29.

ring to the United States, "is like a fine, florid youth, full of fiery impulses, and hard to restrain; his strong hand nobly championing his heart. On all sides, freely he gives, and still seeks to acquire." Such expansiveness tainted with greed threatened to transform a once noble eagle into a "bloody hawk." Personally confident of America's future, Melville urged that America proceed patiently toward its destiny rather than violate its true mission of freedom by grasping for a continental empire through the force of arms:

It is not freedom to filch. Expand not your area too widely, now. Seek you proselytes? Neighboring nations may be free, without coming under your banner. And if you cannot lay your ambition, know this: that it is best served by waiting events.

Time, but Time only, may enable you to cross the equator; and give you the Arctic Circles for your boundaries.[32]

A theme present in the thoughts of Parker, Fuller, Emerson, and Melville, then, was their common fear that this once "model republic" had forsaken its true mission. The champion of freedom and justice was now characterized by the unceasing quest of its citizens for material wealth, by its continued toleration of slavery and acquiescence in the schemes of the southern Slave Power, and most recently by its avarice for neighboring territory. In this context they viewed the Mexican War as a symptom rather than a cause of what was wrong with the republic. Never primarily an evil in itself, the war embodied a virulent malady afflicting American society.

---

32. Herman Melville, *The Works of Herman Melville,* vol. 4, *Mardi,* 2 (New York, 1963 [reissue of Standard Edition, 1922]), 240, 241, 245. For an analysis of *Mardi,* see Merrell R. Davis, *Melville's Mardi: A Chartless Voyage* (New Haven, Conn., 1952) ; also pertinent on Melville is Alan Heimert, "Moby Dick and American Political Symbolism," *American Quarterly* 15 (1963): 498–534.

8

★ *Antiwar Strategy
and "All Mexico"*

AS DISSENTERS OUTSIDE THE POLITICAL arena sharpened
their critiques and pondered the meaning of the war, politicians continued
their bitter partisan dispute throughout 1847. Between March and early
December, when the newly elected Thirtieth Congress convened, both
familiar themes and new developments characterized the political debate.
As they had since May 1846, both conservative and radical Whigs hurled
the old charges and new allegations at the administration, while they remained at odds with each other over the war. Whig intraparty differences
during mid-1847 centered on a disagreement over the "true" strategy for
ending the conflict: the No Territory plan endorsed by the conservative
Whigs or the Wilmot Proviso now endorsed by the antislavery radicals.
Then autumn brought to the war debate a new element for Whigs of all
shades to attack: a vocal and growing movement to end the war by annexing the whole of Mexico.

Crucial in shaping the domestic political debate was the frustrating situation on the Mexican front. "We are in the predicament of a man who has a
wolf by the ears," observed the *New York Tribune* in June; "It is dangerous
to hold on, and may be fatal to let go."[1] Since mid-April 1847, when he departed for Mexico, word of the supposedly secret peace mission of Nicholas
Trist had been widely reported. But news of peace negotiations did not follow
Trist's arrival in Mexico or his advance with Scott's army. Even with the
Americans militarily victorious and in possession of Mexico City, the Mexicans remained intransigent and refused to discuss peace terms. In short, by the
fall of 1847 with Mexico City conquered, fighting virtually had ceased but a
treaty seemed as remote as ever. In response to this frustrating situation, national enthusiasm for the war, which had been invigorated by Scott's victory,
continued to wane. Whatever their view of the conflict, most Americans were

---

1. *New York Tribune,* 15 June 1847.

120

disconcerted by a president who could not terminate a war despite his generals' brilliant victories. At this point, both political and nonpolitical critics of the war demanded anew and even more vigorously an immediate and just peace. At the same time, a significant minority of Americans added their support to a proposal espoused by rabid expansionists to end the war by subjugating and absorbing the whole of Mexico.

The events of the spring and summer reinforced Whig fears that America's true mission was being perverted by the war. In March came news of a rebellion by the inhabitants of New Mexico in January and February 1847 against the harshness of American rule and the excesses of undisciplined, rowdy, and drunken American volunteers stationed there. Although the insurrection was suppressed and order restored, the *New York Tribune* and other Whig journals made these events in New Mexico examples in their attacks on the "imbecility" of the administration's conduct of the war and its disregard for sacred American ideals. Not only was it pure folly to expect to conquer and hold the enemy province of New Mexico by issuing a proclamation of annexation enforced by only a few untrained American volunteers, it was also a blatant violation of the principle of the consent of the governed. Never doubting that "nine-tenths, probably ninety-nine hundredths, of the people of New Mexico choose to be Mexicans and loathe the supremacy of the United States," the *Tribune* asked how any man could "pretend to be a Republican and yet insist that New Mexico . . . shall be compelled to unite with us when it emphatically chooses to fraternize with Mexico?"[2]

The same month, acting under his war-making power and through Secretary of the Treasury Robert Walker, the president reopened Mexican ports then under American control to international trade, subject to a new schedule of custom duties established by the administration without the approval of Congress. Immediately, the *National Intelligencer* assailed the "NEW 'ORDER IN COUNCIL' " as the act of a self-proclaimed "conqueror." The authority to establish a tariff was distinctly a legislative power, not an executive war power, and Polk's exercise of that prerogative was fit only for the king of an empire, not the president of a republic.[3] By August, the *Intelligencer,* reviewing Polk's war policies, sarcastically marveled at the endless and diverse feats of the president: "Here, there, every where at once; civil, military, legislative, judicial, and executive; dove of peace, thunderbolt of war, and a perfect serpent of diplomacy, who was ever so various or amazing?"[4]

---

2. Ibid., 18 March, 19 March 1847.

3. *National Intelligencer* (Washington, D.C.), 3 April 1847; see also excerpts from the *Courier and Enquirer* (New York, N.Y.) and the *Daily Republican* (Springfield, Mass.), ibid., 10 April 1847.

4. Ibid., 5 August 1847.

PLUCKED:

THE MEXICAN EAGLE BEFORE THE WAR!

OR.

THE MEXICAN EAGLE AFTER THE WAR!

Appearing in the spring of 1847, before Polk's war objectives were precisely known, this cartoon predicted the extent of the president's territorial goals. *Yankee Doodle* 2 (1847–48): 55. *Courtesy of the Newberry Library, Chicago.*

As American troops drove toward Mexico City and vocal expansionists demanded greater chunks of Mexican soil, the Whigs constantly repeated and extended their already sharp attacks on Polk's territorial objectives. Denying that American destiny dictated the permanent conquest of Mexican territory, the *Ohio State Journal* pleaded for the nation to return to "the principle that Righteousness—not *conquest*—exalteth a nation."[5] The Whig press was increasingly alarmed by expansionists who argued that annexation would contribute to the progress of civilization, the mission of the American republic, and the regeneration of the backward Mexicans. How could a supposedly Christian nation, professing a "paramount duty" to love its enemies, ravage its neighbor's territory and, with each new victory, rejoice to hear that more Mexicans had "been maimed, wounded, or killed?"[6]

Speaking at the University of Virginia in July 1847, former Virginia Whig Senator William Cabell Rives defined the true mission of the American people as he understood it. Rives emphasized that the country had "no mission to interfere with the institutions of other countries." Other people should be as free to pursue their own destiny as "we are to pursue our happiness in the modes we judge best for ourselves." To extend the nation's borders by "violence and conquest is a low and discredited ambition," unworthy of the United States, but "to extend the moral empire of Law, of Peace, of Liberty, of Religion . . . is an ambition worthy of the age and worthy of America."[7] In June, the *Providence Journal* warned that the war had already "planted the seeds of corruption and decay, which will spring up and bear bitter fruits for many generations to come."[8] The evil influences of a war of conquest, once unleashed, could not be "arrested for a long time, but must flow on in a deep, full, overflowing stream, corrupting the future generations of young men and poisoning the future literature of our country," claimed the New Jersey *Fredonian*.[9] Instead of understanding war as barbarous, men would now glorify it, supplanting the honest pursuits of peace with the bloody spectacle of desolation and war.

Along with their distress over the war's effect on the political morality of the republic went pressing practical considerations of race and slavery. The Whig press emphasized that it wanted neither Mexican soil nor the "wretched population" which went with it.[10] The addition of a people alien "in lan-

---

5. *Ohio State Journal* (Columbus), 22 April 1847.
6. Lebanon *Star* (Ohio), cited in *National Intelligencer*, 29 May 1847.
7. "Address of William Cabell Rives at the University of Virginia," quoted in *National Intelligencer*, 17 July 1847; see also Rives to John J. Crittenden, 5 February 1847, John J. Crittenden Papers, Manuscript Division, Library of Congress.
8. *Providence Journal* (Rhode Island), quoted in *National Intelligencer*, 5 May 1847.
9. New Jersey *Fredonian* (New Brunswick) quoted in *National Intelligencer*, 15 May 1847.
10. *Richmond Whig* (Virginia), 19 May 1847.

guage and race, in habits, usages and associations" would only be "repugnant" to Americans and contrary to the spirit of their institutions.[11] But the slavery question remained a more urgent concern to Whigs than the prospect of adding alien races to the Union. Like their representatives in Congress, Whig editors understood the resolve of each section on the issue and shied from the prospect: "nothing appears plainer to us," stated the *Augusta Chronicle and Sentinel*, "than that the North is united on the Wilmot proviso. The South is united against it. Hence rises a question of lurid and fearful portent." Conservative Whigs appealed to the administration to recognize that the cost of acquiring territory was dear, the Union itself: "Can a contest be imagined more frightful and furious than that which this very acquisition of Mexican territory will excite between the North and South?"[12]

While denouncing Democratic war policy, the Whigs debated within their own ranks on a "true" strategy for terminating the war. Although superficially a debate over how best to oppose the war, the dispute clearly exposed other deep party divisions. Important in the dispute, of course, was the slavery question. To conservative Whigs, No Territory remained as much a way of avoiding the ominous slavery question and preserving party unity as it did a viable tactic to end the war. On the other hand, radical Whigs objected to this evasion and determined to confront the issue directly. Also connected with this Whig dispute was the coming presidential contest. With numerous aspirants available, the two Whig factions sought very different qualities in the nominee. The conservative majority wanted a man who could lead the party to victory; his ability to appeal to voters of all sections was considered a more important qualification than his political convictions on such issues as the war. The radical minority, on the other hand, was determined that the Whig standard-bearer be a man who would forcefully espouse its antislavery convictions and endorse the principle of the Wilmot Proviso.

Defending the party's already accepted position, the conservative majority of Whigs argued that No Territory was the only realistic opposition tactic which would end the war, preserve the nation's republican honor, avoid the slavery question, and maintain party harmony. On it all Whigs and all sections could unite "with consistency and with justice." If the United States did not dismember Mexico, neither "Freedom nor Slavery" would be compromised, while the republic would be rescued "from the imputation of wishing to rob Mexico of her soil."[13] "We want no more territory," cried the *Ohio State Journal*, "NEITHER WITH NOR WITHOUT THE WILMOT PROVISO."[14] If Polk

---

11. Baltimore *American*, 26 April 1847.

12. *Augusta Daily Chronicle and Sentinel* (Georgia), 17 June, 18 May 1847.

13. *Boston Atlas*, 24 May 1847.

14. *Ohio State Journal*, 3 April 1847. Previously in June 1846, this paper had endorsed the principles embodied later in the Wilmot Proviso.

sincerely sought peace, he need only reassure Mexico that "her rights, her national domain, shall be respected. Tell her this, and offer the olive branch, and our word for it, [and] her hills and valleys so will resound with the carol of peace. . . ."[15]

Although a few Whig politicians and newspapers, like the *Baltimore American,* refused to hold the line and professed a willingness to accept a limited territorial indemnity from Mexico, including San Francisco Bay and the Rio Grande as the border of Texas, the great majority of Whigs stood firm on No Territory. As they had since 1846, politics, necessity, and the specter of slavery combined to dictate this course for conservative Whigs. The No Territory strategy continued to allow Whigs to denounce Polk's war policy, and to strengthen their own position in anticipation of 1848. Although they were critical of a war for territory, they were still patriots who supported the war effort and refused to endorse a troop withdrawal.

The antislavery Whigs, however, refused to accept either conservative Whig reasoning or its antiwar position. Men like Giddings, Charles Sumner, and Charles Francis Adams believed that No Territory was unworkable. In rejecting No Territory, the radicals doubted the sincerity and the dependability of conservative Whigs from both the North and the South. With American troops already occupying New Mexico, California, and several other Mexican provinces, No Territory was but a hollow phrase unless implemented by the withdrawal of American troops. But the same conservatives who mouthed the phrase No Territory had refused to support resolutions in the previous Congress demanding immediate troop withdrawal from Mexico. Giddings asked *"will they withdraw the troops?* No Sir, it is not probable that more than fifty Whigs will be found in the next Congress who will vote to withdraw the army."[16] In this case, the fighting would continue until President Polk could negotiate a treaty embodying his territorial designs. Once such a treaty came before the Senate, the radicals feared that enough southern Whigs would acquiesce, as they had previously on the annexation of Texas, so that Senate approval would be assured. *"Southern Whigs,"* wrote Giddings, "deserted us at the time of trial and will again."[17]

More important, No Territory was escapism, according to the radicals, who wanted to meet the war and its motivating force head-on. They argued simply that because the war represented a scheme of the Slave Power to extend slave territory, the fighting would end quickly and without Mexican territory

---

15. *Augusta Daily Chronicle and Sentinel,* 2 June 1847.

16. Giddings to Oran Follett, 26 July 1847, in "Selections from the Follett Papers, III," ed. Belle L. Hamlin, *Quarterly Publication of the Historical and Philosophical Society of Ohio* 10 (1915): 4–33; see esp. 31.

17. Giddings to C. F. Adams, 12 August 1847, Adams Family Papers, Massachusetts Historical Society, Boston.

only if that objective were denied the president and his southern supporters by expressly prohibiting slavery from the new territories. Previously, Giddings had argued that even if the No Territory plan should succeed and a peace without territory should be concluded, the basic problem would not be resolved. Slaveholders would continue to migrate into the Southwest with their chattels, stage a Texas-style revolution at some future date, and then request admission to the Union as a slave state. Unless the proviso were approved, therefore, as many as fourteen slave states the size of Ohio might eventually be admitted to the Union in this manner, thus reducing the power of the free states to "insignificance" in Congress.[18]

Ever an optimist, Giddings personally believed that the proviso strategy might well succeed in the coming Congress. Once it again became apparent that conservative Whigs were unwilling to implement their No Territory plan by voting troop withdrawal, the proviso might be presented as an alternative. Giddings predicted that the proviso would pass and would receive support from northerners of both parties; not even timid conservative Whigs from the North would "dare vote against it."[19] Congressional passage of the proviso would give clear warning to all southerners that any Mexican territory acquired by the war would be free territory. And once the administration realized the determination of the free states, Polk would quickly conclude an honorable peace without territorial indemnity. For the radicals assumed that the administration and its southern supporters in Congress would not expend one dollar or one southern life to add free territory. According to Giddings, the proviso strategy would go beyond the demand that American troops be withdrawn: it would insure their removal and expedite a just peace.[20]

Publicly the radical position was echoed and expanded by a small minority of Whig presses like the Boston *Daily Whig,* the *Ashtabula Sentinel* and the Boston *Courier.* These papers decried the No Territory position as unrealistic, imprecise, and motivated by "a vehement desire to evade the issue of slavery in order to save the slaveholding wing of the party." In addition, defenders of the proviso charged that No Territory might well bind the Whig party to a principle which precluded honorable and peaceable annexations of free territory in the future.[21]

Proponents of No Territory were disturbed by the radical strategy as a threat to the Union and party cohesion, and criticized it sharply. While Giddings and his colleagues wanted to ignite the explosive slavery question, the conservatives doggedly practiced the tactics of evasion. The *Boston Atlas,* a

18. *Cong. Globe,* 29th Cong., 2nd Sess., 1847, Appendix, 404.
19. Giddings to C. F. Adams, 12 August 1847, Adams Family Papers.
20. Ibid.; Giddings to Oran Follett, 26 July 1847, "Follett Papers, III," 30–33.
21. Boston *Daily Whig,* 30 July, 4 August 1947; Boston *Courier,* 18 September 1847.

Cotton Whig organ, termed the proviso strategy unwise and destructive. Professing its abhorrence to slavery the *Atlas* argued that No Territory, which did not necessarily compromise antislavery principles, should be the banner of all Whigs. Even if the No Territory approach failed, northern opponents of the war could then retrench and stand on the proviso with northern Democrats when Mexican territory was acquired.[22] "We do not conceive," concurred the *Ohio State Journal,* that "we sacrifice one iota of Whig principle, or concede a hair's breadth from the principle of the Wilmot Proviso. Our Whig brethren of the South come and propose to sacrifice with us at a common altar."[23]

As the Whigs sought the "true ground" for opposing the war, a new element surfaced in the war debate during the autumn of 1847. Despite American military victories in previous months, by October it was apparent that negotiations had broken down. This frustrating situation compelled some disappointed war supporters to join zealous expansionists in arguing that the absorption of all of Mexico was a prerequisite to peace. Scattered suggestions to this effect had appeared earlier in 1847, but it was not until the American army had occupied Mexico City in September that the so-called All Mexico movement began to catch fire. For the first time, the assimilation of Mexico seemed both defensible and militarily possible. The expansionist penny press of the eastern seaboard led numerous editors across the nation in this chorus. While bringing an end to the war, the subjugation of Mexico would help America to achieve her territorial destiny and fulfill her mission of regenerating and uplifting her backward neighbors until they might be qualified to enter the "Temple of Freedom" as equals. By the end of 1847, the All Mexico movement was in full voice and seemed to enjoy broad national support. In fact, however, this primarily Democratic movement was always more vocal than potent. Although its exponents were outspoken, vigorous, and articulate, the strength of its popular support is questionable.[24]

A curious advocate of All Mexico was the antiwar *National Era* edited by Gamaliel Bailey. Thirty-nine years old when the paper was founded in 1847,

22. *Boston Atlas,* 28 July, 19 August, 27 August 1847. Other defenses of this predominant Whig position in the Whig press were numerous. For example, *Augusta Daily Chronicle and Sentinel* (Georgia), 15 September 1847; *Richmond Whig* (Virginia), 25 August 1847; *Louisville Journal* quoted in *Ohio State Journal,* 27 September 1847; *National Intelligencer,* 7 September, 19 October 1847; and *Albany Evening Journal* quoted in *Ohio State Journal,* 2 Septmber 1847.

23. *Ohio State Journal,* 3 September 1847.

24. The standard monograph on the movement is John D. P. Fuller, *The Movement for the Acquisition of All Mexico, 1846–1848* (Baltimore, Md., 1936). An incisive evaluation of the movement which questions its strength and actual influence with the public is Frederick Merk, *Manifest Destiny and Mission in American History: A Reinterpretation* (New York, 1963), 157–201.

Bailey had been a confirmed abolitionist since 1835 and a prominent political abolitionist during the 1840s as editor of the Liberty party paper, the *Cincinnati Herald and Philanthropist*. Among such associates as James G. Birney and Lewis Tappan, Bailey earned a deserved reputation for sound principles, good judgment, discretion, and editorial ability. These qualities made him the logical choice for editor when Liberty party leaders created a journal in Washington, D.C. Once established, the *National Era* quickly became an influential newspaper with a weekly circulation of 15,000 copies by 1850. In its first edition in January 1847, Bailey avowed his faith in the "doctrines and measures" of the Liberty party, his conviction that slavery should be constitutionally abolished, and his adherence to the "State-rights school" of government. The war position of the *National Era* was similar to that of the antislavery Whigs. Bailey attacked several targets: the administration which had provoked war; the Democrats, who supported it; and the Whigs, who sustained a conflict they assailed. Like the followers of Giddings, Bailey declared the war to be a tactic of the southern-controlled administration "to obtain a large portion of her [Mexico's] territory, and to establish therein human slavery," and affirmed his support for the Wilmot Proviso.[25]

But on August 19, 1847, the *National Era* espoused an imaginative and bold plan to advance America's territorial destiny, prevent the extension of slavery, and successfully terminate the war. The United States should immediately cease all fighting and in "all good faith" submit to every state in Mexico "the proposition to enter, if it so choose, into the American Union, upon a footing of equality with the original States." The advantages of this "startling" proposal, it stated, were manifest:

The annexation of the Mexican States on the plan proposed, always, of course, *with their own free will and consent,* would complete our continental boundaries, South, secure a basis of 4,000,000 of square miles for our empire, establish Freedom as the fundamental and unchangeable Law of the North American continent, and give Republicanism the perpetual ascendency over all other forms of Government. The United States would appear then before the world, not as the robber of a sister Republic, but its greatest benefactor. . . .[26]

This plan, argued Bailey, was just, constitutional, and expedient. Both the United States and Mexico would benefit. The commerce and industry of both countries would be protected; perpetual peace would be ensured by ending the war without humiliation or animosity to either side. With the end of military rule, stability would be restored to Mexico, and the United States would realize its southern territorial limits.

But, most important to Bailey, the dispute over the extension of slavery

25. *National Era* (Washington, D.C.), 7 January, 18 March 1847.
26. Ibid., 19 August 1847.

would be solved by establishing a buffer of as many as nineteen free Mexican states. The South could hardly object to the entry of these Mexican provinces into the Union, since their entry would be voluntary and each would be free to determine its own status in regard to slavery, a principle long advocated by southern politicians. Naturally, Bailey assumed that since the individual Mexican states had abolished slavery, they would remain free states.

There could be only one practical alternative to this "Plan of Pacification and Continental Union." If the whole of Mexico was not to be absorbed, American armies must be withdrawn immediately and all Mexican soil forsworn. Rejecting any proposal which fell between these extremes, the *National Era* attacked the No Territory proposal as "antiAmerican," impractical, "delusive," shortsighted, and a "cowardly concession to an impudent demand of Slavery." Such a proposal sacrificed the future growth and destiny of the nation in an attempt to preserve the unity of a political party, avoid an explosive issue, and "quell the rising spirit of Freedom among the people." No Territory was especially detestable to Bailey because it prevented a coalition of free-state citizens on the subject of slavery by dividing them on the question of expansion. Obviously antislavery Democrats who supported territorial expansion would be in opposition to antislavery Whigs who denounced forceful expansion if the war question were argued in terms of territory versus no territory by conquest. Although adhering to its own pacifistic program, the *Era* firmly asserted that the Wilmot Proviso was a truer ground than No Territory on which to confront the extension of slavery.[27]

The newspaper anticipated a sympathetic response to its ingenious plan from both expansionist northern Democrats and antislavery Whigs. But none was forthcoming. Only the most fervent expansionist papers embraced the proposal, while No Territory Whigs from both free and slave states bitterly condemned all proposals, Democratic or otherwise, to incorporate the whole of Mexico, or to acquire any portion of Mexican soil by force. Across the nation, Whig editors restated their aversion to the permanent conquest of any territory. Willing to accept only the Bay of San Francisco, they demanded that it must be acquired on a voluntary and honorable basis.

The *National Era's* singular project went largely ignored as the Whigs vigorously attacked the vocal All Mexico movement which was gaining momentum during the fall of 1847. Previously the *Ohio State Journal* had labeled the Mexicans "a miserable race of beings" and denounced the growing prospect of unrestrained conquest and subjugation of Mexico as "a pity ineffable, a shame past endurance" should "our young Aurora . . . run like an idiot for such withered wreaths. . . ."[28] Likewise, the Baltimore *American,* one of

---

27. Ibid., 16 September; see also ibid., 23 September 1847.
28. *Ohio State Journal,* 15 June, 1 May 1847.

the few Whig papers to endorse a limited territorial indemnity, decried the
All Mexico proposal as a "phantasy as revolting as it is absurd!" Though "a
moderate morsel" of territory might well "be swallowed without difficulty,"
this journal cautioned that "an immoderate one might choke [the Union] to
suffocation."[29] To those wild-eyed expansionists who incessantly ranted about
the destiny of the United States to subjugate Mexico, the *Cincinnati Atlas*
replied that if "it be our destiny to conquer and rob Mexico, it will assuredly
be our destiny to be conquered and robbed in turn."[30]

Just as northern Whigs feared that the whole of Mexico, if annexed,
would become slave territory, a number of southerners feared that it would not.
By this time, some southern Whigs and Democrats were convinced that the
institution of slavery could not be extended beyond Texas or below the Rio
Grande because the institution was unfit for a vast portion of the Mexican
soil.[31] The acquisition of such necessarily free territory would only harm and
weaken southern interests and power. In fact by late 1847, responding in part
to antislavery expansion proposals like that advanced by the *National Era,*
some southern Whigs openly feared a conspiracy of the free states to isolate
and weaken the South by creating a huge buffer of free states along the southwestern frontier. The *Augusta Chronicle and Sentinel* urged fellow southerners to renounce the reckless All Mexico scheme as a "Remedy . . . Worse than
the Disease." All true southerners, it pleaded on October 25, must know and
protect their section's interests by rejecting "these death-robed schemes" for
subjugating Mexico, schemes which could only assure the South's eventual iso-
lation and political demise. The *Chronicle* continued: "You know that our
peculiar institutions have no existence in Mexico. Do you wish to be placed at
the mercy of ten millions, hostile to you, as enemies and conquerors, in the
first place, and as supporters of that institution in the next?"[32] Increasingly,
then, during the final months of 1847, political attention and debate shifted to
meet the All Mexico movement. Both antislavery and proslavery critics shud-
dered at the thought of a subjugated Mexico, a prospect which both northern
and southern Whigs believed would be not only politically disastrous and
morally outrageous but also devastating to their own respective sectional interests.

---

29. Baltimore *American,* 12 October, 15 October 1847.

30. *Cincinnati Atlas* quoted in *Richmond Palladium* (Indiana), 5 October 1847.

31. For a discussion of the idea held by some important southern leaders of both
parties that slavery was not suited for expansion into the Southwest, see Fuller, *The
Movement for the Acquisition of All Mexico,* 73–74; Chaplain W. Morrison, *Democratic
Politics and Sectionalism; the Wilmot Proviso Controversy* (Chapel Hill, N.C., 1967),
52–53; and "Remarks of Gen. W. Thompson," quoted in *National Intelligencer,* 21 October 1847.

32. *Augusta Daily Chronicle and Sentinel,* 20 October, 25 October 1847; also *Richmond Whig* (Virginia), 4 December 1847.

At the same time that controversy raged over the war, slavery, and eventually the All Mexico movement during 1847, both Democratic and Whig politicians had already begun to position themselves for the 1848 presidential race. A significant, but never dominant, element in the early campaign was the war and its related issues. Although the slavery extension question would eventually dwarf the war as an election issue and become crucial in determining the presidential nominees, the war issue helped shape the nomination contests until the Senate ratified the peace treaty in March 1848.[33]

Because President Polk was an unlikely candidate for reelection, a number of Democrats emerged as aspirants in 1847. Most prominent were Vice-President George M. Dallas, Secretary of State James Buchanan, Michigan Senator Lewis Cass, John C. Calhoun, and former New York Governor Silas Wright. With the exception of the Van Buren wing and Calhoun, most Democrats were, of course, prowar and proexpansion, and anxious to avoid the related slavery and Wilmot Proviso questions. But the dissident positions of the Van Burenites and Calhoun on slavery and the war complicated the Democratic picture.

Until October 1847, the Van Burenites continued to reaffirm their party loyalty, to support the war effort, to endorse Polk's expansionist program, but to pledge their commitment to the Wilmot Proviso. As it had been since 1846, their political position was dictated by their anticipation of regaining control of the party and winning the presidential nomination for Silas Wright. But unexpected developments in New York forced a change in strategy. First, Silas Wright died suddenly in August, leaving his supporters without a candidate of comparable strength or appeal. Then, in October, the antislavery Van Buren or Barnburner wing, as it was known in New York, lost control of the state party to the conservative Hunker Democrats. In the convention at Syracuse, the Hunkers selected a slate of their own candidates and defeated adoption of antislavery resolutions supported by the Barnburners. Frustrated and irate, the Barnburners bolted the convention. Several weeks later they reconvened at the village of Herkimer where they proclaimed their antislavery principles and pledged to support no candidate who was not committed to the principles of the Wilmot Proviso. At this time they still considered themselves loyal Democrats, and would until their final defeat at the National Convention the following May. But the Barnburners had already embarked on the road which would lead them into a new political party in the summer of 1848.

Equally troublesome for the party was John C. Calhoun, the only antiwar Democratic aspirant. Until early 1847, his restrained antiwar position won

33. For a recent monograph on this topic see Joseph Rayback, *Free Soil: The Election of 1848* (Lexington, Ky., 1970).

praise and seemed to be helping his candidacy. Then, in February, Calhoun's attractiveness to many southern Democrats was shattered when he broke openly with the administration by voting against the Ten Regiment Bill and by subsequently supporting the expulsion of administration editor Thomas Ritchie from the Senate floor. After his dramatic public break with the administration, Calhoun attempted to regain his momentum by assuming leadership of a nonpartisan southern rights movement. First, he introduced a series of proslavery resolutions in the Senate on February 19. Then in Charleston, on March 9, Calhoun fully developed his theory of southern rights. In his address, he declared that southerners of both parties must henceforth defend their rights by refusing to support any party or candidate who courted the abolitionists. To guarantee the election of an acceptable president, southerners should absent themselves from the party conventions and unify in support of a proslavery candidate.[34] Initial response among Democrats in the Deep South was enthusiastic. Some Whigs even joined the chorus, among them Representatives Henry Hilliard of Alabama and Robert Toombs of Georgia. On April 30, Toombs reported his state's wide approval of Calhoun's speech and noted that southern leadership was now in Calhoun's hands.[35] However, a large number of southern Democrats still loyal to the administration resented Calhoun's proposed southern rights movement as merely a selfish attempt to splinter the Democratic party. In private and in the press, they accused Calhoun of trying to unite the South behind him in one final push for the presidency. Amid this increasing criticism and rising southern enthusiasm for the candidacy of slaveholding General Zachary Taylor, Calhoun's presidential hopes began a steady decline in the summer of 1847.

No longer a viable candidate by mid-1847, Calhoun now confirmed his political independence by reasserting his hostility to Polk's war. "Free of all responsibility, and independent of both parties, and their entanglement with the war," Calhoun scorned the Democrats, as well as the "folly and weakness" of the Whigs, while looking to the outcome of the war with gloom.[36] Whether "victorious or defeated," the United States seemed to hold an untenable position. If military defeat were now improbable, victory promised only the subjugation of Mexico. But to annex Mexico, reminded Calhoun, "would be to overthrow our Government, and, to hold it as a Province, to corrupt and

34. Richard Cralle, ed., *The Works of John C. Calhoun,* 6 vols. (New York, 1854–58), 4: 382–96.

35. Toombs to Calhoun, 30 April 1847, in *Correspondence Addressed to John C. Calhoun, 1837–1849,* ed. Chauncey Boucher and Robert Brooks, *Annual Report of the American Historical Association* (Washington, D.C.), 373–74.

36. Calhoun to T. G. Clemson, 15 June 1847, in *Correspondence of John C. Calhoun,* ed. J. Franklin Jameson, *Annual Report of the American Historical Society for the year 1899,* vol. 2 (Washington, D.C., 1899), 2: 734.

destroy it. The farther we advance, the more appearant [*sic*] the folly and wantonness of the war. . . ."[37]

Despite his pessimism, Calhoun did note a bright spot in the storm of war. By waging war in order to preserve the power of his Hunker Democrats, Polk had only insured their political demise. Taylor's brilliant military victories and his great popularity now seemed to promise defeat for the Polk Democrats in 1848. As a lesson in practical politics, Taylor's probable election augured well for the nation's future because it would likely create a vital precedent: "the party in power, which makes war, will be sure to be turned out of power by it;—if successful, by the successful General; and if not, by the opposition. When that comes to be understood, as it will be, if Taylor should be elected, we never again shall have a war, when it can be averted. . . ."[38] Although personally opposed to "military chieftains" as presidents, Calhoun viewed Taylor with favor. Privately he wrote that it might "be our duty to support him. . . . The fact, that he is a slaveholder, a Southern man, a cotton planter, is one of no little importance at the present moment." But even as Taylor's prestige grew and his own confidence died, Calhoun refused to abandon all hope. Because the slavery issue promised "great confusion & breaking up of parties," he might yet emerge from such chaos as a serious candidate.[39] As late as July 1847, Calhoun noted that his position was the "most eligible of all of the publick [*sic*] men of our country. It is the only independent one; and I can see symptoms, that it begins to be felt."[40]

In the Whig party, meanwhile, the war and related slavery issues complicated presidential politics and continued to increase factional tension just as these same issues did among Democrats. By 1847, the Whigs could survey a number of able, experienced, and eminent presidential possibilities, including Henry Clay, Daniel Webster, John J. Crittenden, Thomas Corwin, and John McLean. In spite of their individual attributes, however, none of these men possessed the inherent popular appeal necessary to capture the imagination of voters and ensure victory. In addition, the war issue was potentially fatal to all of these politicians. Because they opposed the war with varying degrees of intensity, none could identify with or share its military glory. And all were potentially vulnerable to Democratic political attacks on their loyalty and patriotism. To the Whigs, the nomination of a military figure offered one means of surmounting these obstacles. Most obvious as a choice was General Win-

37. Ibid.; also, Calhoun to Mrs. T. G. Clemson, 10 June 1847, ibid., 730–31.

38. Calhoun to T. G. Clemson, 6 May 1847, ibid., 728–29; also, Calhoun to T. G. Clemson, 11 April 1847, ibid., 727–28; Calhoun to H. W. Conner, 14 May 1847, Henry W. Conner Papers, Manuscript Division, Library of Congress.

39. Calhoun to H. W. Conner, 14 May 1847, Henry W. Conner Papers.

40. Calhoun to T. G. Clemson, 24 July 1847, *Calhoun Correspondence*, 2: 735.

field Scott, who by early 1847 was commanding the invasion of Mexico. But despite his Whig orthodoxy, his long record of service, and his military achievements, Scott's pomposity and querulousness weakened his stature. In addition, Scott's frequent bickering with the administration further diminished his public image.

A more attractive possibility was General Zachary Taylor. Although he was without political experience and had never even voted in a presidential election, here was a roughhewn, unpretentious, and gallant general who had long served his country with modest and unfailing devotion. He might lack personal flamboyance, but Taylor's strong quiet sense of duty personified the patriotic qualities exemplified in an earlier age by George Washington. Not a man of strong political convictions, Taylor was known to hold Whig-like sentiments, and hungry Whig professionals quickly sensed his potential.[41] Taylor's initial triumphs over the Mexicans had enhanced his popularity in 1846. Then in February 1847, his astonishing victory against an overwhelming Mexican force at Buena Vista catapulted him into the political limelight. During the spring and summer, southern Whigs spearheaded the Taylor movement and backed the Louisiana slaveholder for the nomination. In addition to the endorsement of such Whigs as Robert Toombs and Alexander Stephens, the Taylor candidacy even received the quiet, but firm, support of Clay's longtime lieutenant, John J. Crittenden. Although Taylor's association with slavery made him generally less popular in the North, he retained wide public appeal here, as well as the support of numerous Whigs. For example, Abraham Lincoln of Illinois, the politically shrewd Thurlow Weed of New York, and the Cotton Whigs of Massachusetts all favored Taylor. In short, many victory-starved Whigs willingly overlooked the General's obscure politics in favor of his expected voter appeal.

In addition to his popularity, Taylor's association with the war attracted conservative Whigs. Whig opponents of the war, especially those in the South and West where the conflict tended to be popular, realized that their advocacy of Taylor strengthened their own position at the polls. As the war's greatest hero, Old Rough and Ready was in no way tainted with disloyalty. Thus the Whigs, while continuing to assail the war and expansion, could nullify Democratic attacks on their patriotism and share in the glory of the war by rallying around the gallant General.[42] Viewing the war primarily as a political issue and eager to gain political capital from it, most conservative Whigs were **not**

---

41. Among the first to recognize Taylor's presidential potential was Thurlow Weed in the initial weeks of the war. *Albany Evening Journal*, 18 June 1846.

42. This point is well made in Brian G. Walton, "Elections for the Thirtieth Congress and the Presidential Candidacy of Zachary Taylor," *Journal of Southern History* 35 (May 1969): 186–202.

disturbed by Taylor's role as one of the war's most destructive agents.

Despite Taylor's strong support among the Whigs, his opponents within the party remained numerous. Committed followers of Clay, McLean, and Webster tended to be unsympathetic to the General. But the most vehement opposition to Taylor came from the staunch antiwar, antislavery radical Whigs. To them, Taylor embodied everything the Young Whigs abhorred. As an attempt to extend slavery and southern power, the war was a moral crime which they refused to countenance in any way, much less could they accept the nomination of the war's most eulogized hero. Giddings, for example, charged that the Taylor movement merely dramatized another of the "palpable absurdities" of the conservative position: "They oppose the war, but lend their whole energy to prosecute our Conquest in Mexico. . . . They advocate the encouragement of free labor, but pledge themselves to vote a President whose whole interest is vested in slave labor. . . ."[43] Antislavery Whig Columbus Delano treated the Taylor candidacy with sarcastic contempt: "To kill women and children and hurry men unprepared to eternity because they refuse to give us their land now free in order that we may cover it with slaves, are certainly high qualifications, for the highest office in the gift of a free nation of professing christians."[44]

Because they believed that the war would be the "great political subject" that would "swallow up all others" in 1848, and because they predicted that the nomination of a slaveholder would be "fatal" to the future of the Whig party, the radicals had begun to search for a genuine antiwar candidate of their own by late 1846.[45] Unsuccessful at first, their quest suddenly seemed over on February 11, 1847, when Thomas Corwin bitterly indicted the war and declared that he would no longer vote to support it. That same evening, Giddings happily reported that the "Young Whigs" in Congress now regarded Corwin "as their man for President."[46] From Massachusetts, Charles Francis Adams related that a "very large part of the people is ready to rally round him at once,"[47] an opinion in which Henry Wilson concurred: "I hear it said all around that we must have him for our candidate . . . if he will

43. Giddings to C. F. Adams, 23 December 1846, Adams Family Papers. For an abolitionist indictment of Taylor, see Henry C. Wright, *Dick Crowingshield the Assassin and Zachary Taylor the Soldier: The Difference Between Them* (Hopedale, Mass., 1848). Crowingshield had committed a particularly notorious murder in Salem, Mass., in 1830.

44. C. Delano to Giddings, 25 May 1847, Giddings Papers, Ohio Historical Society, Columbus.

45. Giddings to C. F. Adams, 23 December, 26 December 1847, Adams Family Papers.

46. Giddings to Sumner, 11 February 1847 in George W. Julian, *Life of Joshua Reed Giddings* (Chicago, 1892), 199.

47. C. F. Adams to Giddings, 22 February 1847, Giddings Papers.

maintain his position with firmness . . . we can carry him into the chair of State with a rush."[48]

At this time, the radicals were not troubled by Corwin's silence on slavery. They believed that his sentiments approximated their own and that, when the occasion arose, he would forcefully express them. In April, Giddings confidently assured Adams that the antislavery Whigs of Ohio had "no doubt as to his position concerning slavery nor have they any fears that he will shrink from an expression of those veins at the proper time."[49] The antislavery Whigs, however, had badly mistaken Corwin's antiwar resolve for a corresponding, but nonexistent, commitment on slavery. Because of his intense love for the Whig party, Corwin's views on slavery resembled the position of other conservative Whigs. He sought not to confront the issue, but to avoid it. Accordingly, in his speech of February 11, he had recommended that Congress end the war without Mexican territory by refusing to vote further supplies. Unlike the radicals who denounced the war as a scheme of the Slave Power, Corwin opposed the conflict because of his moral disgust at its aggressive nature.[50] In short, while he confessed that he would be "content to see" the Whig party "uprooted to its foundation" if it continued to sustain a war it purported to abhor, Corwin refused to endanger party unity by agitating the slavery question.[51]

In this context, Corwin was reluctant to allow his name to be advanced as a presidential candidate. He realized that the Young Whigs were using his name as a foil to defeat the Taylor candidacy, a course which could only contribute to antagonism within the party he loved so much. For this reason, he refused in the summer of 1847 to travel to Boston and Buffalo to speak as his antislavery supporters had requested. In spite of his "strong repugnance" to being a candidate, however, Corwin did not withdraw his name from consideration. To do so would only weaken the antiwar movement he had helped stimulate. If he withdrew his name, war supporters would proclaim the move as "an abandonment" of his position, or "a craven fear of public opinion. . . ."[52] Largely for this reason, Corwin continued to allow his name to be used throughout 1847, and late in the summer, during the state election campaign in Ohio, he took the stump to assist the Whig effort there.

---

48. H. Wilson to Giddings, 24 February 1847, Giddings Papers.

49. Giddings to C. F. Adams, 16 April 1847, Adams Family Papers.

50. This misunderstanding and Corwin's candidacy are discussed in Norman Graebner, "Thomas Corwin and the Election of 1848: A Study in Conservative Politics," *Journal of Southern History* 17 (May 1951): 162–79.

51. Corwin to William Greene, 11 April 1847, and Corwin to Greene, 25 July 1847, in "Selections from the William Greene Papers, I," ed. Belle L. Hamlin, *Quarterly Publication of the Historical and Philosophical Society of Ohio* 13 (1918): 19, 22.

52. Corwin to Giddings, 12 October 1847, Giddings Papers.

It was during this Ohio campaign that Corwin reaffirmed his stand on the war and clarified his widely misunderstood position on slavery. Speaking at Lebanon, Ohio, on August 28, Corwin emphasized that the only means of ending the war and avoiding a bitter struggle over the extension of slavery was to add "no more territory." To implement this strategy he again stressed that it was the constitutional duty of Congress to withhold further supplies.[53] Then at Carthage, Ohio, three weeks later, Corwin termed the Wilmot Proviso a "dangerous question" which "ought not to receive the serious consideration of any man. . . ." Only if it became impossible to prevent the acquisition of territory should the proviso be adopted. "If we owned territory to which it could be applied, it should be applied," Corwin stated, but to advocate the proviso before it became applicable was "infatuated folly" at a time when No Territory offered "the only safe policy of the nation."[54]

The widely publicized Carthage speech surprised and "disheartened" Corwin's antislavery followers. In Massachusetts, the Conscience Whigs had only recently resolved on the proviso strategy. That their supposed leader would endorse the No Territory proposal espoused by conservative Whigs had not entered their minds. Recognizing now that Corwin was not "an Anti-Slavery man," Charles Sumner charged that Corwin seriously blundered by "shrinking from the Wilmot Proviso, as a *dangerous* question," when in fact, the proviso "when rightly understood, is a source of safety. It is the beginning of the rally against the Slave-Power which will save the Union."[55] By November, after recovering from their initial shock, the Conscience men came to realize that Corwin's antiwar fervor was not to be translated into antislavery dedication. "He is against War which is not in its nature a permanent evil and he hesitates about Slavery which is," wrote Adams. "He has taken up the chain at the wrong end."[56]

Corwin, meanwhile, was upset by the uproar which his speeches had created among antislavery Whigs, and he sought to clarify his position on the war and slavery even though he disavowed any intention of being a candidate. In several letters, Corwin argued that he had been misunderstood and denied that to oppose the "further extension of territory" was necessarily to forsake the Wilmot Proviso: "I cannot see how we abandon the latter by trying the former."[57] The best course was to "take the sure ground *first* of no more terri-

53. For excerpts of the Lebanon speech, see Daryl Pendergraft, "The Public Career of Thomas Corwin" (Ph.D. diss., State University of Iowa, 1943), Appendix H, 793–96.

54. Ibid., Appendix I, 796–97, contains excerpts from the Carthage speech.

55. Sumner to Giddings, October 1847; Sumner to Giddings, 1 November 1847, Giddings Papers.

56. C. F. Adams to Giddings, 2 November 1847, Giddings Papers.

57. Corwin to Sumner, 25 October 1847, Charles Sumner Papers, Houghton Library, Harvard University, Cambridge, Mass.; also, Corwin to ——— in *Cincinnati Atlas,* 27 September 1847, quoted in Pendergraft, "Corwin," Appendix J, 797–98.

tory, if we succeed in this even with the aid of a few southern votes, *then* we *know* Slavery cannot be extended—*then* we *know* the War will be terminated for want of a motive to prosecute it, *then justice* will be done to Mexico & Mexicans. . . ." When and if the No Territory plan failed, opponents of the war and slavery might unite on the proviso, for "by attempting the one, we do by no means abandon the other—If we fail in the first we only cling with more tenacity to the second. . . ."[58] Some antislavery Whigs like Giddings and Indiana's Caleb Smith accepted Corwin's position. In fact, the ever-sanguine Giddings predicted that troops would be withdrawn from Mexico and Corwin elected president after his "boldly" advocating that the federal government be divorced from "all support of slavery."[59]

But if Giddings and Smith were satisfied, the Conscience Whigs of Massachusetts remained unmoved and dejected. They continued to maintain that No Territory was only meaningless verbiage with American troops occupying most of Mexico. Only a position guaranteeing troop withdrawal could prevent territorial indemnity, and only the adoption of the proviso could insure troop withdrawal.[60] If they were now without a suitable candidate, the Conscience men were also pessimistic about their future within the Whig party. In September their efforts to bind the Massachusetts Whig party to antislavery principles had failed again at the state convention in Springfield. Here the conservatives defeated a Conscience effort to prevent the nomination of Webster as a favorite son and rejected a resolution stipulating that the party support for president and vice-president only "those who are known by their acts or declared opinions to be opposed to the existence of slavery. . . ."[61]

In a speech to the convention Daniel Webster made a dramatic attempt to enlist the support of the party's antislavery elements. First, to the delight of the radicals, Webster reversed his position on the withholding of supplies. Previously Webster had maintained that whatever the causes of the war, the military effort must be sustained. Now he asserted that Congress did have the right and duty to refuse supplies for a war which it deemed unjustifiable. To the surprise of many, Webster also declared that he had supported the principles of the proviso for at least a decade and he even intimated that credit for the doctrine should rightfully be his.[62] Although Webster's speech won a fa-

---

58. Corwin to Giddings, 12 October 1847, Giddings Papers.

59. Giddings to C. F. Adams, 25 October 1847, Adams Family Papers. It was in this same letter that Giddings summarized Smith's opinions.

60. See for example, Sumner to Corwin, 7 September 1847, in *Memoir and Letters of Charles Sumner*, ed. Edward L. Pierce, 4 vols. (Boston, 1848), 3: 142–43.

61. For a discussion of the convention, see Kinley J. Brauer, *Cotton versus Conscience: Massachusetts Whig Politics and Southwestern Expansion, 1843–1848* (Lexington, Ky., 1967), 216–18.

62. "The Mexican War," 29 September 1847, in *The Writings and Speeches of Daniel Webster*, ed. Fletcher Webster, 18 vols. (Boston, 1903), 13: 363–64, 359.

vorable reception from the Conscience men, they knew his true colors well and did not consider endorsing the conservative Senator.

In the wake of the convention and Corwin's Carthage speech, the Conscience Whigs realized that continued cooperation with the Cotton Whigs within the framework of the party was impossible. Once outspoken in their party loyalty, Adams and Sumner now conceded that political reorganization was necessary to advance their principles. For example, Charles Francis Adams reported to Giddings that he leaned "more and more to the conviction that little or nothing can be done with the Old Whig party." In the future, "we must disregard organizations where we cannot bend them," confided Adams to his diary; "the only question is one of time."[63] Although they were unsympathetic to the Liberty party, the Conscience men viewed the Democratic party split in New York with hope. Particularly heartening were the antislavery pronouncements of the Herkimer Convention in October. In response to these developments, Sumner, who envisioned a future coalition of Van Burenites and antislavery Whigs, predicted that "anti-slavery sentiment will be the basis of a new organization."[64] And Adams notified Giddings that he leaned "to the selection of a democrat, if such can be found to head the movement party."[65]

During the autumn of 1847, the Whig presidential outlook was further complicated by the revitalization of the Clay movement. In the spring rush for Taylor, the seventy-year-old Clay had been almost forgotten. But in mid-1847, enthusiasm for the General began to lag. In the North, Taylor's lack of political experience and his unfortunate propensity for writing embarrassing and damaging letters, as well as his identification with slavery and the war, combined to weaken his viability as a candidate. In the South, some Whigs who had boomed Taylor's name to assist them in the 1847 congressional elections were disappointed with the results and questioned whether the General's voter appeal was as strong as had been originally assumed. In the meantime, Clay's supporters began to mount another serious drive for the nomination. Clay himself remained publicly uncommitted on his candidacy, but attracted wide attention on November 13 in Lexington, Kentucky, with a major attack on the war. Although he was an opponent of the war which had claimed the life of a son at Buena Vista, Clay had not spoken on the issue until his Lexington speech. This silence prompted observers to interpret the address as Clay's opening move in the presidential race.[66]

63. C. F. Adams to Giddings, 19 October 1847; C. F. Adams Diary, 12 October 1847; also, C. F. Adams to Giddings, 2 November 1847, and C. F. Adams to Giddings, 28 November 1847, Adams Family Papers.

64. Sumner to Giddings, 2 November 1847, in Pierce, *Memoir of Sumner*, 3: 157.

65. Adams to Giddings, 2 November 1847, Adams Family Papers.

66. See Clay to S. Schenck, 8 April 1847 quoted in *Richmond Whig* (Virginia), 24

At Lexington, Clay attempted to reassert his party leadership by carefully constructing a platform based on the war and slavery questions that would be acceptable to Whigs of all sections and all persuasions. As expected, he assailed the administration's war with standard Whig indictments sure to win approval within the party. But Clay also hoped to enhance his stature as a statesman by offering a viable solution. Claiming for Congress the "full and complete war-making power," Clay, like Webster and Corwin before him, argued that Congress should declare the ends for which the war was to be fought and then take whatever action was necessary to hold the president to these stated objectives. Personally, Clay believed that the United States should renounce all intentions "to conquer and annex . . . Mexico, or any part of it," a course which he believed would result in a prompt and honorable settlement.[67]

While embracing No Territory, Clay attempted to walk a tightrope on the slavery issue by assuaging antislavery Whig discontent without alienating southern Whigs. As a longtime member and officer of the American Colonization Society, Clay assured his listeners that he regarded slavery as "a great evil, a wrong . . . an irredeemable wrong for its unfortunate victims." But since it already existed and involved thousands of blacks who in some states outnumbered whites, emancipation was an unworkable solution. Its result would be bloody racial conflict ending in either the ultimate "expulsion or extinction" of the black race. While accepting the permanence of slavery, Clay hoped to relieve antislavery misgivings about the war by proposing that the nation "positively and emphatically, disclaim and disavow any wish or desire . . . to acquire any foreign territory whatever, for the purpose of propagating slavery, or of introducing slaves from the United States into such foreign territory."[68]

As the sentiments of an elder statesman demanded, Clay's speech attracted immediate national attention, and in subsequent weeks his address and resolutions were reprinted, discussed, and reevaluated. A series of antiwar rallies in Louisville, Cincinnati, Philadelphia, New York, and Trenton enthusiastically adopted the resolutions which accompanied the address. Whig papers around the country praised Clay's logic, force, and eloquence and jubilantly pro-

---

April 1847; also, Clay to John M. Clayton, 16 April 1847, John M. Clayton Papers, Manuscript Division, Library of Congress; Clay to [a citizen of New York], 8 April 1847, quoted in *National Intelligencer,* 27 April 1847. Early in 1847, during a banquet in New Orleans and before his son's death, Clay had created a mild stir by reportedly saying that he was " 'half inclined to ask for some nook or corner in the army. *I have thought that I might yet be able to capture or slay a Mexican.'* " Quoted in Calvin Colton, *The Last Seven Years of the Life of Henry Clay* (New York, 1856), 46.

67. Henry Clay, *Speech of Henry Clay at the Lexington Mass Meeting, 13th November 1847 . . .* (New York, 1847), 13.

68. Ibid., 11–12, 14.

nounced their willingness to unite once again behind Old Harry. In Alabama, the *Mobile Advertiser,* previously a Taylor paper, declared its determination to " 'stand by the doctrines of that speech to the LAST, simply because THEY ARE RIGHT.' " With Clay now in the field, the *Advertiser* stated that we " '*cannot,* we WILL NOT, support any one else.' "[69]

But Whig praise was not unanimous. Taylor's followers did not view the speech as an eloquent, statesmanlike address but as a calculated political maneuver. At the same time, some Whig papers opposed the basic principle of No Territory, favoring instead limited acquisitions of territory. For example, the New York *Courier and Enquirer* sought San Francisco Bay and the area north of the Missouri Compromise line, as did the Baltimore *American* and the *Richmond Times.*[70] In addition, Clay was suspect in both the North and the South because of his statements on the slavery question. The abolitionist *Liberator* observed that what Clay had said "about slavery will alienate the South, while it will disgust the North."[71] In the South, Clay was widely accused of pandering to rising northern abolitionist sentiment, while in the North, antislavery Whigs remained unsatisfied.[72]

Thus, by the end of 1847, as response to Clay's Lexington address and the strength of the Taylor movement indicated, neither opposition to the war nor advocacy of No Territory was an important criterion for the Whig nomination. While the antislavery Whigs continued to seek a man who would stand on antislavery principle and endorse the Wilmot Proviso as the best strategy for ending the war, the majority of Whigs were less concerned about issues, such as war, than they were with victory in 1848. To most Whig politicians, power at the polls was the most important qualification for the nomination.

---

69. *Mobile Advertiser,* quoted in *Chicago Daily Journal,* 21 December 1847.

70. Baltimore *American,* 14 September 1847.

71. *Liberator,* 3 December 1847.

72. See, for example, Iverson L. Harris to John M. Berrien, 15 December 1847, John M. Berrien Papers, Southern Historical Collection, University of North Carolina, Chapel Hill, North Carolina; and Boston *Daily Whig,* 25 November 1847.

9

★ *A Flawed but Acceptable Peace*

THE PRESIDENT WAS BOTH perplexed and frustrated by events in Mexico as the Thirtieth Congress prepared to convene in December 1847. After occupying Mexico City in September, the American forces controlled not only the capital but also Mexico's key seaports and all of her northern provinces. Yet the defeated and seriously divided enemy remained recalcitrant. Peace negotiations had broken down in September and had not been resumed. Furthermore, the conduct of General Scott and peace commissioner Nicholas Trist vexed President Polk. After an initial quarrel, Trist and Scott had become fast friends, and in August, just as the army neared Mexico City, Scott had agreed to an armistice with Santa Anna in order to open peace negotiations. The subsequent discussions proved completely unsatisfactory because the Mexicans refused to consider terms which reflected their hopeless military situation. Willing to concede Texas, the Mexicans still claimed the Nueces River as the border, refused to cede either the provinces of California or New Mexico, indicated that they would consider compensation for only a tiny portion of Upper California encompassing San Francisco Bay, and demanded payment for damages committed by American troops upon private Mexican property.

When Polk received word of these events, he was angered that Scott would agree to an armistice with the faithless Santa Anna at the gates of Mexico City and that Trist would violate his diplomatic instructions by even entertaining the Mexican proposal. When commissioned, Trist had been ordered to demand not only the Rio Grande, but also the provinces of New Mexico and California. Polk responded by ordering Trist's recall in October and by December was weighing Scott's removal from command.

Handicapped by an unsettled war, an insolent general, and a refractory diplomat, Polk faced additional political problems on the domestic front. Because he was surrounded by unreliable cabinet members, a divided Democratic party, an angry Whig opposition in Congress, and growing public sentiment to end the war, the president could look ahead only to months of bitterness, conflict, and turmoil. He could not depend upon the counsel of James Buchanan because the secretary of state's personal presidential aspirations were now a dominant element in his thinking.[1] Nor could he depend on Congress for vital support; the Whigs now controlled the House, and the Democratic majority in the Senate was a shaky one. Political developments around the nation during 1847 had exacerbated rather than assuaged party differences. In New York, the Hunkers and Barnburners had split openly in October. In addition, John Calhoun returned to Congress determined to defend southern rights at all costs and to attempt actively to halt the war. Finally, Thomas Hart Benton, an erstwhile but erratic supporter of the president, also fell from the ranks. The Missouri Senator's hostility was occasioned by the War Department's impending court-martial of his adventurous son-in-law, Colonel John C. Fremont.

Nor could the president rely on public opinion to sustain his Mexican policy. After nineteen months of fighting, most Americans were battle weary. A growing concern in commercial circles was the nation's financial condition, which seemed to be headed for disaster, with war expenses steadily increasing, the government deficit multiplying, and another war loan impending.[2] Frustrated by Mexico's obstinacy, more and more war supporters argued that the only way to end the conflict was to subjugate, either permanently or temporarily, the entire Mexican nation. Rabid expansionists with their eyes on the vast reaches of Mexico encouraged such suggestions. Given the continuation of the war and the agitation of the expansionists, the All Mexico movement continued to gain momentum during December 1847 and the early months of 1848.[3]

But other Americans, deeply disillusioned with the war, hardened their opposition. For example, the *Richmond Palladium* of Indiana, a paper which had early supported the war, now even suggested that Congress impeach the president "as an indemnity to the American people for the loss of the 15,000 lives, which have been sacrificed in Mexico. . . ."[4] A particularly eloquent critic, moved by the urgency of the crisis to take up his pen, was eighty-six-

---

1. See, for example, Milo M. Quaife, ed., *The Diary of James K. Polk, 1845–1849,* 4 vols. (Chicago, 1910), 3: 359–60.

2. See, for example, Justin H. Smith, *The War with Mexico,* 2 vols. (New York, 1919), 2: 489; D. Outlaw to Wife, 1 February, 2 February 1848, David Outlaw Papers, Southern Historical Collection, University of North Carolina, Chapel Hill, North Carolina; Albert Gallatin, *War Expenses* (New York, 1848); John McLean to ———, 7 January 1848, quoted in *National Intelligencer,* 1 February 1848.

3. See John D. P. Fuller, *The Movement for the Acquisition of All Mexico, 1846-1848* (Baltimore, Md., 1936), 91–136; and Frederick Merk, *Manifest Destiny and Mission in American History: A Reinterpretation* (New York, 1963), 180–201.

4. *Richmond Palladium* (Indiana), 30 November 1847.

year-old Albert Gallatin. At one time an able secretary of the treasury under presidents Jefferson and Madison, the former Jeffersonian statesman and diplomat had long been out of public life. During the 1840s, Gallatin had actively pioneered the study of American ethnology, and his brilliant mind remained as sharp and vigorous as ever. And although Democratic supporters of the war disparaged him as old, decrepit, and still an alien at heart, the wisdom of his years and the breadth of his experience entitled Gallatin's views to serious consideration.

In *Peace with Mexico,* a pamphlet published in the fall of 1847, Gallatin pleaded for the nation to reach an immediate and just peace. The only object of any settlement should be "peace, immediate peace, a just peace." Although he himself staunchly opposed the cession of territory and suggested that, as the guilty party, the United States should indemnify Mexico by assuming the outstanding claims owed to American citizens, Gallatin was willing to accept a treaty which adjusted the Texas border and required Mexican payment of her outstanding claims.[5]

Central to Gallatin's antiwar criticism was his intense conviction that, by waging aggressive war against Mexico, the United States was betraying and perverting its true mission as a "model for all other governments and for all other less-favored nations. . . ." That "mission," Gallatin emphasized, was "to improve the state of the world, to be the 'model republic,' to show that men are capable of governing themselves, and that this simple and natural form of government is that also which confers most happiness on all. . . ."[6] But instead, America's noblest virtues had been perverted as the country had embarked on a career "of unjust aggrandizement by brutal force" against a weak sister republic. Gallatin was particularly alarmed by those expansionists who attempted to justify the war by arguing that the American people "have an hereditary superiority of race over the Mexicans which gives them the right to subjugate . . . the inferior nation" as a "means of enlightening the degraded Mexicans. . . ." To Gallatin, such arguments represented flagrant violations of the sacred American principle "that no one man is born with the right of governing another man." And even if one admitted the superiority of "the Anglo-American race" over the Mexicans, it gave the "Americans no right to infringe upon the rights of the inferior race." Although the United States might "rightfully . . . exercise a most beneficial moral influence over the Mexicans and other less enlightened nations of America," it had "no right" to go beyond this moral example.[7] Around the nation, newspapers critical of the

5. Albert Gallatin, "Peace with Mexico," in *The Writings of Albert Gallatin,* ed. Henry Adams, 3 vols. (1879; reprint ed., New York, 1960), 3: 590, 588.

6. Ibid., 583, 581–82.

7. Ibid., 582, 585, 586.

war reprinted this essay and acknowledged the wisdom of its sentiments.[8] And American readers, confounded by what seemed an interminable war, were receptive to the thoughtful views of Gallatin and other men sharing his fears.

Polk's thorny path was eased, however, by the continuing division and vacillation of his Whig opponents. More determined and vituperative than ever by December 1847, the Whig majority in the House was nevertheless unreliable, and they disagreed among themselves on the proper mode of ending the war. Controlling the House, they remained a distinct minority in the Senate. With a narrow margin of, at most, seven votes in the House, the party would have to maintain strict party discipline if it expected to do anything more than impede the president. But, like the Democrats, the Whigs suffered from internal divisions which prevented substantial unity on explosive issues like the war and the slavery question.

In fact, some dedicated war opponents considered the newly won Whig majority in the House to be a "calamity." The Whigs would now be obligated either to take steps to end the war, or to assume "the responsibility of continuing the war. . . ."[9] As Columbus Delano of Ohio prophesied in August, "If this war goes on until Congress meets—it will become necessary for the Whigs to adopt it, and '*fight it out*' or to repudiate it, and give the country peace. Have the Whigs courage enough to do right? Courage enough to give the country peace without *Conquest?* I fear for the result."[10]

In the months preceding the opening of the Thirtieth Congress, Whig editorial comment clearly forecast the lack of a clear consensus on any concrete antiwar strategy during the coming session. The immediate question in dispute was whether the slim Whig majority in the House should continue to vote supplies. On one side of the issue, a number of Whig papers, representing a variety of positions on the expansion question, advocated continued support. For example, the Baltimore *American,* already committed to a "limited" territorial indemnity including New Mexico and California, suggested that 25,000 additional troops be raised to allow General Scott to impose peace

---

8. For example, *National Era,* 16 December 1847; Boston *Courier,* 3 December 1847; *Ohio State Journal,* 6 December, 7 December 1847; *Nashville Republican Banner,* 22 December 1847; *New York Tribune,* 2 December, 18 December 1847; *Richmond Whig* (Virginia), 7 December, 24 December, 31 December 1847; *National Intelligencer,* 4 December 1847; C. F. Adams to J. G. Palfrey, 3 December 1847, Adams Family Papers, Massachusetts Historical Society, Boston, Massachusetts; William Underwood to John M. Berrien, 19 December 1847, John M. Berrien Papers, Southern Historical Collection, University of North Carolina, Chapel Hill, North Carolina.

9. Delano to Giddings, 22 August 1847; C. B. Smith to Giddings, 21 May 1847, Giddings Papers, Ohio Historical Society, Columbus, Ohio.

10. Delano to Giddings, 22 August 1847, Giddings Papers.

terms on Mexico, unless Mexico signed a treaty before Congress reconvened.[11] In a more moderate vein, the mildly antiwar New York *Courier and Enquirer,* which favored taking San Francisco Bay in return for outstanding damage claims, and the staunchly antiwar, No Territory *Richmond Whig* argued that the Whigs should "place at the disposal of the Executive all the men and all the money he may ask, for the prosecution of the war. If they refuse this, they must assume the responsibility which he [Polk] will thus escape."[12]

While southern Whigs tended to share this view, most northern Whig editors, whether they espoused the No Territory or the Wilmot Proviso strategy, agreed with the views already expressed by Clay, Corwin, and Webster. That is, the duty of the Whig House majority in the next Congress was to demand that the president state his war objectives explicitly and then, if Polk refused or if Congress disapproved of his stated goals, to withhold supplies and stop the fighting. But even those editors who argued that Congress might be forced to withhold supplies could not agree on the precise conditions under which this action was to be taken. While the *New York Tribune* now expressed a willingness to accept the cession of a small amount of territory along the southern border of Texas to end the war, other journals like the *Ohio State Journal* demanded that any further fighting "for conquest and the mere lust of power" be abandoned.[13] No supplies to add more territory should be voted. Declaring that neither Webster nor Clay had gone far enough in his views, the Boston *Daily Whig* urged "an unconditional withholding of supplies for purposes of aggression—to an immediate withdrawal of troops, and thus to an ending of the war."[14] In short, the Whig press debate foreshadowed party differences which would surface once Congress convened.

Whig division was also highlighted and intensified by presidential politics. Backers of Taylor, Clay, and John McLean maneuvered constantly for their favorites during the session. This jockeying not only continued to frustrate the president but distressed some Whigs as well. Representative David Outlaw of North Carolina noted that the presidential question seemed to absorb all else and complained that "intellectually great" men could no longer win the office: "It is the age of mediocrity, of schemers and intriguers, or . . . men who are surrounded by the glare of a brilliant military reputation."[15]

---

11. Baltimore *American,* 6 September 1847.

12. New York *Courier and Enquirer* quoted in *New York Tribune,* 25 August 1847; also, *Richmond Whig* (Virginia), 20 October 1847.

13. *New York Tribune,* 16 November 1847; *Ohio State Journal,* 27 October 1847; see also, *Boston Atlas,* 31 August 1847; *Richmond Palladium* (Indiana), 26 October 1847.

14. Boston *Daily Whig,* 4 December 1847.

15. Quaife, *Polk Diary,* 3: 366; Outlaw to Wife, 6 January 1848; also, Outlaw to Wife, 3 February 1848, Outlaw Papers; W. Mangum to David Swain, 12 January 1848, in *Papers of Magnum,* ed. Henry T. Shanks, 5 vols. (Raleigh, N.C., 1950), 5: 91.

Obviously, differing opinions among Whigs on the respective candidates were inevitable and not necessarily divisive, but the presidential question continued to expose the deep differences which existed between the radical and conservative Whigs. Unsuccessful in their search for a suitable candidate to replace Corwin, the radicals vowed to "support no man who is not in favor of the Wilmot Proviso. . . ."[16] This meant that by early 1848, as a Taylor or Clay nomination loomed, these Whigs prepared for their coming separation from the party. The only real obstacle to cooperation with the antislavery Democrats remained the continued war, which the radical Whigs were now more eager than ever to see terminated so that the central issue of slavery might be met.[17] In sharp contrast was the conservative majority of Whigs who continued to believe that the most important qualification for the nomination was not a candidate's views on the war or slavery but his ability to win in 1848. For example, during the session, Taylor's growing number of supporters seemed more intent on waging a successful presidential campaign than on ending the war.

Once Congress convened and tried to select a Speaker of the House for the session, Whig disunity quickly surfaced. After aged Samuel Vinton of Ohio declined the nomination, the Whig caucus selected Robert Winthrop, who recognized quickly that his party did not stand unanimously behind him: " 'while I am not enough of an anti-slavery man for some of our Northern friends, I am too much of a Wilmot Proviso man for some of our Southern friends.' "[18] With the Whigs holding a narrow margin, Winthrop won only after three ballots. On the first two ballots, three southern Whigs and two antislavery Whigs voted against Winthrop, and it was only after Democrat Isaac Holmes of South Carolina left the House floor that Winthrop received the necessary majority by one vote.[19] Although most antislavery Whigs accepted the decision of the party caucus, both Joshua Giddings and John Gorham Palfrey refused to acquiesce. Giddings found particularly offensive Winthrop's vacillating course on the war, his weak stand on the slavery question, and his role as a leading Cotton Whig of Massachusetts, which had pitted Winthrop against the Conscience Whig friends of Giddings. As a close friend of both Charles Francis Adams and Charles Sumner, Palfrey felt obligated to stand with Giddings although Palfrey quickly congratulated Winthrop upon

16. Giddings to C. F. Adams, 2 February 1848, Adams Family Papers.

17. C. F. Adams to J. G. Palfrey, 12 February 1848; Giddings to C. F. Adams, 2 February 1848, Adams Family Papers.

18. Winthrop to a friend, quoted in Kinley J. Brauer, *Cotton versus Conscience: Massachusetts Whig Politics and Southwestern Expansion, 1843–1848* (Lexington, Ky., 1967), 219.

19. *Cong. Globe,* 30th Cong., 1st Sess., 1848, 2.

his election.[20] Although this incident seemed minor, it increased tension between conservatives like Winthrop and radicals like Giddings and again demonstrated that the Whig party in Congress would find it impossible to agree on any positive course of antiwar action.

Confronting a stubborn enemy, a divided Democratic party, and an angry opposition, the president nevertheless sustained his attack on opponents of the war and refused to yield his territorial objectives. Polk's third annual message to Congress clearly signified his determination. After reiterating his view of the causes and conduct of the war, the president emphasized that the United States required indemnity as an indispensable condition of peace. By indemnity, Polk, of course, meant territory from the bankrupt Mexicans for outstanding claims and war expenses. To reject indemnity, argued Polk, "would be to abandon all our just demands" and to have waged war "without a purpose or definite object." To agree to the Whig doctrine of No Territory, which meant "no indemnity," would be to acknowledge publicly that "our country was wrong . . . [that the war was] unjust and should be abandoned—an admission unfounded in fact and degrading to the national character." The president also claimed that Congress itself had approved the principle of indemnity by passing the Three Million Bill in 1847.[21]

The *sine qua non* of any settlement was to be the Rio Grande and the cession of New Mexico and California. Having won control of these valuable provinces, the president declared "that they should never be surrendered to Mexico." Polk also issued a thinly veiled warning to the Mexicans. If they maintained their obstinate perseverance and the war continued, Mexico might expect harsher terms of peace. As expenses continued to rise, so must the indemnity be expected to increase. Should the enemy remain intransigent, the United States would have no alternative but to "continue to occupy her country . . . taking full measure of indemnity into our own hands. . . ."[22]

Polk rejected both the withdrawal of American troops and the defensive line alternatives suggested by his various critics. To withdraw troops after their victory and great sacrifices "would be to degrade the nation in its own estimation and in that of the world." Similarly, to fall back and defend a predetermined line would be to "protract" the war indefinitely by encouraging the enemy to persevere. In the absence of Mexican willingness to negotiate on reasonable terms, the United States must therefore exert still greater pressure

20. Palfrey to Winthrop, 6 December 1847, Winthrop Family Papers, Massachusetts Historical Society, Boston. For an excellent discussion of the whole episode see Frank Otto Gatell, "Palfrey's Vote, the Conscience Whigs and the Election of Speaker Winthrop," *New England Quarterly* 31 (June, 1958): 218–31.

21. James D. Richardson, ed., *A Compilation of the Messages and Papers of the Presidents, 1789–1902*, 10 vols. (Washington, D.C., 1903), 4: 533, 537, 538.

22. Ibid., 545.

on the enemy. To this end, Polk requested that Congress provide him additional volunteers and a loan of "about" $18.5 million.[23]

Response to the message was predictable. Democrats praised and defended; Whigs condemned. Characteristically, to the *National Intelligencer* it was a " 'stereotyped falsehood,' " to the *Boston Atlas* an "utterly perverse and unblushing" document.[24] Just one year earlier Polk had denied any view to conquest, but now he asserted that he would never surrender New Mexico or California and warned that he might demand "additional indemnity" and "additional annexation" unless Mexico came to her senses and accepted his supposedly reasonable terms.[25] Many opponents read the president's warning as an omen of Mexico's pending absorption and America's doom. John Calhoun wrote that the administration now "intended to conquor [*sic*] and subject the whole country . . . as a conquered Province or incorporate it into the Union. Either will overthrow our system of Government."[26] Immediately the *National Intelligencer* renewed its argument against the annexation of Mexico, a course which promised to swell the nation's population with motley and "unknown" tribes, fill the legislatures with "many-colored representatives," necessitate a perpetual standing army, and subvert the most basic ideals of the republic.[27]

Like his message to Congress in December 1846, Polk's report to the Thirtieth Congress not only drew a shower of criticism but again became the focal point of debate during the session. In both houses, formal debate centered on the president's recommendations for additional war measures. Senator Cass introduced two bills to increase the size of the army: one to raise ten additional regiments of regular troops and the other to allow the President to call for 20,000 volunteers if he deemed it advisable. Neither bill was enacted. The volunteer bill never passed the Senate, and the Ten Regiment Bill passed the Senate only to be tabled in the House after the ratification of a peace treaty rendered it unnecessary.[28] The House concentrated largely on the president's request for money to finance the war. His suggested duty on tea and coffee

---

23. Ibid., 543, 553. Polk suggested that the loan might be reduced to $17 million if Congress would approve a duty on tea and coffee and a graduated scale for public land prices.

24. *National Intelligencer,* 8 December 1847; *Boston Atlas,* 15 December 1847.

25. See, for example, Baltimore *American,* 9 December 1847.

26. Calhoun to Andrew F. Calhoun, 11 December 1847, in *Correspondence of John C. Calhoun,* ed. J. Franklin Jameson, *Annual Report of the American Historical Association for the Year 1899,* vol. 2 (Washington, D.C., 1899), 2: 741.

27. *National Intelligencer,* 18 December 1847.

28. The Ten Regiment Bill passed the Senate 29 to 19 but never reached a final vote in the House; *Sen. Journal,* 30th Cong., 1st Sess., 1848, 219–20. Introduced into the Senate in December, the volunteer bill never reached a vote.

and his proposal for a graduated price for public lands were both rejected, but the loan bill passed almost unanimously after being limited to a maximum of $16 million rather than the $18.5 million the administration had requested.[29]

Despite the administration's failure to win prompt approval for its war measures, developments in Mexico helped to cripple congressional opposition to the war. Unknown to Congress at the time was Nicholas Trist's refusal to return to the United States and his reopening of negotiations with a new Mexican regime in early January, which eventually resulted in the treaty signed at Guadalupe Hidalgo in February. Meanwhile in Washington, with the fighting completed, viable means of opposing the president were not available. While Congress might withhold supplies intended for further conquest and might refuse additional troops, such actions were now irrelevant. The president did not need additional troops and he was eventually granted the loan authorization he did need. A more direct alternative was a demand for immediate troop withdrawal, but only a few Whigs supported this proposal. In January Whig Charles Hudson's resolution to examine "the expediency of requesting the President" to withdraw American troops to the Rio Grande and to propose peace on terms establishing the border as the area between the Nueces and the Rio Grande without any indemnity was defeated in the House by an overwhelming 41 to 137 count.[30]

In addition to the reality of the situation in Mexico, continued disagreements among congressional critics guaranteed the failure of possible alternatives. A tiny portion of Whigs continued to support the war. In the Senate, Reverdy Johnson repeated that the war was both "just and honorable" and could best be terminated by being fought. Though critical of Polk, the Maryland Whig declared: "I am for fighting it out in order . . . to have American rights recognized, and American honor vindicated, so as to furnish full and complete security against any subsequent violation."[31]

At the other extreme, Senator John P. Hale of New Hampshire, a heretical Democrat, added his voice to the antislavery chorus. Not only did Senator Hale and Representative Giddings vote against supplies and demand American withdrawal, they even voted against innocuous resolutions of thanks to Generals Scott and Taylor. "I cannot," declared Hale, "by any possibility, by any sophistry, separate in my mind a vote of thanks to those officers for the agency which they have had in the war, from an approval of the war in which they are engaged."[32] When Senator Crittenden challenged his reasoning, Hale

---

29. The loan bill passed 192 to 14 in the House and 34 to 2 in the Senate; *H.R. Journal,* 30th Cong., 1st Sess., 1848, 426–28; *Sen. Journal,* 30th Cong., 1st Sess., 1848, 242.

30. *Cong. Globe,* 30th Cong., 1st Sess., 1848, 94.

31. Ibid., Appendix, 64, 67.

32. Ibid., 341.

scornfully rebuked the contradictory stance of the Whig conservatives: "I have not sufficient skill in splitting hairs—to enable me, without uneasiness, to denounce the war as a war of robbery, as unconstitutional and unjust, as begun by the President, and at the same time, thank the agents who have been engaged in carrying out this unjust and unconstitutional war."[33] But despite its consistency, Hale's position never gained many followers. Only Giddings and Hale voted against the resolutions of thanks; only fourteen votes in the House and two in the Senate could be mustered against the loan bill; and Hudson's resolution recommending American withdrawal received only forty-one affirmative votes.

Somewhere between the extremes of Reverdy Johnson and John Hale fell most war opponents in the Thirtieth Congress. Democrat John Calhoun continued to advocate the practical alternative of a defensive line, which he had first suggested during the previous session of Congress. Although no longer a presidential possibility, Calhoun remained independent and critical of both major parties while working to end the war.[34] In a dramatic speech before a packed Senate chamber on January 4, 1848, Calhoun spoke again in support of his defensive-line strategy which, he believed, the events of the past eleven months had made more advisable than ever. The protracted war against a stubborn Mexico must eventually lead to the subjugation of an alien people rather than a satisfactory peace and limited indemnity. "I protest against the incorporation of such a people," declared Calhoun. "Ours is the government of the white man." In short, the United States would become an "imperial power. . . ." He again rejected the Whig position of No Territory, arguing that the American public supported a territorial indemnity and reminding the Whigs that, despite their protests, they had also endorsed this objective by their consistently supportive votes: "The people are not able to understand why you would vote money so profusely to get indemnity, and refuse to take it when obtained; and hence public opinion has been brought so decidedly to the conclusion not to terminate the war without territorial indemnity."[35]

Because it voiced objections shared by many Democrats and Whigs who feared the absorption of all of Mexico, Calhoun's speech received favorable comment from both Democratic and Whig sources. The *Charleston Mercury* praised it and again warned that Mexico was "forbidden fruit."[36] The Whig press generally applauded Calhoun's views but either rejected his strategy or labeled it a temporary procedure inferior to a No Territory, no indemnity

---

33. Ibid., Appendix, 364.

34. Calhoun to Waddy Thompson, 27 October 1847, *Calhoun Correspondence,* 2: 739.

35. *Cong. Globe,* 30th Cong., 1st Sess., 1848, Appendix, 51, 53.

36. *Charleston Mercury,* 30 December 1847, 10 January, 11 January 1848; for anti-slavery praise, see *National Era,* 13 January 1848.

policy. Papers like the Boston *Courier* and the *Richmond Whig* agreed that the defensive line was a proper step in the right direction of changing "from an *offensive* to a *defensive* war."[37]

In Congress, Calhoun's plan quickly became the subject of debate. Administration supporters termed it an impractical proposal which would actually lengthen, not shorten, the war. But some Democrats began to embrace his suggestions. On February 9, Senator John Niles, a Van Buren Democrat from Connecticut, echoed many of Calhoun's arguments when he proposed one final attempt at negotiation. Then, if it failed, the United States should assume a defensive line along the Rio Grande and hold New Mexico and California as indemnity, subject to a treaty with Mexico. Among northern expansionists, Niles stood alone, but Calhoun's proposal received a favorable response from a number of southern Democrats.[38] Speaking in the Senate on February 7, R. M. T. Hunter, a Calhoun supporter from Virginia, urged the adoption of a defensive-line strategy along the so-called Sierra Madre Line and spoke against the annexation of Mexico.[39] In the House, such southern representatives as Robert Barnwell Rhett of South Carolina expressed their opposition to All Mexico. In fact, by the beginning of 1848, proannexation feeling in the older slave states waned as more people realized that slavery was not suitable for the soil of the southwest beyond the Rio Grande. The promised land would turn into ashes if it became free territory and then free states strangling the South. Among the most prominent men who held this view were a former minister to Mexico, Waddy Thompson of South Carolina, John C. Calhoun, and Justice John A. Campbell of Alabama, whose growing reluctance to engulf Mexico represented an attempt to preserve the strength of the slave South.[40]

While Whigs in Congress endorsed Calhoun's antiwar criticisms, only a few like Kentucky's Senator Joseph R. Underwood and Indiana Congressman Caleb Smith actually endorsed the defensive-line strategy. To most Whigs, of course, the key drawback in Calhoun's plan was its acceptance of the principle of limited war indemnity, an idea which contradicted their own No Territory, no indemnity position. But even among the conservative, No Territory majority of Whigs, basic disagreement existed. While most agreed with Dela-

---

37. Boston *Courier,* 10 January 1848; *Richmond Whig* (Virginia), 10 January, 11 January 1848.

38. *Cong. Globe,* 30th Cong., 1st Sess., 1848, Appendix, 278–85.

39. Ibid., Appendix, 272–78.

40. For example, see John Campbell to Calhoun, 20 November, 30 December 1847, *Calhoun Correspondence,* 2: 1139–42; Campbell to Calhoun, 1 March 1848, in *Correspondence Addressed to John C. Calhoun, 1837–1849,* ed. Chauncey Boucher and Robert Brooks, *Annual Report of the American Historical Society for the Year 1929* (Washington, D.C., 1929), 430–34.

ware's John Clayton that Congress should prevent a territorial indemnity by refusing to vote for more supplies and troops, some did not.[41] For example, Senator John J. Crittenden, who was manifestly more interested in making political capital of the war and advancing Taylor's candidacy, professed his willingness to vote for needed war measures.[42] The No Territory position was further weakened by other Whigs now willing to compromise on the question of territorial indemnity. Confronting the reality of a president who refused to make peace without an indemnity, these Whigs feared that all Mexico might eventually be annexed unless the war was ended quickly with a limited territorial settlement. Better the lesser evil of New Mexico and California than the entire country. Like Clayton, Senator John Bell of Tennessee announced that he would vote against more troops. But because he feared total subjugation, Bell pleaded for immediate peace on available terms: "If you must have the territories of New Mexico and California, get a cession of them; if you cannot do that, come back to the Rio Grande. . . ."[43] Senator S. S. Phelps of Vermont acquiesced in a "reasonable and just" indemnity: "infuse a little moderation into your counsels. . . . Show a disposition to preserve instead of destroying the nationality of Mexico . . . be satisfied with a reasonable provision for your claims."[44]

Unable to agree on positive action, the Whigs acted as they had during the previous two congressional sessions by persistently scheming to embarrass and discredit the administration. Indicative of Whig activity were the resolutions and speech of Abraham Lincoln. Although he willingly voted supplies, this first-term Congressman from Illinois authenticated his Whig credentials by introducing a series of resolutions requesting that the president submit information showing "whether the particular spot on which the blood of our citizens was so shed was or was not at that time *our own soil*. . . ."[45] And in a subsequent speech in support of his resolutions, Lincoln concentrated, not on the crucial issue of ending the war, but rather on a partisan and tightly reasoned examination of the war's causes and Polk's responsibility.[46] Throughout the session, the Whig opposition introduced resolutions condemning the war and calling on Polk to provide Congress with confidential official documents from the executive and war departments. The Whigs were particularly interested in information related to peace terms and the potentially embarrassing documents pertaining to Polk's dealings with his generals and Santa Anna. In

---

41. *Cong. Globe,* 30th Cong., 1st Sess., 1848, Appendix, 73–77.
42. Ibid., 367.
43. Ibid., Appendix, 201.
44. Ibid., Appendix, 238.
45. Ibid., 64.
46. Ibid., Appendix, 93–95.

the House, the highpoint of the session for Whigs came on January 3, when George Ashmun of Massachusetts moved to amend a resolution of thanks to General Taylor to read "in a war unnecessarily and unconstitutionally begun by the President of the United States."[47] By a margin of 85 to 81 along partisan lines, the amendment carried in that form before being rejected by the Senate.

In debate, the Whig opposition continued to level an unceasing political attack on the administration by endlessly denouncing a culpable and inept president, reexamining the war's causes, and reaffirming their own loyalty and patriotism. An important part of the Whig attack was an increasing emphasis on the nation's financial condition. Charging the administration with financial bungling, the opposition argued that Secretary of the Treasury Walker had been devious in reporting on war finances by consistently overestimating government receipts and grossly underestimating its expenses. Estimates of the deficit now ran anywhere from forty to seventy million dollars, a high price, the Whigs thought, for what was supposed to have been a short and inexpensive war. Furthermore, the president had refused to go before the people and ask candidly for the duties and taxes necessary to finance the war. Instead, the administration had chosen the evasive technique of issuing treasury notes and assuming huge loans, a policy which camouflaged the real cost of the war and endangered America's credit standing and its economy. Like Calhoun and Gallatin, the Whigs now predicted financial disaster if the flow of currency from the country were not stemmed. "The prospect now before us," declared Samuel Vinton of Ohio in February, "is full of gloom and fearful foreboding. While the war with Mexico continues, species must be constantly exported there to pay the war expenditures . . . specie must also be sent to England to pay the balance against us there . . . the unhappy country is like a strong man bleeding at both arms. He will faint and sink at last; and when he does fall, he will sink to rise no more. . . ."[48]

During the final months of war debate, slavery was not so prominent an issue as it had been during the Twenty-ninth Congress. In early December, Senator Daniel Dickinson, a Hunker Democrat from New York, introduced a series of resolutions designed to reconcile North and South on the slavery question. The resolutions reaffirmed the desirability of acquiring new territory and stipulated that all questions of "domestic policy" be left to the individual legislatures selected by the people of the various territories.[49] Later, debate would rage over this principle of popular sovereignty, but heated discussion on Dickinson's proposal did not develop until after the peace treaty had been

47. Ibid., 95.
48. Ibid., Appendix, 337
49. Ibid., 21.

ratified. However, in the early months of 1848, northern antislavery radicals continued to demand the adoption of the Wilmot Proviso just as resolute southerners zealously protected slavery's future status in the new territory.

An important reason for the slavery issue's receding in early 1848 was the continued rise of a more immediate and pressing question—the All Mexico movement. Whigs now joined Calhoun and other Democrats in a frantic attempt to block what appeared to be the impending annexation of all Mexico. By early 1848, this movement had reached its height in the expansionist press. In addition, Buchanan and Walker in Polk's cabinet were known to favor the project, public support appeared to be growing rapidly, and administration requests for more troops seemed to indicate Polk's desire to annex the whole country.[50] In Congress, opponents of the All Mexico coalition tried to prevent passage of Polk's request for 30,000 additional volunteers and regulars, because to them this seemed a naked admission of the president's designs.

Debate on All Mexico centered largely in the Senate, where the bills to raise troops were introduced. On January 4, Calhoun's speech recommending the defensive-line strategy and enumerating the manifest dangers of subjugating the whole of Mexico offered an able example for others to follow. In the following weeks, a procession of Whig and Democratic speakers repeated and expanded upon Calhoun's arguments that the addition of that entire nation was "contrary to the genius and character" of American institutions and threatened the spirit and letter of the Constitution itself. Democrats like Niles of Connecticut and Hunter of Virginia endorsed the defensive line in their desire to prevent annexation. Concerning Mexico and Mexicans Hunter stated: "'We wanted no such race as hers in the midst of ours—we wanted not her people in our councils—we wanted them not to fight our battles—we wanted not their habits, manners, and customs, alien as they were to ours—we wanted not their lands—we wanted them not with their debts. . . .'"[51] Whig John Bell of Tennessee argued that any project to annex and absorb Mexico was both unworkable and destructive. "All history, all experience" demonstrated that any attempt to regenerate the Mexicans so that they might enter the Union on an equal basis was doomed to miserable failure.[52]

To expansionist arguments that the nation's destiny and Anglo-Saxon superiority demanded the annexation and regeneration of Mexico, Kentucky's Joseph R. Underwood replied that in such schemes he had no faith: "I am unwilling to enter upon military crusades with a view to teach our politics or

---

50. On the widespread Whig fear that the acquisition of all of Mexico was imminent, see, for example, W. Mangum to David Swain, 12 January 1848; W. Mangum to William Graham, 23 January 1848, in Shanks, *Papers of Mangum,* 5: 91, 95.

51. *Cong. Globe,* 30th Cong., 1st Sess., 1848, Appendix, 272.

52. Ibid., Appendix, 197.

religion to the other nations of the earth. . . . Sir, it is not in the nature of man to be taught true religion, or the true principles of civil liberty and republican government, at the point of the bayonet."[53] Senator George E. Badger of North Carolina warned that the unjust subjugation of Mexico would leave indelible stains on America's history: "No oblivion that thousands of years could throw over it, no darkness with which the lapse of ages could surround it, would ever prevent the flagrant enormity of such a measure from being apparent to posterity."[54]

Suddenly, in late February, amidst continuing controversy over the war and the threat of All Mexico, debate was cut short by unexpected news. A treaty of peace had been concluded and had arrived in Washington for Polk's consideration. The treaty came as a surprise, not only because the Mexicans appeared to be as recalcitrant as ever in early 1848, but also because it had been negotiated by a man without authority. After evaluating the situation in Mexico in November 1847, Trist had refused to return to the United States as ordered by the president, but had decided instead to remain in Mexico and, under his original instructions, to reopen negotiations with a newly elected Mexican regime. After a month of discussion, the treaty was signed on February 2 at the village of Guadalupe Hidalgo, just outside Mexico City. By the terms of the settlement, Mexico agreed to relinquish all her claims to Texas above the Rio Grande and to cede New Mexico and California to the United States. In return the United States would pay $15 million and assume the outstanding claims, which totaled some $3.25 million, of its citizens against the Mexican government. Upon its arrival in Washington, the treaty was considered by a hesitant president who doubted the legitimacy of the settlement. But because the terms of the treaty were within Trist's original instructions and because he feared rising opposition to the war, Polk on February 23 sent the treaty to the Senate for ratification.[55]

Relief rather than jubilation marked the nation's response to the reported treaty, which went to the Senate on the day of venerable John Quincy Adams' death. Collapsing at his desk in the house, Adams died within hours. News of his death added a somber tone to the national mood as Americans united in praise of a dedicated, if irascible, statesman and began to evaluate a flawed treaty of peace. Objections were numerous. Visionary expansionists and war critics alike charged that either too little or too much territory had been ceded. Furthermore, could Mexicans be trusted to honor the settlement?[56] But more important than its defects was the fact that the treaty would terminate an enervating war.

---

53. Ibid., Appendix, 308.
54. Ibid., Appendix, 120.
55. Quaife, *Polk Diary*, 3:347–50.
56. For a summary of reaction to the treaty, see Fuller, *All Mexico*, 148–50.

Although terms of the agreement were supposedly secret, they were well known and widely discussed in the press. A long editorial in the *National Intelligencer* on February 29 cited the settlement's defects and became a harbinger of national Whig press reaction. The acquisition of vast areas of Mexican territory, argued the *Intelligencer,* was to be regarded with "distrust and apprehension" because of the sectional controversy which would follow. A crucial objection was the absorption of "people who are for the most part in a state of moral degradation, and are unfit . . . to sustain a free government." Finally, the cost of almost $20 million was much too great for a region not worth more than $5 million. "But, momentous as these considerations are," stated the *Intelligencer,* "we view them as dust in the balance in comparison with those which force themselves upon us, in contemplation of the rejection of the Treaty."[57] If the war continued, it would surely spread, the military establishment would be vastly increased, the cost would skyrocket, and the "fatal" annexation of all of Mexico would surely follow.

One attractive feature to war critics in the otherwise objectionable settlement was the agreement to pay $15 million for the ceded territory. Although the cost was high, to the *Intelligencer,* the fact that *"we take nothing* BY CONQUEST . . . is alone worth far more to a Christian Nation than the sum we shall pay. The lust of Conquest is as unjust and ruinous in a Republic as in any other form of government. . . . Thank God, we shall be saved from the curse of this blighting principle!"[58] Because the United States had demanded only a limited territory and had agreed to compensate Mexico for it, the *Intelligencer* believed that both the true honor of the United States and the national pride of Mexico had been preserved.

By preventing the complete humilation of Mexico and protecting her independence, the *Richmond Whig* asserted that "we neutralize much of the bitterness which never fails to attend upon conquest, and lay a broad foundation for future harmony." At the same time, the treaty agreement for the purchase of the ceded territory meant necessarily that the president had relinquished his own demands that Mexico indemnify the victors for the war's expenses. Since Polk had claimed "Indemnity" as a condition of peace, the *Richmond Whig* noted the "marvellous promptitude" with which this demand was abandoned, "a circumstance which obviously indicates that it was without foundation from the beginning."[59] Even those Whig papers which most vehemently denounced the settlement never urged its rejection. The *Richmond Palladium* called the treaty "disastrous to the true interests of the country" and complained anew, once it was ratified, but never suggested that it should be defeated.[60]

---

57. *National Intelligencer,* 29 February 1848.
58. Ibid.
59. *Richmond Whig* (Virginia), 1 March 1848.
60. *Richmond Palladium* (Indiana), 2 March, 22 March 1848.

When the treaty was first submitted to the Senate, its ratification seemed doubtful. It was known that almost every senator had his own objection. On the Foreign Relations Committee several Democrats and Whigs protested that the treaty had been concluded by an unauthorized agent. They suggested that a duly authorized peace commission be dispatched to Mexico to renegotiate the settlement. At the same time, an unlikely coalition of No Territory Whigs and expansionist Democrats seemed prepared to prevent ratification. Democrats like Sam Houston of Texas and Jefferson Davis of Mississippi sought much more territory, while Whigs like Corwin and Webster demanded that none be taken. But as debate continued in secret Senate session, the mood gradually changed and the restoration of peace superseded the document's numerous flaws. "The desire for peace," wrote Calhoun on March 8, "and not the approbation of its terms, induces the Senate to yield its consent."[61]

First, Webster's proposal to appoint a new peace commission met overwhelming defeat.[62] Then Whig amendments renouncing the cession of any territory were voted down, Democratic motions to expand the area to be acquired were rejected, and an attempt to attach the Wilmot Proviso was easily quashed.[63] Finally, after more than two weeks of secret deliberations, the Senate ratified the treaty by a 38 to 14 margin, in a vote which was neither partisan nor sectional. Twelve Whigs joined Calhoun and twenty-five other Democrats in the affirmative; seven Whigs and seven Democrats voted in the negative; and one Democrat and three Whigs did not vote.[64]

The impetus behind Whig support for ratification in the Senate was an intense desire for peace, even on objectionable terms. Although each Whig would undoubtedly have liked to register a negative vote on its terms, the opposition feared that unless the settlement was then approved, the war would continue and consume Mexico. In fact, if ratification had been seriously in doubt during the final vote, it is probable that more Whigs would have registered ayes.

When news of Senate ratification spread, the *National Intelligencer* spoke for all war opponents when it declared the settlement to embody *"a Peace which every one will be glad of, but no one will be proud of."*[65] On March 19, the New Orleans *Picayune* responded with a panegyric on the restoration of peace:

There is something cheerful in the sound of peace. There is a charm in the word which soothes the chafed and bruised spirit. Kinder and more charitable thoughts

61. Calhoun to T. G. Clemson, 7 March 1848, *Calhoun Correspondence*, 2:746.
62. *Senate Executive Documents*, No. 52, 30th Cong., 1st Sess., 1848, 4, 9.
63. Ibid., 5–6, 18, 22–23, 24–25.
64. Ibid., 36.
65. *National Intelligencer*, 14 March 1848.

displace the revengeful fancies which usurped the mind of the nation, and gentle reveries succeed the rude impulses which possessed the people. After all, battles are hard purchasers and glory the luxury of cruelty. We have heard so much of the cannon's roar, that the tinkling bell is a welcome change.[66]

In, New York, Horace Greeley implored that the lessons of aggressive war might now be well remembered: "Shall not our People be cured of a passion for that Glory which only idiots or demons can soberly prize and exult in? . . . O let us resolve henceforth to treat as a public enemy the man who dare propose the sending of a single regiment, on any pretext beyond the limits of our own country!"[67] And writing to Joshua Giddings, former Congressman and war critic Garrett Davis still hoped that the injustice of the war might someday be undone: "If just men should ever again come into power, I believe they ought not to hesitate to retrocede to Mexico the country of which we have mostly injustly despoiled her. That would be some atonement for our great inquity [*sic*]."[68]

Frequently expressed fears in the United States that the Mexican Congress would never accept such an agreement proved unfounded. In May, the treaty was ratified and both nations exchanged official ratifications. American troops were evacuated from Mexico City in June and on July 4, 1848, President Polk proclaimed the treaty to be in effect. The war, as well as the hostilities, was now concluded.

---

66. New Orleans *Picayune,* 19 March 1848 as quoted in Merk, *Manifest Destiny and Mission,* 189 n.

67. *New York Tribune,* 26 February 1848.

68. Davis to Giddings, 18 March 1848, Giddings Papers.

10

★ *Conclusion*

BORN ABRUPTLY IN MAY 1846 in Congress, as a frantic though futile attempt to prevent or delay formal war with Mexico, war opposition grew until, by the time peace came in 1848, it had become a vocal, diverse, and determined attempt to block the absorption of the whole of Mexico. During the initial three months of fighting, the political opposition, composed of Whigs and Calhoun Democrats, remained unorganized and diffident. Once the war bill had become law and military provisions for the crisis had been voted, interest soon reverted to other subjects, international and domestic: the Oregon question, the tariff, fiscal policy, and internal improvements. At this time, Calhoun and most Whigs treated the war as just another partisan issue and evinced little understanding of the administration's ultimate objectives. Though some editors and politicians gave them cursory treatment, the territorial goals of the administration went largely ignored amidst a barrage of partisan indictments and immediate apprehensions. Both Calhoun and the Whigs feared that war with Mexico would endanger the pending Oregon settlement with Great Britain and might well induce European intervention on Mexico's behalf. In the summer of 1846, the antislavery Whigs alone charged that this would, indeed, be a war of conquest for the extension of slavery.

Only by the fall of 1846, in response to new developments, did the war debate move into its second stage. The Two Million Bill, the invasion of New Mexico, California, and northern Mexico, and the establishment of civil governments in New Mexico and California now confirmed the verbalized fears of antislavery Whigs and the silent ones of conservative Whigs. Even if the president had not yet declared his precise objectives, obviously he was fighting for Mexican territory. War debate was further complicated in early 1847, when the controversy over the Wilmot Proviso intensified in Congress. Now the issues of expansion, war, and slavery became inseparable. In response, the radical Whigs demanded immediate troop withdrawal and passage of the proviso while John Calhoun advocated the adoption of a defensive line strat-

egy, a limited territorial indemnity, and equal rights for slaveholders in territories. Finally, conservative Whigs from the North and the South united on
the principle of No Territory to end the war, preserve Whig party unity, and
escape the fearful slavery issue.

But while they disagreed over how the war could best be opposed, Calhoun and the Whigs readily agreed on the manifest evils of Polk's war of
conquest. Clearly this drive into the Southwest presaged a dreadful struggle
over slavery which could endanger existing political parties, as well as the
Union itself. The war also promised a dangerous growth in presidential power
and the strength of the executive branch. These fears, frequently expressed by
the opposition, were sharpened by Polk's control over wartime patronage, as
well as by the administration's establishment of tariff duties for Mexican
ports, without congressional approval, and the creation of civil governments
in New Mexico and California by military officers. But beyond these more
immediate apprehensions, antiwar politicians evinced deeper concerns. Whatever its results, the war with Mexico represented a perversion of the basic
ideals and the true mission of the United States. While the so-called "progres-
sive Democracy" of Polk and his supporters blustered expansively about extending the "area of freedom" and enlarging the "Temple of Freedom," their
critics understood that such language was mere political "Clap-Trap."[1] Conceding the importance of continued territorial expansion, critics demanded
that this goal be achieved honorably. The United States must not violate her
basic republican principles in her hunger for land and frontage on the Pacific.
If the principles of republicanism were to be fostered across the western hemi-
sphere, the forceful imposition of civil governments and American institutions on the reluctant people of New Mexico and California could only destroy these principles by violating the basic right of self-determination.

In the final months of the war, a new element dominated war debate as
Calhoun and the Whigs resisted the so-called All Mexico movement. The subjugation of the whole of Mexico appeared to be increasingly imminent by
early 1848 because the idea was nourished by a sense of national frustration,
as well as by buoyant expansionism. For although General Scott's army had
invaded central Mexico in the spring of 1847 and occupied Mexico City in
September, the enemy remained intransigent. The slavery extension issue itself
lost center stage as war opponents ceased to question merely whether Mexican
territory would be ceded, but began to fear that the entire country would be
engulfed. This fear does explain, in large part, why both Whig and Democratic critics of the war supported the objectionable Treaty of Guadalupe Hidalgo. Should the treaty be rejected, they saw as probable the annexation of all
Mexico.

---

1. *National Intelligencer* (Washington, D.C.), 15 January 1848.

A host of public critics centered in New England lent support to political critics of the war, though the critiques of these pacifists, abolitionists, clergymen, and publicists differed from those of the politicians. Agreeing that Polk and his Democratic supporters were guilty, public dissenters also condemned hypocritical antiwar politicians who voted support for a conflict they professed to abhor. To the nonpolitical dissenters the war was not a partisan issue to be utilized to oust the Polk administration but a moral question, an outrageous national crime. By fighting a war of conquest against a weak and distracted neighbor in the name of national honor, the United States perpetrated a national lie. Was it not, they asked, unchristian for soldiers of a Christian republic to seize Mexican land and slaughter its innocent inhabitants? Thus, enemies of the administration's policy attempted to awaken the nation's conscience and create an irresistible tide of antiwar opinion.

But Americans and their servants in the government were more concerned with the reality of territory than with the abstractions of republican virtue, and the antiwar movement was swept aside by the relentless tide of expansionism. By the mid-1840s, with the United States surging toward the Pacific Coast, most Americans, like their president, viewed the Mexican War as auspicious. Ebullient and determined to realize their territorial "destiny," most Americans did not understand, nor did they care about, the broad implications of an aggressive war. In the initial months of fighting, few Americans doubted that Mexico had to be chastised for her continued insults and provocations of recent years, and thousands of eager young men rushed forth to seek military glory. When Polk's territorial ambitions became clear, most did not question them. Only later in 1847, largely because of the administration's conduct of the war, did disillusionment become widespread. Its policies marked by frequent blunders, intense partisanship, and disturbing attempts to undermine leading American commanders, the administration seemed more intent upon crushing its political rivals than the Mexican foe. Casualties rose and the fighting dragged on month after month, yet without enemy defeat.

Though disillusionment was rife in all but the southwestern and northwestern states by late 1847, it did not translate into actual antiwar sentiment upon which longtime dissenters could call. A concerted movement to terminate the war without territory or to demand the withdrawal of American troops never emerged. Instead, numerous Americans joined with ardent expansionists during late 1847 to argue that the war could be satisfactorily concluded only by a temporary or a permanent subjugation of the whole of Mexico. Finally, in 1848, it was an illegally negotiated treaty rather than the aroused conscience of the nation which saved Mexico from losing a much larger portion of her territory.

In conclusion, it must be said that the antiwar movement had little effect on the war's duration, outcome, or final terms. In Congress, Calhoun and the conservative majority of Whigs saw no other alternative but to sustain the military effort, while denouncing the administration. In addition to being a minority for almost the entire conflict, the opposition never was able to agree upon a viable alternative to administration policy. The effectiveness of Calhoun's and the conservative Whigs' opposition was further weakened by their respective presidential hopes which tended to take precedence over their desire to end the war. In addition, antiwar politicians were subjected to persistent Democratic charges that their dissent offered "aid and comfort" to the enemy. Angrily ridiculing these allegations, the great majority of political critics, nevertheless, were unwilling to give credence to the charges by refusing to vote military supplies. A minority of radical Whigs, of course, assailed this political hypocrisy and voted as well as spoke their dissent. But, for the most part, these radical antiwar, antislavery Whigs represented sympathetic northern districts.

Thus President Polk received almost everything he requested from Congress. Only his most controversial recommendations, such as the Lieutenant General Bill and temporarily the Two and Three Million Bills, were denied him. At various times, a combination of Whig determination, Democratic factionalism, and congressional preoccupation with the slavery controversy paralyzed Congress and delayed action on Polk's requests. But such delays were merely thorns in the path of a resolute president.

Nor were dissenters outside Congress any more potent. A small army of editors, clergymen, reformers, and publicists worked incessantly to mobilize antiwar sentiment and force the administration to reverse its policy. But since they were concentrated in the northeastern states, they lacked broad national support. Elsewhere along the eastern seaboard, decisive opposition failed to materialize, while in the West, men tuned to the expansionist cry were unreceptive to the quibbling of the war critic.

Despite its previous impotence, the Whig opposition appeared to enjoy a strong position as the Thirtieth Congress convened with a Whig majority in the House. But with their majority paper-thin and unable to agree on any alternative strategy, the Whig opposition still represented a negative rather than a dynamic force. They could obstruct and paralyze but not reverse the president's policy. Fearing the intense partisanship of his opponents, Polk believed that the Whigs might tie his hands by withholding further appropriations and eventually force him to withdraw American troops from Mexico. In February, this apprehension was central to his submitting to the Senate for ratification the treaty negotiated without authority. Despite Trist's illegal conduct and Polk's own desire for a greater cession of territory from the enemy, the president finally decided to accept the document because it conformed to Trist's original instructions and because Polk feared that his territorial goals might be lost if the war continued:

If I were now to reject a Treaty made upon my own terms, as authorized in April last . . . the probability is that Congress would not grant either men or money to prosecute the war. Should this be the result, the army now in Mexico would be constantly wasting and diminishing in numbers, and I might at last be compelled to withdraw them, and thus lose the two provinces of New Mexico & Upper California, which were ceded to the U.S. by this Treaty.[2]

Polk's fears were not well founded. The administration could expect that a number of Whig critics would do as they had since May 1846. That is, they would vote with the Democrats to sustain the military effort while denouncing the administration verbally. Interestingly, Whig Senators and politicians who reluctantly supported ratification of the Treaty of Guadalupe Hidalgo had a much more modest estimation of their own strength. A common argument advanced for ratifying the treaty was that, unless the agreement was accepted, the acquisition of a much larger portion of enemy territory, possibly the whole of Mexico, would ensue. Another inducement to Whigs to ratify the treaty was the $15,000,000 payment to Mexico, a figure arguing that the territory had been purchased rather than seized.

The Mexican War, then, ended as it had begun, with political opponents denouncing a treaty of peace which they voted to ratify, just as they had assailed the original war bill in May 1846 before voting its passage. But if the Whigs had failed to defeat or alter the administration's war goals, they did succeed in turning the issue to their immediate political advantage. Their vacillating antiwar position allowed them to oppose the war without committing political suicide. In short, they had avoided the political disaster of the Federalists in the War of 1812. In addition, the Whig No Territory stance, combined with the subsequent nomination of war hero Zachary Taylor, allowed the Whigs to evade the slavery issue temporarily and place a Whig in the White House in 1848.

This victory was not, of course, without its price. Conscience Whigs refused to suffer the final indignity of a Taylor nomination and bolted the party rather than countenance the candidacy of a slaveholding warrior of conquest. Moreover, by aggravating the slavery issue, the Mexican War had a similar divisive effect on the Democratic party as antislavery Democrats joined Conscience Whigs and former Liberty men to form the Free Soil party in 1848. In retrospect, the Whig party's ability to evade the political ramifications of the Mexican War and the ensuing presidential victory were fleeting. The Whigs had predicted well during the war when they warned that victory over Mexico and the addition of new territory would unleash an issue ominous for both national parties and for the Union itself.

---

2. Milo M. Quaife, ed., *The Diary of James K. Polk, 1845–1849*, 4 vols. (Chicago, 1910), 3: 348.

Reference Matter

★ *Essay on Sources*

THIS BRIEF ESSAY will describe the sources which were most useful in the preparation of this study. It is not an attempt to list or discuss every source consulted or every source cited in the footnotes. For a complete listing of sources, readers should consult the bibliography in my dissertation, "To Give 'Aid and Comfort': American Opposition to the Mexican War, 1846–1848" (Ph.D. diss., University of Virginia, 1971).

Mr. Polk's War is based largely on a variety of primary source materials, including unpublished manuscripts, official documents, congressional debates and proceedings, newspapers, periodicals, and printed writings. Basic to the research were the many unpublished manuscript collections consulted. At the Manuscript Division of the Library of Congress substantial material was pertinent. Particularly revealing of John C. Calhoun's opposition were the Henry W. Conner Papers, as well as the John C. Calhoun Papers. Informative for Democratic politics during the war were the extensive Martin Van Buren Papers which include correspondence both to and from Van Buren. Although the Giddings-Julian Papers contained a limited number of items for this period, they relate directly to the dissent of Joshua Giddings. Of the collections which focus on Whig politics and maneuvering for the presidency during the war years, the most valuable were the John J. Crittenden Papers, the John McLean Papers, and the Caleb B. Smith Papers. The extensive Salmon P. Chase Papers were more useful for antislavery politics than for opposition to the war.

At the Massachusetts Historical Society, several collections were valuable for opposition to the war, as well as for the controversy between the Cotton and Conscience wings of the Massachusetts Whig party. The Adams Family Papers are an incredibly rich collection which includes the diaries of both John Quincy and Charles Francis Adams in addition to their extensive correspondence during the war years. Also extensive are the Winthrop Family Papers which include the correspondence of Robert Winthrop and fragments of his diary from November 1847 to February 1848. Although the Nathan Appleton Papers and the Edward Everett Papers contain only a few items pertinent to this topic, they were useful. At the Houghton Library, Harvard University, the Charles Sumner Papers are a rich collection containing substantial correspondence pertaining to Massachusetts Whig politics and Sumner's own dissent. Also of use here were the Daniel Webster Papers and the John Gorham Palfrey Papers.

At the New York Historical Society, the Albert Gallatin Papers contain abundant information on Gallatin's antiwar views and activities. At this same repository, the Horace Greeley Papers include useful information on Whig presidential politics. Likewise, the Horace Greeley Papers at the New York Public Library contain similar information. Another useful source here was the Azariah Flagg Papers containing important letters on Democratic politics and on the response of various Van Burenites to the war. At the Ohio Historical Society, Columbus, the Joshua Reed Giddings Papers are a rich collection containing several hundred items of correspondence. The manuscripts include Giddings' political correspondence, as well as revealing personal letters from Giddings to members of his family. At the William R. Perkins Library, Duke University, Durham, N.C., each of the following collections contained useful information on politics during the war: the Armistead Burt Papers, the John C. Calhoun Papers, the John J. Crittenden Papers, the George McDuffie Papers, and the Alexander H. Stephens Papers. The same was true of the John M. Berrien Papers in the Southern Historical Collection, University of North Carolina, Chapel Hill. Here also are the David Outlaw Papers which provide an interesting first-hand view of the Thirtieth Congress. As an unexceptional Whig representative from North Carolina, Outlaw regularly criticized Congress in candid letters to his wife.

Another essential source was provided by official documents. The standard collection of presidential messages to Congress is James D. Richardson, ed., *A Compilation of the Messages and Papers of the Presidents, 1789–1902,* 10 vols. (Washington, D.C., 1903). Although the reporting was uneven and, at times, inadequate, the only nearly complete record of congressional debates for this period is the *Congressional Globe,* 46 vols. (Washington, D.C., 1834–1873). For the actual proceedings and votes in Congress, useful sources are the *Journal of the House of Representatives of the United States . . .* [1846–1848] (Washington, D.C., 1846–48) and the *Journal of the Senate of the United States . . .* [1846–1848] (Washington, D.C., 1846–48). The proceedings and votes of the Senate in executive session on the peace treaty are available in *Senate Executive Documents,* 30th Cong., 1st Sess., 1848, No. 52.

Newspapers were an invaluable source for this study. Not only did they express a wide variety of editorial opinions on the war issue, they also contained important articles on state elections and leading politicians, as well as reprinted speeches, pamphlets, and letters. Useful because of the primary information it contained was the *Niles' Weekly Register* (Baltimore, Md.). The Washington *Daily Union,* edited by Thomas Ritchie, acted as the public spokesman for the Polk administration on the war. In contrast, a southern Democratic paper of antiwar views was the *Charleston Mercury* (S.C.), which consistently warned that the Mexican War would injure southern interests.

Of the many Whig newspapers consulted for this study, the *National Intelligencer* (Washington, D.C.) was the most important. It consistently reprinted a variety of antiwar material and editorials from other Whig papers; in addition, its editorial opinions were influential and widely cited in many Whig journals. A number of other Whig newspapers from different regions of the nation were used to supplement the *Intelligencer.* In the middle Atlantic area, the *New York Tribune* and the *American and Commercial Daily Advertiser* (Baltimore, Md.) provided two very different shades of antiwar opinion. In New England, the *Boston Daily Advertiser* and the *Boston Atlas* expressed the conservative Cotton Whig view of the war and Whig politics; in contrast, the Boston *Daily Whig* and the Boston *Courier* demonstrated a more radical or Conscience Whig position. In the South, the *Augusta Daily Chronicle and Sentinel* (Georgia), the Nashville *Republican Banner* (Tennessee), and the *Richmond Whig* (Virginia) were authentic voices of Whig sentiment. In the western states, the *Chicago Daily Journal,* the Saint Louis *Missouri Republican,* the Columbus *Ohio State Journal,* and the *Richmond Palladium* (Indiana) expressed a variety of Whig antiwar sentiments. For various shades of antislavery and abolitionist opinion, several journals were useful. The *Cincinnati Herald and Philanthropist* (Ohio) in 1846 and the *National Era* (Washington, D.C.) in 1847 and 1848 were voices of political abolitionism. Likewise, two abolitionist papers, the *Liberator* (Boston) and the *National Anti-Slavery Standard* (New York), consistently condemned the war.

In addition, a number of periodicals were useful because of their antiwar articles and opinions. Among these were *The American Review: A Whig Journal of Politics, Literature, Art, and Science, Brownson's Quarterly Review,* the *New Englander,* and the *Massachusetts Quarterly Review. Yankee Doodle* presented a satirical view of the war and politics of the day through various sketches and numerous cartoons.

Many printed collections of speeches, writings, and correspondence are available for the 1840s; these publications include edited collections for the great majority of the public figures of the day. Here I shall mention only those of greatest importance for this study. Invaluable for President Polk is Milo M. Quaife, ed., *The Diary of James K. Polk, 1845–1849,* 4 vols. (Chicago, 1910). The following three publications are important for John C. Calhoun: J. Franklin Jameson, ed., *Correspondence of John C. Calhoun, Annual Report of the American Historical Association for the Year 1899,* vol.

2 (Washington, D.C., 1899); Chauncey Boucher and Robert Brooks, eds., *Correspondence Addressed to John C. Calhoun, 1837–1849, Annual Report of the American Historical Association for the Year 1929* (Washington, D.C., 1929); Richard Cralle, ed., *The Works of John C. Calhoun,* 6 vols. (New York, 1848–54).

Although numerous, published primary sources for Whig politicians were of limited importance. The most important were Edward L. Pierce, ed., *Memoir and Letters of Charles Sumner,* 4 vols. (Boston, 1893); *Charles Sumner: His Complete Works,* 20 vols. (Boston, 1900); C. H. Van Tyne, ed., *The Letters of Daniel Webster* (New York, 1902); Fletcher Webster, ed., *The Private Correspondence of Daniel Webster,* 2 vols. (Boston, 1857); Fletcher Webster, ed., *The Writings and Speeches of Daniel Webster,* 18 vols. (National Edition, Boston, 1903); Robert C. Winthrop, *Addresses and Speeches on Various Occasions,* 4 vols. (Boston, 1852–86). For antiwar politics pertinent to Thomas Corwin and Joshua Giddings, the following brief collections of correspondence edited by Belle L. Hamlin were important: "Selections from the Follett Papers, II," *Quarterly Publication of the Historical and Philosophical Society of Ohio* 9 (1914): 72–100; "Selections from the Follett Papers, III, "*Quarterly Publication of the Historical and Philosophical Society of Ohio* 10 (1915): 4–33; "Selections from the William Greene Papers, I," *Quarterly Publication of the Historical Society of Ohio* 13 (1918): 3–38. Useful for the opposition of young Abraham Lincoln, then a first term congressman from Illinois, is Roy P. Basler, ed., *The Collected Works of Abraham Lincoln,* 10 vols. (New Brunswick, N.J., 1953). The antiwar views of Philip Hone, an aristocratic and conservative New York Whig, are expressed in Allan Nevins, ed., *The Diary of Philip Hone, 1828–1851,* 2 vols. (New York, 1927).

Other printed primary sources of particular interest were Henry Adams, ed., *The Writings of Albert Gallatin,* 3 vols. (1879; reprint ed., New York, 1960) for useful correspondence on Gallatin's antiwar activities. Edward Waldo Emerson and Waldo Emerson Forbes, eds., *Journals of Ralph Waldo Emerson,* 10 vols. (Boston, 1909–14) are especially informative for Emerson's thoughts on a wide variety of topics including the war and politics. For the writings of an eloquent dissenter, see Theodore Parker [*The Works of Theodore Parker*], 15 vols. (Centenary Edition, Boston, 1907–11). Among the most useful antiwar volumes used in this study were the following: William Jay, *A Review of the Causes and Consequences of the Mexican War* (Boston, 1849); Abiel A. Livermore, *The War with Mexico Reviewed* (Boston, 1850); James Russell Lowell, *The Biglow Papers* (Cambridge, Mass., 1848); and [Seba Smith] Major Jack Downing, *My Thirty Years Out of the Senate* (New York, 1859).

Although few secondary sources related directly in any depth to the subject of the present book, I did rely upon the abundant studies which exist for background and general information. For example, solid, and often outstanding, biographies exist on most of the major figures of the 1840s. In addition, a substantial body of secondary literature is available on the military and diplomatic conduct of the war itself, on expansionism of the period, on state and national politics, on the Ante-Bellum reform movement, and on intellectual currents. When these studies related directly to this book, I have indicated my debts in the footnotes.

★ Index

Abolitionists: and war, 36, 99–105; sign antiwar pledge, 99–100; frustrated by war spirit, 100; denounce Cassius M. Clay, 101; denounce George Briggs, 104; on political parties and participation, 104–5; Emerson on, 106; mentioned, xiv, 33, 92, 94, 107, 141, 162

Adams, Charles Francis: editor of Boston *Daily Whig*, 40, 59n; criticizes Abbott Lawrence, 59; on antiwar strategy, 125; on Corwin, 135, 137; mentioned, 136

Adams, John Quincy: votes against war bill, 29n; on Two Million Bill, 45; praised by abolitionists, 104; death of, 156; mentioned, 6, 11, 15, 29–30, 78

Advocate of Peace and Universal Brotherhood: title changed, 97n; mentioned, 95, 96, 97, 98, 99

All Mexico Movement: rise of, 120, 127–30; proposal of Gamaliel Bailey, 127–29; and slavery issue, 128–29; response to, 129–30, 155n, 155–56; mentioned, 89–90, 143, 152, 161, 162

Allen, William, 4, 16

American Anti-Slavery Society: adopts antiwar resolution, 99; mentioned, 36

American antiwar dissent: characterized, ix–xiv

American Colonization Society, 140

American Peace Society: and war, 36, 94–99; pacifism of, 94; antiwar tactics, 95–99; factions in, 95–96

American Revolution, 113

Antislavery Whigs. *See* Radical Whigs

Antiwar rallies, 90n, 140

Appleton, Lawrence, 59, 60

Ashmun, George: votes against war bill, 29n; resolution on war in 30th Congress, 154; mentioned, 31

Ashtabula Sentinel (Ohio): on origins of war, 40; on Wilmot Proviso, 126

Atocha, A. J., 52

Augusta Daily Chronicle and Sentinel: on origins of war, 41; on conquest, 53; on slavery issue, 124; on All Mexico, 130

Badger, George E.: on All Mexico, 156

Bailey, Gamaliel: editor of *National Era,* 127; mentioned, 105. *See also National Era*

Baker, Edward, 77

Ballou, Adin, 94

Baltimore, Maryland: prowar rally in, 33

Baltimore American: initial view of war, 40; on Two Million Bill, 48; on

173

DESIGNED BY TED SMITH GRAPHICS

MANUFACTURED BY GEORGE BANTA CO., INC., MENASHA, WISCONSIN

TEXT LINES ARE SET IN INTERTYPE GARAMOND

DISPLAY LINES IN FRANKLIN GOTHIC AND GARAMOND

Library of Congress Cataloging in Publication Data
Schroeder, John H.   1943–
Mr. Polk's War.

Bibliography: p. 167–71
1. United States—History—War with Mexico,
1845–1848—Public opinion. I. Title.
E415.2.S3   973.6′2   73–2049
ISBN 0-299-06160-4